GARDENING ACROSS THE POND

Anglo-American Exchanges from the Settlers in Virginia to Prairie Gardens in England

Richard Bisgrove

PIMPERNEL
PRESS LTD
www.pimpernelpress.com

Pimpernel Press Limited
www.pimpernelpress.com

Gardening Across the Pond
Anglo-American Exchanges from the Settlers in Virginia to Prairie Gardens in England

A catalogue record for this book is available from the British Library.

Designed by Anne Wilson
Typeset in Minion and Filosofia

ISBN 978-1-910258-24-8

Printed and bound in China
by C&C Offset Printing Company Limited

9 8 7 6 5 4 3 2 1

ENDPAPERS Pages from *Sutton's Amateur's Guide and Spring Catalogue for 1881*.
HALF-TITLE The frontispiece from Andrew Jackson Downing's *Treatise on the Theory and Practice of Landscape Gardening adapted to North America*, first published in 1841.
TITLE PAGE John Bartram's line drawing, dated 1758, of his botanic garden in Philadelphia, from which many boxes of plants came to enrich English gardens.

Contents

Foreword

A MERICA AND ENGLAND have long had a special relationship in matters political, cultural and economic. *Gardening across the Pond* explores one aspect of a cultural relationship of particular significance to the English and to Anglophile Americans: their gardens. What started as a life-supporting flow of familiar plants from England to sustain the new settlers and a return flow of exciting new plants to furnish the parks and gardens of the English aristocracy developed into a two-way flow of ideas: in the nineteenth century, on the role of parks and gardens in two civilized but industrializing democracies and, in the twentieth century, to a joint seeking for solutions to the global problems of sustainability – social and environmental. Now, in the early decades of the twenty-first century, exchanging ideas and inspiration has never been easier, and the horticultural ties between the two countries and their people are as strong as ever.

The early chapters of the book are arranged more or less chronologically, accepting that history does not organize itself in neat slices, but as the twentieth century approaches and examples of American–English exchanges and parallel developments proliferate, the treatment is of chronologically overlapping themes.

To some extent this book is autobiographical. After my horticultural science degree at the University of Reading in England I spent four years in the United States as a research and teaching assistant and student of landscape architecture at the universities of Illinois and Michigan. Illinois had its own separate library for architecture and landscape with a very helpful librarian. My year there could not have been more fortuitous as it coincided with the republishing of George Perkins Marsh's mammoth tome *Man and Nature* (1965) on the centenary of its first publication in 1864. In Michigan I read Frederick Law Olmsted's newly republished *Walks and Talks of an American Farmer in England* (1967), first published in 1852, and Albert Fein's compendium of Olmsted reports in *Landscape into Cityscape* (also 1967). Olmsted became my American hero as Gertrude Jekyll was later to become my English heroine. Studying in America also made me see much more clearly what England was about. Coming to a vast country where front gardens, or 'yards', were of open lawn and the back usually had little more than a tree, a bird feeder and a barbecue, and where everyone travelled by car rather than by bus and train as in the crowded little island I had left, put England into sharper focus.

Back home and at the University of Reading once more, this time as a lecturer, it was some years before I saw the US again, although American friends came to visit. In England I lectured at Reading for 40 years, and for most of that time I was involved with

GARDENING ACROSS THE POND

the Garden Club of America Interchange Fellowship, interviewing English candidates for the fellowship and often hosting the American students in Reading. Some of those students have remained good friends so I am able to keep in touch with their activities. I have also been involved in summer schools at Oxford with various American universities, currently Berkeley and Michigan State and in the past Florida, Iowa State and Duke, as well as the Smithsonian Institution. Oxford courses are very much two-way exchanges, and I have gained more from the widely travelled and widely read American participants on the courses than they have gained from me. Recently I have had fleeting visits to New York and a study tour of Boston and Philadelphia. I also been involved with making a 'Gertrude Jekyll' garden in southern California for someone who admires the architecture of Edwin Lutyens and has designed his own 'Lutyens' house, so I have dug in American dirt, or soil as the English would say.

Throughout the text I have written in 'English' English except when quoting from American texts, with occasional translations into American where it seems necessary. I hope this will add a cute English accent for American readers, and it will probably pass unnoticed by English readers, who will be familiar with 'gardens' rather than 'yards', 'motorways' rather than 'freeways' and so on. After my four years in America I am more or less bilingual. Perhaps controversially, I have also referred, on my side of the Atlantic, to England rather than to Britain, unless this is patently inaccurate, but only because 'Britain' and especially 'British' sound so frightfully stiff upper lip. I sincerely hope this does not give offence to fellow Britons. I definitely do not see England as in any way superior to Ireland, Scotland or Wales. It is undoubtedly much bigger but obesity is no indicator of merit.

Gardening across the Pond cannot be a complete account of gardening links between the United States and the United Kingdom. It is not possible in 80,000 words to document the many thousands of garden-minded people, plants and ideas that have crossed and often recrossed the Atlantic, but I hope there is enough information to illustrate the major moments in the exchange and that it creates enough interest to encourage readers to explore further. The subject matter has sometimes strayed beyond gardens in the narrow sense of the word to include parks, parkways and even town planning, because in these areas the transatlantic exchange of ideas has been most fruitful in creating that paradise on earth, the Garden of Eden, we all consciously or subconsciously crave.

Introduction

T HE 'SPECIAL RELATIONSHIP' between the US and England has had a turbulent history spanning more than 400 years. Beginning with a tiny group of settlers on the island of Roanoke in 1585, the colonists relied almost completely on the mother country to supply its essentials. By 1700, there were 12 flourishing colonies trading tobacco, cotton, indigo and other products of the soil in exchange for manufactured goods from England. Less than a century later, the lively young child became a truculent adolescent reacting angrily to its domineering parent until the adolescent stormed out and the United States of America became an independent nation in 1783. Relations with the old country were fractious, leading to the War of 1812, but family ties on both sides of the Atlantic remained. English Whig sympathy with the young nation as it faced oppression by an essentially German king and a Tory government was strong, and the two countries resumed peaceful relations and, perhaps most importantly, the new nation retained the language of the old – more or less.[1]

Despite the hopes of George Washington and Thomas Jefferson, first and third presidents of the United States, that America would develop into a land of farmers, the rich natural resources of the country and the innovative character of its citizens resulted in spectacular growth of industrial might and wealth in its cities. By 1900 the truculent adolescent had grown into a strong and vigorous adult. The 1898 *New York Journal* cartoon of a lofty Uncle Sam looking down on a tiny, rotund and top-hatted John Bull aptly captured the relationship which would develop throughout the twentieth century.

Ironically, as America – and especially the immensely wealthy upper stratum of American society – grew in power, it seemed to develop something of an inferiority complex. The one thing the new Americans lacked was history, so with the now routine crossings of the Atlantic by scheduled ships and later by aeroplanes, second and third generation inheritors of industrial wealth sought that history in Europe, especially in England, France and Italy. The novelist and gardener Edith Wharton, whom Henry James described as 'the pendulum woman' for her repeated crossing and recrossing of the Atlantic, said scathingly that American gardens had no foreground and Americans had no background.[2]

In the twenty-first century the flow across the Atlantic has become a little more even, albeit with the greater wealth of a larger American population creating some imbalance. English tourists to America seek out the phenomenal natural beauty of its national parks, the climate of Florida or California, the ski slopes of the Rockies, the towering buildings of New York and the recreational wonders of Disney Worlds and Las Vegas. Visitors from America delight in the old cultural centres of London, Oxford, Cambridge and medieval cores of a dozen other cities, in the smaller scale comfortable landscapes of the Cotswolds, Lake District or South West, and in the ancient lineage of so many English families in so many country houses. Many of these great houses have beautiful gardens, and to paraphrase the eighteenth-century words of Horace Walpole, it is possible to leap the garden fence and to see the whole of the English landscape as a beautifully tended garden.

The garden is a powerful barometer of social evolution, involving, as it does, so many facets of art, science, technology, economics and philosophy. It is not surprising, therefore, that the potted history of Anglo-American relations sketched above is mirrored in the development of gardens on both sides of the Atlantic. For much of the twentieth century the garden was seen by the majority of people as a mundane – literally a down-to-earth – subject, its maintenance a necessary chore, but as the twenty-first century progresses the much wider role of the garden and the metaphor of the Garden of Eden have awoken more and more people to the many functions that the garden can and should fulfil in creating a better life.

The early settlers took with them all the tools, equipment, seeds, plants and books that they needed to establish small pockets of English life – hopefully free from the religious or economic strictures which had forced them to flee – on the edges of a vast, unknown and hostile land. Brave pioneers nibbled away at the edge of the continent and many died in the process.

In England this early period of American colonisation coincided with religious turmoil and battles with France, but there was growing wealth, created at least in part by international trade, and much of that wealth was spent in making splendid new houses and gardens. The untold botanical wealth of a new paradise across the Atlantic exerted great attraction. The seventeenth and eighteenth centuries were marked by a flow of new plants from the New World to the Old, not least thanks to the activities of the John Tradescants, father and son. (That flow continued well into the

John Bull and Uncle Sam: a nineteenth-century cartoon.

9

A dapper Washington Atlas Burpee (1858-1915), founder of Burpee Seeds in Pennsylvania, meets the elderly Scotsman Henry Eckford (1823-1905), famed for his sweet pea breeding.

nineteenth century, with David Douglas becoming a national hero because of his plant collecting explorations on behalf of the Horticultural Society of London.) However, the source of those new plants was changing rapidly. America was no longer a cluster of small settlements but a nation beginning to exert international influence. While Thomas Jefferson negotiated treaties for his new country in France in 1786, he found time for a tour of English gardens in preparation for the creation of his own garden at Monticello in Virginia.

By the nineteenth century the industrial might of America had spawned a new aristocracy of business giants seeking an appropriate setting for their lives. They turned to English precedents but even more to the grandeur of Louis XIV's France and the spectacular terraced gardens of Renaissance Italy. As the century progressed, wealth filtered down in both nations to a growing middle class seeking to demonstrate their respectability and good taste. In England Humphry Repton adapted the great parks of Lancelot 'Capability' Brown to a smaller compass and struggled to meet his patrons' desires to have more and more new plants in smaller and smaller gardens. John Claudius Loudon then extended Repton's advice for the innumerable small suburban gardens which were multiplying across the country. In turn, Andrew Jackson Downing adapted their writings to North America, convinced that good taste in architecture and gardening would create a civilized nation. Sadly, he died when the steamer he was sailing on exploded and sank, but not before he introduced his English architectural partner, Calvert Vaux, to the young American Frederick Law Olmsted.

In some ways Olmsted was America's Capability Brown, but his influence was far more pervasive. The creator of Manhattan's Central Park, in collaboration with Vaux, he went on to campaign for national parks, to design university campuses and suburban communities, and to invent the profession of landscape architecture, providing its first generation of young members trained in his office.

While Olmsted was reshaping America, wealthy Americans were discovering the delights of England – and especially the tumbledown but charming honey-coloured cottages of the Cotswolds gathered in picturesque clusters in tiny villages. They repaired and modernized the houses and created appropriate cottagey garden settings for them. To a significant degree the flower-filled English cottage garden of the late nineteenth and early twentieth centuries was an American invention.

In the latter part of the twentieth century a new triangle formed between America, England and Germany with America's efforts to save and recreate its vanishing prairies, England developing its Robinsonian wildflower meadows and Germany developing new ecologically inspired perennial gardens. The peak of achievement in that sphere in England was surely the much acclaimed profusion of prairie landscape planting at the London Olympic Park in 2012.

The need to reconnect with nature evident in this 'New Wave' planting movement has been expressed in very different ways in the tightly packed cities of North America, beginning in New York, in the creation of community gardens – made even more valuable as the health benefits of exercise, contact with nature and feeling part of a community have become increasingly recognized. Allied to this in the twenty-first century is the need to rethink the structure of society in a post-industrial age. The collapse of the car industry in Detroit following the 2008 financial crisis and the growth of the urban farming movement in the industrial wastelands of former factory sites are indicative of the fact that over-civilisation has its perils. We lofty humans are still products of the natural world. We need food, clean air and clean water to survive, as does every other living animal. The garden is a metaphor for the natural world. This is all serious stuff, but by sharing our hopes, ambitions and experiences in the search for the paradise that the garden represents we will surely help to create a better world.

1

The seventeenth century and the Tradescants

E NGLAND'S FIRST INVOLVEMENTS with the New World were in the nature of a persistent fly trying to settle on a human nose and meeting constant rebuff. In 1563 Francis Drake sailed to the Americas with his second cousin John Hawkins to attack Spanish ships. He returned again in 1568 and 1572, capturing 20 tons of gold and silver. Sent by Queen Elizabeth to attack the Spanish fleet in the Pacific Ocean, Drake rounded the Cape in September 1578 and, after months of raiding along the coast of Chile and Peru, landed on the coast of California, declaring it 'Nova Albion' on 17 June 1579. In September 1580 he returned to Plymouth and was knighted in 1581.

On 25 March 1584 Elizabeth granted Walter Ralegh (now usually spelled Raleigh) a charter to colonize North America. Ralegh sent Philip Amadas and Arthur Barlowe to explore the east coast, and they landed on Roanoke Island (off the coast of what is now North Carolina) on 4 July. A second expedition of five ships led by Sir Richard Greville set off in 1585, but the ships were scattered in bad weather. Greville left Ralph Lane and 107 men to establish a colony on the island, but his return with more supplies was delayed for three years. In 1586 an attack by Indians was repelled but Francis Drake arrived, after attacking Spanish colonies in Colombia and Florida, to take most of the colonists back to England, famously introducing tobacco, maize and potatoes to the Old World.

After several other failed attempts to establish a Roanoke colony, in 1607 the Virginia Company of London sent a party of settlers to establish a colony of Virginia, arriving at what became James Fort on 4 May. Poorly equipped, poorly qualified to survive in the new environment and with food supplies severely diminished by delays in the voyage, 60 of the 104 members of the party died in the first summer. The arrival of Captain Samuel Argall in 1609 drove off a Spanish attack, but it was the demand of Captain John Smith that the Company in London send *useful* people to populate the colony that ensured its survival. Nevertheless, a combination of Native American unrest, defection of German and Polish members of the colony to join the Native Americans, Spanish threats and bad weather resulted in the loss of 80 per cent of the new inhabitants in the 'starving winter' of 1609–10.

By 1614, though, Captain Smith was able to write, in his *Description of New England*, of 'sandy cliffes and cliffes of rock, both which we saw so planted with Gardens and Cornefields'. He 'made a garden in May producing sallets in June and July.'[3] The Reverend Francis Higginson, who arrived in Salem, Massachusetts, in 1629, also recorded an 'abundance of grass and corn. The Governor has pease as good as in England.' There were 'turnips, parsnips and carrots bigger and sweeter … Herbs and fruits galore'.[4]

The hazardous adventures into a new world resulted in part from political and religious unrest in England, but they were also signs of England's growth as a major mercantile nation. The formation of the East India Company in 1600 and the Virginia Company in 1607 reflected a growing thirst for international trade which, when successful, brought enormous wealth. In the successive reigns of Elizabeth I, James I and Charles I, much of that wealth was spent on new houses and gardens. In 1607, as the first settlers landed in Virginia, Robert Cecil, Earl of Salisbury, exchanged his father's opulent house at Theobalds, in Hertfordshire, for James I's run-down house nearby at Hatfield, together with 16 other properties. Cecil pulled down three-quarters of the old Tudor palace and started on a magnificent new building within sight of the old. By 1610 the work was sufficiently under way to start on the gardens. For the kitchen gardens Cecil engaged John Tradescant (c.1570–1639), who later played a major role in introducing plants from the New World to England.

Little is known of Tradescant's early life. He was probably born in Suffolk and is first recorded as marrying Elizabeth Day in 1607. He moved to Hatfield at the age of about 40, already a respected plantsman, at a very substantial wage of £50 per annum. Under Cecil's patronage he travelled to Flanders to buy vines, then to Flushing, Rotterdam and Delft to buy apples, pears, quinces, cherries, currants and flowering plants before going on to Paris, where he began a life-long friendship with Jean Robin, director of the king's Jardin des Plantes, and his son Vespasian.

At home in England he travelled regularly between the Cecil country houses at Hatfield and Cranborne Manor in Dorset and the London home, Salisbury House, on the Strand. Always keenly interested in plants and curiosities, he spent many hours in the London docks, talking to ships' captains and acquiring from them seeds and 'rarities'. He became well acquainted with Captains Samuel Argall and John Smith, and listened eagerly to their tales of adventure in the New World. In 1617, when Argall was allowed by the Virginia Company to issue Bills of Adventure, Tradescant bought two shares for £25. Each entitled him to send 24 people to Virginia where they would each be granted 100 acres of land, with Tradescant receiving 50 per cent of the proceeds. He was, though, interested as much in plants from the New World as in potential farming profits.

Cecil died in 1612. In 1615 Tradescant moved to Canterbury to work for Edward, Lord Wotton, where he became famed for his cultivation of melons. In 1624 Tradescant moved again, to work for George Villiers, 1st Duke of Buckingham, the favourite of James and Charles I, at New Hall in Essex, a former summer residence of Henry VIII. The gardener became an important member of the household. When Buckingham's visit as proxy groom for Charles's marriage to the French princess Henrietta Maria was postponed because of James's death, Tradescant was sent to bring back the duke's spectacular wardrobe. He took advantage of his journey to visit the Robins, father and son, in Paris. More importantly, when the duke decided to assemble a cabinet of rarities, Tradescant was appointed overseer of the collection. With his many connections in the docks he set to work on the cabinet, retaining for himself any overspill and duplicates. When Buckingham was assassinated in 1628, Tradescant moved to Lambeth, south of the Thames from London, leasing a house in 1629 with an acre of garden, 2 acres of orchards and 20 acres of fields nearby. He added a high-ceilinged room with elegant Venetian windows to accommodate his museum which, with its collection of curiosities from all parts of the world, became known as the 'Ark'. Visitors paid a shilling (5 pence in today's currency) to be shown the collection, which quickly became a major attraction.

In 1630 came a royal appointment: Tradescant was made Keeper of the Gardens, Vines and Silkworms to Charles I at Oatlands Palace in Surrey at £100 per annum, but he continued to develop his nursery and to enlarge the museum until his death in 1639. During his life his reputation as a gardener and collector of plants was unparalleled. He was a friend of John Parkinson (1567–1650), Charles's royal botanist, whose *Paradisi in Sole Paradisus Terrestris* (Park-in-Sun's Earthly Paradise, a pun on his name) of 1629, with Gerard's *Herball* (1593 and 1633) and Culpeper's *Complete Herbal* of 1653, were mainstays of the colonists' libraries. In *Paradisi* Parkinson made many references to plants introduced from America by 'my good friend' John Tradescant.[5] Among these plants were the red mulberry *Morus rubra*, shagbark hickory *Carya ovata*, black walnut *Juglans nigra*, stag's horn sumac *Rhus typhina*, Virginia creeper *Parthenocissus quinquefolia*, and *Tradescantia virginiana*.

Tradescant was succeeded by his son, also John. Born in 1608, John junior went to school in Canterbury until 1623, then worked with his father. He married Jane Hurte in 1628, but she died of the plague in 1635. John junior left for Virginia, returning to finalize his father's estate in 1639. He succeeded to his father's position at Oatlands, but working for the king was increasingly hazardous. Opposition to the king's dictatorial government of the country led to increasing discontent and finally to civil war. After the 1642 Battle of Edgehill, the first pitched battle between the Parliamentarians opposing the king and his supporting Royalists, John left again for Virginia, returning for his daughter's wedding in 1645 but going to Virginia once more in 1653. Much of his time in Virginia was spent exploring and plant collecting, living at times off the land like a Native American. Among the many plants introduced to the Lambeth nursery were the Virginia snakeweed *Aristolochia serpentaria*, two 'shrubby starworts' (perennial asters or Michaelmas daisies) including

Aster tradescantii, and poison ivy *Rhus toxicodendron* in 1632.[6] The spiky *Agave americana* and tall, elegant, daisy-like *Erigeron annuus* were introduced in 1633. (Amusingly, the erigeron has recently become a must-have plant among discerning English gardeners only 380 years after its introduction.) In 1634 Tradescant's list included *Locusta virginiana arbor*. Seeds arrived in England in 1635, and seeds of this and other plants were sent to Jean Robin in Paris. *Locusta virginiana arbor* later became *Robinia pseudoacacia*, the black locust or false acacia, named after Robin. Among the plants brought back from later visits were the tulip tree *Liriodendron tulipifera*, red maple *Acer rubrum*, hackberry *Celtis occidentalis*, Adam's needle *Yucca filamentosa*, and fox grape *Vitis vulpina*, while Parkinson's *Theatrum Botanicum* of 1640 records the American plane (sycamore or buttonwood in America) *Platanus occidentalis*, swamp or bald cypress *Taxodium distichum*, the tiny fern *Adiantum pedatum*, and the curious, insectivorous *Sarracenia purpurea* as Tradescant introductions.

Back in England once more, Tradescant met Elias Ashmole (1617–1692) in 1658. Ashmole's wealthy third wife was a friend of Tradescant's second wife, Hester, and she stayed at the Ark from time to time when her husband was being particularly difficult. Ashmole paid for the publication of a catalogue of the contents of the Ark, *Musaeum Tradescantium*, and in 1659 Tradescant was inveigled into bequeathing his museum to Ashmole. A second edition of the *Musaeum* in 1660 was dedicated to the newly crowned Charles II. During the Great Fire of 1666 Ashmole's own library was ferried across the Thames for safe lodging with Hester. In 1674 Ashmole moved next door to the Ark to watch over 'his' museum, and after Tradescant's death in 1662, he hounded Hester, who was found drowned in the garden pond in 1678. The museum was moved to Oxford and on Ashmole's death in 1692 was bequeathed to the University of Oxford, where it formed the early nucleus of the Ashmolean Museum.

The Tradescants, father and son, played a key role in introducing plants from the New World at a time when the development of English gardens was about to explode.

2

A new king and a firm foothold

⌒

THE BEHEADING of Charles I in 1649 was followed by the Commonwealth and the Protectorate under Thomas Cromwell, but the English eventually decided that monarchy was the lesser of two evils and Charles's son, also Charles, returned from exile in France in 1660. The restoration of the monarchy led to a surge of new building and gardening in England on a grand scale. Estates sequestered during the Commonwealth were given back by a grateful king, while other Royalist supporters received new lands, not only in England but in the colonies.

After often perilous beginnings, the colonies flourished as the seventeenth century advanced. In 1675 John Josselyn, after visiting his brother Henry, wrote *An Account of Two Voyages to New England* in which he described 'Boston ... the south side adorned with Gardens and Orchards ... Charles-Town ... the market place not far from the waterside is surrounded with houses, forth of which issue two streets orderly built and beautiful with Orchards and Gardens ... New-Town ... now called Cambridge where there is a colleg [*sic*] for Students of late.' In his *New England's Rarities* (1674) he boasted, 'The plants in New England for the variety, beauty, number and vertues, may stand in competition with the plants of any country in Europe.'[7]

Less enthusiastic was Robert Beverly, a strident anti-monarchist highly critical of the royal governors visited on the planters by the Crown with the single exception of Sir William Berkeley. Berkeley was Governor of Virginia from 1641 to 1652, and then, after the Restoration, from 1660 to his death in 1677. A favourite of Charles II, he was given a vast tract of land for his own use, and he farmed experimentally to try to reduce Virginia's reliance on the single crop of tobacco. He tried silkworm cultivation and grew maize ('corn' in the US), wheat ('corn' in England), oats, barley, rye, sugar, oranges and grapes. In the twentieth century his descendants sold their Virginian lands to restore Berkeley Castle on the borders of England and Wales.

Berkeley's experiments obviously failed to impress his fellow landowners. In *The History and Present State of Virginia* (1705) Robert Beverly castigated the lazy Virginians:

They have their Cloathing of all sorts from England, as Linen, Woollen, Silk, Hates and Leather. Yet Flax and Hemp grow no where in the World better than there; their Sheep yield mighty increase and bear good Fleeces, but they sheer them only to cool them.

The Mulberry tree, whose leaf is the proper food of the Silk-Worm, grows there like a Weed, and Silk-Worms have been observed to thrive extremely well and without any hazard … Nay, they are such abominable ill-husbands that tho' their Country be over-run with Wood, yet they have all their Wooden Ware from England; their Cabinets, Chairs, Tables, Stools, Chests, Boxes, Cart-Wheels and all other things, even so much as their Bowls and Burchen Brooms, to the Eternal Reproach of their Laziness.[8]

Like Berkeley, he thought the Virginians relied too heavily on the wealth derived from tobacco.

In England one of the loyal supporters of the future Charles II in exile was the writer, gardener and diarist John Evelyn (1620–1706). On Charles's restoration as king of England, Evelyn persuaded him to bring together the leading thinkers of the day to form the Royal Society: still, in the twenty-first century, the country's most distinguished scientific community. The first material result from its deliberations was the publication in 1664 of Evelyn's weighty book, *Sylva, or A Discourse on Forest-Trees and the Propagation of Timber*.

The arguments in *Sylva* were threefold. In an England impoverished of tree cover as a result of an expanding population requiring more food and of the destruction of woodlands during the Civil War, tree planting represented an investment in the future: a young landowner planting trees would pass on the economic benefits to his heirs. Second, by creating extensive woodlands the landowner would be helping to create a greener and more pleasant land, Parkinson's 'Earthly Paradise', and would therefore further ennoble himself. He would become a more worthy being. Third, as paradise did not have a winter season, Evelyn encouraged growing evergreen plants. In his own garden in Deptford, on the Thames five miles south-east of the City of London and home to the first royal naval dockyard, he had a huge holly hedge of which he was very proud, but England's range of evergreen plants was very sparse: holly and yew, Scot's pine, juniper and, if one can include a climber which assumes tree-like stature in old age, the ivy.

His first and second arguments encouraged the aristocracy, nobility and gentry to take an active interest in their estates, an attitude which filtered down over centuries to turn the English into a nation of gardeners. His third stimulated widespread enthusiasm for the cultivation of less hardy evergreen plants from the Mediterranean and beyond: bay and myrtle, *Viburnum tinus* (laurustinus) and cistus, but especially oranges and other citrus trees which were not only evergreen but ever-flowering and fruitful. Shelter was required to conserve tender evergreens in the winter months, thus stimulating the construction of 'conservatories', 'green houses' and 'orangeries' of increasing sophistication.

Evelyn's *Sylva* was much more than a compendium of philosophical ideals. It was a practical handbook on trees and their cultivation. He particularly admired the *Robinia*, a difficult timber to work because of its twisted grain but very durable in contact with the soil, so useful for making fence posts. In 1668 Evelyn wrote to his friend Samuel Pepys, Secretary to the Navy, requesting that the captain he had met at dinner the previous evening 'be asked to send some natural productions of the vegetable kingdom', and listing 40 trees that he wanted to acquire from the colonies.[9]

Another important figure in post-Restoration plant collecting was Henry Compton (1632–1713), Bishop of London from 1675 and tutor to the future James II's daughters Mary and Anne. Compton was responsible for the care of the churches in the colonies and, as a keen plant collector, instructed his missionaries to send plants as well as to save souls. The Revd John Banister was sent to Virginia in 1678, where he established his own botanic garden and helped the William Byrds, father and son, to develop their Westover Plantation. By 1680 he completed the first study of American plants, the catalogue of which was published in John Ray's three-volume *Historia Plantarum*, published between 1686 and 1704. Banister has the dubious distinction of being the first plant collector to die in pursuit of plants while on an expedition with the elder William Byrd in 1692. Whether he died as a result of a fall from a cliff or was accidentally shot in a hunting accident is uncertain, but during his life he sent many plants back to Bishop Compton, including the graceful and aromatic shrubby sweet fern *Comptonia peregrina*. He also sent plants to the Chelsea Physic Garden and to the older Oxford Physic (now Botanic) Garden, including the sweet bay *Magnolia virginiana*, scarlet oak *Quercus coccinea* and sweet gum *Liquidambar styraciflua*.

Compton was suspended from office during the brief reign of James II as the latter attempted to restore the Catholic Church to England, but he returned in 1688, having been a leading figure in the Glorious Revolution bringing the Protestant William of Orange and James II's daughter Mary to the throne. Fifty years later, the Scottish agriculturist, gardener and author John Claudius Loudon considered Compton to be 'the greatest introducer of foreign trees in this century'.[10]

During his temporary fall from grace Compton gave permission to his gardener, George London (c.1640–1713), to leave the Lambeth garden, with many of the bishop's plants, to establish a nursery. London went into partnership with three other gardeners, but when they died or retired he took into partnership the young Henry Wise (1653–1738), who had trained under the royal gardener James Rose, who had himself been trained in France. The London and Wise nursery at Brompton Park rapidly became by far the most important in England, supplying and planting most of the great gardens of the late seventeenth and early eighteenth centuries. Among their most enthusiastic supporters was John Evelyn.

Of George London, one of his later employees, Stephen Switzer, a foreman at the laying out of the vast London and Wise garden at Blenheim in Oxfordshire, wrote:

It will perhaps be hardly believed in times to come that this one person actually saw and gave directions once or twice a year in most of the noblemen's and gentlemen's gardens in England. And since it was common for him to ride fifty or sixty miles in a day he made his northern circuit in five or six weeks and sometimes less, and his western in as little time: as for the south and east they were but three or four days work for him; most times twice a year visiting all the country seats, conversing with gentlemen and forwarding the business of gardening in such a degree as is almost impossible to describe.[11]

It was estimated that, valued at 1*d.* (one old penny) per plant, the nursery would be worth £40,000. As there were 240 old pence in a pound, that puts the holdings of Brompton Park at about 10 million plants. Certainly, they supplied plants by the hundreds of thousands at Blenheim, by barge and by wagon, and many of their other gardens such as Chatsworth in Derbyshire in the north of England and Longleat in Wiltshire in the west were on a similar scale.

One of Henry Wise's notebooks contains 'A Collection of Flowers as they Blow in Each Season of the Year' so that the parterre below the house could be kept in a perpetually colourful condition. In the spring months the flowers were mainly bulbs and English or European spring flowers, but in May the 'Double and Virginian Columbines' appear, with larkspur and lupins from America among the annual flowers. In June there is 'Spider Wort' (*Tradescantia*) and in July French and African marigolds, both from Central America, and Virginia honeysuckle. August brought the cardinal flower (*Lobelia cardinalis*) and trumpet flower (*Campsis*), both flowering into September, and the 'Virginia Martagon' and goldenrod.[12]

The change from the elaborate courtly displays of Charles II and James II modelled on France to the more domestic lifestyle of William and Mary, devoted as they were to each other, did not go unnoticed in the New World. A Puritan ethic and simple common sense in the colonies prevented the emulation of grandiose schemes such as Versailles or the many gardens of London and Wise, but the smaller scale and more colourful Dutch gardens made in England after 1688 found favour among the wealthier inhabitants. Middle Plantation became the temporary capital of Virginia in 1676, being more easily defended than the old capital at James Fort, later James Town (now Jamestown), on the coast. The College of William and Mary was founded in Middle Plantation in 1693, and when the town was made the permanent capital in 1699 it was renamed Williamsburg. It had a spacious layout with the College of William and Mary at one end of Duke of Gloucester Street and the Capitol at the other. Simple gardens of box-edged beds filled with tulips and other flowers embellished with modest topiary lined the street together with the all-important vegetable plots and fruit trees.

In 1681 William Penn (1644–1718) was granted a huge tract of land in America – 45,000 square miles – by Charles II in a complex settlement of the king's debt to Penn's father, Admiral Sir William Penn. The younger Penn had had a very eventful life as a student railing against the authoritarian Church, as a Catholic defending the family's Irish estates and as a Quaker after his conversion in 1666. He was thrown out of the family home by his father, and was imprisoned on several occasions for defending the faith of others and then for adhering resolutely to his own faith. The king probably thought that one way of dealing with him was to remove the problem from English shores.

By 1682 Penn had decided on the site for his new city of Philadelphia (meaning brotherly love) between the Delaware and Schuylkill rivers. Houses were to be sited in the middle of spacious plots, 'every house [to] be placed, if the Person pleases, in ye middle of its place as to the breadth way of it, so that there may be ground on each side, for Gardens, or Orchards, or Fields, yt it may be a greene Country Towne, wch will never be burnt and will allwayes be wholesome.'[13] This plan was perhaps influenced by memories of the 1666 Great Fire of London when Penn was 21. He arrived in October 1682 to lay out the new city, a grid with a public square in the middle of each quarter. He granted 300,000 acres to 250 settlers, mainly wealthy Quakers from London, and set about creating a model democracy. He advocated the formation of a union between the English colonies and the formation of a United States of Europe as means of achieving lasting peace. Sadly, his life continued to be complicated by his lack of financial prudence, his inability to see evil in other people and his unwillingness to pay attention to detail. He shuttled back and forth across the Atlantic and died penniless in England in 1718, but not before Pennsylvania was firmly established as a thriving democratic colony with Philadelphia as its elegant capital.

By 1700, European and especially English settlers were also firmly established in the New World. Boston's 'new-town' of Cambridge had its 'colleg'; Williamsburg had its wide streets lined with charming and productive gardens. A late seventeenth-century map of New York shows a grid street pattern east of the Battery: 15 blocks ringed with houses but with ample gardens of clipped greens, flowers and trees behind the facades.

3

A catalogue of plants and a revolution

N EW YORK, Philadelphia, Williamsburg and other settlements were very small
footprints on an immense continent, closer in spirit to the parent country than to
the wilderness but secure enough to begin to recognize the wealth of plants surrounding
them. In 1712 the artist and keen botanist Mark Catesby from Essex in England visited his
sister in Williamsburg. Enchanted by what he saw, he stayed for seven years sketching and
collecting plants and animals. In 1713 he sent seeds to Bishop Compton, but the latter died
before he could receive them. Catesby continued to send material to his friend Thomas
Fairchild in Hoxton on the northern edge of the City of London. Fairchild was one of a new
breed of nurserymen specialising in ornamental plants to furnish the gardens of wealthy
clients in and around London – many of whom, of course, also had huge estates elsewhere
in the country. It was Fairchild who created the first deliberate plant hybrid, 'Fairchild's
Mule', a cross between a carnation and a sweet william. Troubled by his experiment in
meddling with God's creation, he left a substantial sum of money on his death for prayers
to be said to protect his soul.

Catesby returned home in 1719, but a syndicate of keen plant enthusiasts sent him back
to the south-east of America, where he lived from 1722 to 1726. On returning once again
to England, he worked for Fairchild and for Christopher Gray of the American Nursery in
Fulham, of whom it was said: 'Mr Gray of Fulham has, for many years, made it his business
to raise and cultivate the plants of America, from whence he has annually fresh supplies, in
order to furnish the curious with what they want … through his industry and skill a greater
variety of American forest trees and shrubs may be seen in his garden than in any other
place in England.'[14] In 1730 Gray and a fellow nurseryman, Robert Furber of Kensington,
both of whom had benefited from the dispersal of Bishop Compton's plants after his
death, issued a *Catalogue of Trees, Shrubs, Plants and Flowers by a Society of Gardeners*. The
catalogue was widely distributed on both sides of the Atlantic.

While working for Fairchild and Gray, Catesby taught himself the art of engraving. He
engraved his own plates and supervised their colouring for his mammoth *Natural History of
Carolina, Florida and the Bahama Islands*, published in parts between 1730 and 1747. Over
170 new plant species were illustrated, together with birds, butterflies and small animals.
Financial support for the venture came from the London draper Peter Collinson (1694–
1768), whose interest in plants was thus aroused. On completion of the work, Collinson

An engraving of London draper Peter Collinson, who imported boxes of plants collected by John Bartram and distributed them to an impressive network of subscribers.

wrote to the Swedish botanist Linnaeus, 'Catesby's noble work is finished.'[15]

In order to see the work finished, Collinson had to find correspondents in the colonies who would send fresh specimens of the plants Catesby wanted to illustrate. Through other friends he was introduced to John Custis, a prominent planter and great gardener from Virginia. Letters, plants, seeds and bulbs flowed between the two men – dubbed by Collinson 'Brothers of the Spade' – from 1734 to 1746. In 1737 Collinson wrote to introduce Custis to 'a down right plain country man', a fellow Quaker, John Bartram (1699–1777).[16] Custis in fact already knew Bartram, a farmer turned botanist, having been introduced to him in Philadelphia in 1734. Bartram had established a botanic garden in 1728 and collected extensively along the east coast from New York to Florida. An agreement was reached whereby Bartram would send Collinson consignments of a hundred plants each, for which Collinson paid five guineas. Collinson then distributed the plants to a network of subscribers including the dukes of Richmond, Norfolk, Bedford and Marlborough, the earls of Bute, Leicester, Jersey and Lincoln, Philip Miller at the Chelsea Physic Garden, and Lord Robert Petre, a passionate collector of trees who died at just 30 in 1743. On Lord Petre's death there was a scramble for his plants, the majority going to the dukes of Bedford and Richmond, but some were taken by his gardener, James Gordon, who set up a nursery in Mile End, east of London. The 3rd Duke of Argyll also used Collinson's services to furnish his estates in Whitton in Middlesex and Argyll in Scotland. 'Duke John, the planter' was obsessed with collecting unusual trees. On his death in 1761 many of his young trees were lifted from the Whitton garden by Lord Bute and transferred to the Princess of Wales's new botanic garden at Kew.

John Bartram, a farmer turned botanist who collected extensively along the east coast of America from New York to Florida. He was considered by Linnaeus to be 'the greatest natural botanist in the world'.

Bartram also corresponded with Philip Miller (1691–1771), curator of the Chelsea Physic Garden and author of the weighty *Gardeners' Dictionary* of 1731. Miller was appointed curator of the moribund garden by Sir Hans Sloane in 1722 and stayed in post until a year before his death. He engaged in a vast international correspondence and read papers at meetings of the Royal Society on the cultivation of coconuts, sugar, coffee and cocoa. He also trained many influential gardener/botanists including Joseph Banks (1743–1820), who financed and took part in Captain Cook's voyage to the Southern Continent, William Aiton (1731–1793), who became director of the Royal Botanic Gardens at Kew, and William Forsyth (1737–1804), who succeeded Miller as curator at Chelsea and who, thanks to his 'invention' of 'Forsyth's Plaister', which miraculously restored ancient and hollow trees to full health so they could be used to build ships for the navy, was appointed royal botanist to George III.

Benjamin Franklin (1706–1790) was another of Bartram's many friends. Like so many of his contemporaries Franklin was a man of many parts: author, newspaper proprietor, politician, Postmaster General to the Crown, diplomat and scientist, perhaps best known for his pioneering studies on electricity. He sought to define a society in which Americans would direct their energies to supporting thrift, hard work, education and the development of self-governing institutions in contrast to the political and religious authoritarianism of Europe. A friend of both Bartram in Philadelphia and Collinson in London (who sent him papers from the Royal Society on English experiments with electricity), in 1785 he encouraged the establishment of the Philadelphia Society for Promoting Agriculture. This in turn led to the founding in 1827 of the Pennsylvania Horticultural Society, America's second oldest horticultural society after Massachusetts. Franklin is commemorated in a beautiful small tree with fragrant white flowers, *Franklinia alatamaha*, discovered by John Bartram's sons John and William during a plant hunting expedition to Georgia in 1765 funded by the London physician Dr John Fothergill. It was named by William in honour of 'that Patron of sciences and truly great and distinguished character, Dr. Benjamin Franklin', and a good friend of William's late father.[17] Seeds were collected by the Bartrams in 1773–6, fortunately, because the plant – known only from one small location – subsequently became extinct in the wild.

In 1765 Peter Collinson persuaded the king to appoint Bartram senior as Botaniser Royal in America, at a salary of £50 a year, a post which he held until 1776 when relations between the king and his colonies were at a very low ebb. In the 1770s the Dutch nurseryman Conrad Loddiges also corresponded with Bartram, introducing many American plants from his Hackney nursery in east London. Bartram, described by Linnaeus as the greatest natural botanist in the world, died in 1777, his death perhaps accelerated by fears of what would happen to his garden in the war, but his sons John and William continued his work, enriching English gardens by their explorations.

By the late eighteenth century, with transatlantic communications increasingly frequent and reliable, a network of botanists, nurserymen and collectors had evolved between America and Europe with Bartram, Collinson and Miller at the centre of the web, and Linnaeus giving the communicants a new international language with his binomial system identifying each plant by genus and species.

4
An English paradise

⌒⌒

T HE RAPID GROWTH OF INTEREST in American plants was paralleled almost exactly
by dramatic changes in the English gardens for which those plants were destined and
in the English landscape in its broadest political and social sense. This was the Age of
Enlightenment. In his 1730 'Epitaph intended for Sir Isaac Newton' Alexander Pope, the
witty and perceptive poet, essayist, classicist and gardener, wrote:

> Nature and Nature's laws lay hid in night:
> God said, Let Newton be! and all was light.

Isaac Newton's studies of light, motion, gravitation and mathematics, together with the
work of many other outstanding minds in Europe as a whole, formed the foundations of
modern science and cast a new light on the understanding of nature: no longer a fierce
assembly of gods holding human fate in their hands but a series of laws susceptible to
investigation and to human reason. In aesthetic terms Nature became a beautiful woman,
and the duty of a gentleman was, in the words of Horace Walpole, son of England's first
prime minister, to dress and adorn Nature as she deserved.

Science also extended its methods to the land. The Enclosure Acts – which replaced the
old open field system operating since before Norman times in much of lowland England
by a new pattern of enclosed fields over which manorial tenants had permanent control –
resulted in dramatic changes to the landscape and to society. In the old system, manorial
lands suitable for farming were divided into three large open fields, divided into long,
narrow strips to which tenants had access on a shifting basis. The fields were farmed in
rotation, being left fallow for two years in three to recover their fertility. There was no
guarantee that tenants would return to the same strips in the fourth year, no incentive
to work hard to improve the soil, and little opportunity to divert from the traditional
practices of the community as a whole. The less productive parts of manorial lands – the
wetlands, slopes, woods and heaths – were designated as common land, over which the
inhabitants of the manor had certain rights: to graze animals, collect turf or small branches
for fires or building materials, and so on.

In the new enclosed landscape, diligent farmers were able to invest in their lands
knowing that they would reap the benefits of any improvement. The lord of the manor,

who of course had the largest share of the land, was able to reshape it, to drain and plant trees, to recreate his own paradise with the help of Evelyn's *Sylva* and other sources of wisdom. Those at the bottom of the heap, with too little land to support a family and no longer with access to common land, were reduced to abject poverty, working as labourers for others or leaving to find work in the expanding towns. The social effect was bitterly summed up in an anonymous seventeenth-century folk poem:

> What law is this that hangs the man who steals a goose from off the common
> But lets the greater felon loose that steals the common from the goose?

Other changes in farming followed closely on the heels of the enclosures. Charles, 2nd Viscount Townshend at Raynham, in Norfolk, used turnips, long considered coarse food for the poorest members of the peasantry, to feed his sheep. Sheep ate turnip tops in autumn and turnip roots dug out of the ground in the winter, allowing Townshend to keep his sheep alive through the winter months rather than slaughtering them at Michaelmas and salting down the carcasses. Dung and urine from the sheep also improved the soil rather than impoverishing it. Viscount Townshend went down in history with the less than flattering nickname of Turnip Townshend, but his idea marked the beginning of an agricultural revolution.

Fifteen miles away at Holkham on the north Norfolk coast, Thomas Coke used Townshend's system and from it developed the Norfolk four-course rotation, growing wheat (a demanding crop) in the first year, folding sheep on turnips to allow the soil to recover in the second year, sowing the somewhat less demanding oats or barley in the third year, then sowing ryegrass and clover on which cattle could feed in the fourth year. Dung and urine from the cows, the dense fibrous roots of the ryegrass and nitrogen-fixing root nodules of the clover restored the soil to full fertility, allowing the cycle to start again with wheat. Coke also employed the women on his estate to spread baskets of marl – a heavy, alkaline clay – on Holkham's sandy soil to improve its structure. He employed local children to gather seeds of the better grasses to improve his pastures and planted pines on the coastal dunes to stabilize them, then converted the land between the dunes and the old coastline to sheep grazing, adding large new areas to his estate. In these and many other ways landowners throughout a great swathe of central and southern England improved their estates, dramatically increased their yields, increased the rents on tenanted farms and thus greatly increased their wealth.

Another major influence on the eighteenth-century English landscape was the Grand Tour. Among the aristocracy and gentry it was normal practice for boys to have a private tutor and to receive a classical education in which they would read, in Greek and Latin, of the political and cultural achievements of the ancient Greeks and Romans in evolving democratic societies and of their escapes from the intrigues and power struggles of politics into the simple rural life described by Virgil in his *Eclogues*. That education would be rounded off by the Grand Tour, sometimes lasting two or three years, to the Low Countries, to France, but especially to Italian city-states such as Florence and Rome. Here young men saw the remains of noble classical buildings among the ageing villas of fifteenth- and sixteenth-century Italy, set in dramatic landscapes. The villas were modelled on the mathematical proportions set out in Andrea Palladio's *Four Books on Architecture*, first published in 1570 and translated into English by Giacomo Leoni in 1716–20. The effect of these experiences on young and impressionable minds is difficult to imagine in our modern age of mass tourism, but many returned to England laden with works of art, sketchbooks and diaries and a determination to recreate something of the splendour they had seen in Italy on their own estates. The result was a revolution in taste.

In the late seventeenth century of post-Restoration England, France had been the model of a civilized and cultured existence. The English gardens created by the Brompton Park nurseries of London and Wise and depicted in the engravings of Kip and Knyff were Versailles in miniature. By the end of the century England and France were at war again, the Nine Years' War of 1689–97 being followed after a brief period of calm by the War of Spanish Succession (1702–14). The French-inspired garden had never fitted comfortably into the English landscape: English avenues of newly planted trees rose and fell over the undulating and largely treeless terrain of lowland England, and the impressive vistas which were such a symbol of the king's absolute power at Versailles were obscured, sometimes obliterated, in England by the often misty atmosphere.

With the appointment by Parliament of William and Mary as king and queen of England in 1688, any notion of a king appointed by divine right was finally dead. On William's death in 1702, leaving no heir, Mary's sister Anne came to the throne. On Anne's death in 1714, with all 17 of her children dying before her and with Parliament debarring Catholics from the Crown, a cousin, George Louis of Brunswick-Lüneburg, became king. As George I spoke no English and spent more time in Hanover than in England, power shifted more or less completely to Parliament, headed by the first prime minister, Robert Walpole (1676–1745), and to the aristocracy. Thus, by the turn of the century the ageing French-inspired garden was not only impractical and a product of the older generation, it was undemocratic. Anthony Ashley-Cooper, 3rd Earl of Shaftesbury, encapsulated the feelings of the young English milord when he spoke of the 'formal mockery of [French] princely gardens' versus the 'liberty of wit' which would enable

English trees to grow in their natural forms and in irregular groups rather than being dragooned into clipped avenues.[18]

Charles Bridgeman (1690–1738) began the transition from the grandiose symmetrical gardens inspired by France to the freer lines of the English landscape garden. The main lines of his designs were long, often very long, avenues but these were not symmetrically arranged. Instead, they were directed to key points in the landscape, to distant prospects and to high or low points within the garden. Bridgeman is most noted, though, for his introduction of the 'ha-ha', the sunken boundary wall or fosse (ditch) which enabled the eye to roam out into the park and distant countryside but prevented sheep, cattle and deer from coming into the garden and eating the new shrubs and trees. In Horace Walpole's words, Bridgeman's successor William Kent 'lept the fence and found that all nature was a garden', but it was Bridgeman who lowered the fence so that the somewhat corpulent Kent could make that momentous leap.[19] The effect of these and later eighteenth-century changes in the English garden was to blur the boundary between garden, park, farm and distant landscape and to foster admiration of Dame Nature.

In 1719, the year in which Mark Catesby returned to England after his first visit to Virginia, Richard Boyle, 3rd Earl of Burlington, returned from Italy with a young protégé, William Kent (1685–1748). On this (his third) Grand Tour, Lord Burlington used the volumes of Andrea Palladio's *Four Books on Architecture* that he carried with him to interpret what he saw of the Italian Renaissance, and he returned to England a devout disciple of Palladian architecture. William Kent was born in Bridlington, in Yorkshire. He was a painter, albeit mainly a decorator of coaches with family crests and cartouches. In 1710 he was sent by three patrons to study in Italy. There he progressed from painting to the study of architecture and, in his 10 years in Italy, became a guide, an adviser and agent to many of the young aristocrats visiting Italy for shorter periods on their Grand Tour. Burlington brought Kent back to England to advise on the interiors of Burlington House in Piccadilly, and in 1726–9 the two men collaborated at Chiswick, a little village to the west of London where Burlington designed his Palladian villa and Kent decorated the house with his paintings, designed furniture, and created a garden of numerous vistas terminating with his garden buildings and with statues, obelisks and other focal points bearing classical resonance. It was a garden of great 'sensibilities'. Viewing his obelisk reflected in a pool one moonlit night, Kent was so transfixed by the spirit of the place that he was unable to move until dawn broke the spell. The fact that he was an avid student of Italian wines had no bearing on the situation, of course.

It was also in 1719 that another Burlington protégé, the poet, classicist and self-styled 'gardenist' Alexander Pope, began his classically inspired garden on the Thames at

Twickenham. Pope the poet and Kent the painter wielded huge influence in the evolution of what became the English landscape garden, and Pope distilled the spirit of the new age in his 1731 'Epistle to the Earl of Burlington', in which he advised all who would hear to 'consult the genius of the place in all, that tells the waters or [whether] to rise or fall'. We should not, as the French do, he implied, make paper plans and then bring in the army to make the plans fit on the ground but let the spirit of the landscape direct our designs.

Kent went on to design gardens for other aristocrats, many of them members of Burlington's Society of Dilettanti, followers of Palladio. He designed Coke's new house at Holkham, a palace to contain the many treasures brought back from Italy. At Rousham in Oxfordshire he added wings to General Dormer's Elizabethan house to accommodate his patron's large collection of Italian bronzes, and superimposed on Charles Bridgeman's axial design of the garden his own didactic landscape in which the visitor was presented in turn with classical scenes reminiscent of Italy and scenes of an Arcadian English landscape: views of a dozen church spires and the little river Cherwell 'purling' under an ancient stone bridge over which droves of cattle, ladies in fine carriages, gentlemen on fine horses and carts lumbering to market passed in a regular procession. Linking the statue by the great Flemish sculptor Scheemakers of a lion devouring a horse, another of a dying gladiator, a Temple of the Echo and an octagonal pool with a cold bath house, there were green walks where, in the words of Dormer's gardener John Macclary, 'their [sic] you see the deferant sorts of Flowers, peeping through the deferant sorts of Evergreens, here you think the Laurel produces a Rose, the Holly a Syringa [Philadelphus or mock orange], the Yew a Lilac, and the sweet Honeysuckle is peeping out from under every Leafe, in short they are so mixt together than youd think every Leafe of the Evergreens, produced one flower or a nother.'[20]

From Rousham William Kent moved on to Stowe in Buckinghamshire, again embellishing a severely axial Bridgeman landscape with a plethora of symbolic temples and statues. Horace Walpole, whose father represented the enemy in Stowe's fiercely political landscape, later suggested that the garden would be twice as good if it had half the number of temples, but Kent created a landscape to suit his Whig patron, Lord Cobham, and his 'Company of Patriots', determined to fight what they saw as the increasing oppression and corruption of Walpole's Tory government.[21]

At Rousham the viewer oscillated between the classical and the Arcadian. At Stowe the two cultures fused. At the lower end of his Elysian Fields, a small valley near the house with an 'ancient' river Styx flowing from the underworld (a grotto at the upper end of the valley), Kent designed his Temple of British Worthies, a long, curved arcade populated with the busts of great soldiers, politicians, poets and philosophers – all Whigs, of course.

As the visitor's eye roamed across this panoply of worthies, it continued across the river Styx to a Temple of Ancient Virtue, a classical rotunda inhabited by four figures from the classical Greek world: the poet Homer, the philosopher Socrates, the soldier Epaminondas and the lawgiver Lycurgus. By turning to Greece for its inspiration the message was clear: we have recreated the grandeur which was the great republic of Rome before it became a tyrannical empire. The only difference is that Rome lasted a mere thousand years. England will last for ever.

It was at Stowe that Lancelot Brown (1716–1783) really began his meteoric career. Born in Northumberland and apprenticed in the large scale transformation of the landscape on the estate of the local landowner, Sir William Lorraine of Kirkharle, Brown travelled south, first to Lincolnshire, where he was involved in some of the drainage schemes in East Anglia, and then in 1741 to Stowe. 'Capability' was a nickname given to Brown late in his life, resulting from his remarks to his many patrons that their estates had capabilities for improvement, but 'Capability' also applied in large measure to Brown himself. He arrived at Stowe as a gardener – with letters of introduction from Lady Lorraine – but soon rose to a position of authority, implementing the designs of William Kent and showing the new gardens to an international stream of important visitors. In the latter stages of his time at Stowe, with Kent increasingly absent, Brown and his employer, Lord Cobham, continued to work on the gardens together, most notably in the Grecian Valley to the north-east of the house. Cobham had intended to create another lake, but it proved impossible to hold water on the site, so Brown moulded the land into gentle undulations topped with trees which seemed to accentuate the depth of the valley, an effect much praised 40 years later by an American visitor, Thomas Jefferson.

After Kent's death in 1748 and Lord Cobham's in 1749, Brown decided it was time to move on. In 1751 he moved to the small Thames-side village of Hammersmith and began an independent career as an architect, although it was for his transformation of the extensive landscapes as sublime settings for the house that he was, and remains, much better known. His practice was vast: 80 known commissions, many of those many thousands of acres in extent, and many more where he is reputed to have worked. He reshaped hills, rerouted or created lakes and rivers, and planted millions of trees. At one of his earliest commissions, Croome in Warwickshire, he remodelled the house and transformed the low marshy ground into undulating parkland watered by a new serpentine river. His patron Lord Coventry said of Brown that he consulted his purse as well as his taste so as not to bankrupt him. At Blenheim, the Duke of Marlborough's great estate in Oxfordshire, where Sir John Vanbrugh and London and Wise's Brompton Park Nursery had created the nearest English equivalent to Versailles, the formal gardens were swept away and the little river Glyme which flowed under Vanbrugh's great bridge was dammed to create the two majestic lakes which survive today. At Claremont, not far from Hampton Court in Surrey, Brown demolished the old house, built anew on rising ground and transformed the muddled landscape into a serene park for the fabulously wealthy Lord Clive of India. Brown worked on some of his commissions for many years, even decades. In 1783, that all-important date in American history, Brown was returning to his London home after dinner with his early patron Lord Coventry when he collapsed in the street and died. Coventry placed a stone casket beside Brown's lake at Croome with the inscription:

> To the Memory of
> Lancelot Brown
> Who by the powers of
> His inimitable
> And creative genius
> Formed this garden scene
> Out of a morass.

Despite, or perhaps because of, Brown's remarkable success he has often been attacked. Sir William Chambers wrote of a country (England) 'where peasants emerge from the melon grounds to commence professors', and he complained that 'the ax has often, in one day, laid waste the growth of several ages; and thousands of venerable plants, whole woods of them, have been swept away, to make room for a little grass, and a few American weeds.'[22] Later critics of Brown's work assume that his mature landscapes of lofty trees represent his original designs, overlooking the fact that the more intricate elements of his more ephemeral plantings have long since disappeared. An otherwise splendid garden history exhibition at the Victoria and Albert Museum in 1979 devoted only one small panel to Brown, denigrating his work as 'an aberration lasting only half a century, depriving the English of the sort of complicated flowery garden that they love. *Le Jardin anglais* refers to the time, when the English lost their heads and scrapped their gardens.' There were, though, many more supporters than enemies.

In his characteristically flippant manner Horace Walpole wrote to the Countess of Upper Ossory to tell her of Brown's death: 'Your dryads must go into black gloves, Madam, their father-in-law, Lady Nature's second husband, is dead!'[23] The epitaph on Brown's tombstone at Fenstanton in Cambridgeshire, however, conveys more fittingly the qualities of England's most famous landscape gardener as a designer and as a man.

Ye sons of elegance, who truly taste
The simple charms that genuine art supplies,
Come from the sylvan scene, his genius grac'd
And offer here your tributary sighs
But know that more than genius slumbers here.
Virtues were his, which arts best powers transcend.
Come, ye superior train, who these revere
And weep the Christian, Husband, Father, Friend.

The result of these changes throughout the eighteenth century was the creation of expansive parks, often covering thousands or tens of thousands of acres, planted with shelter belts, copses and woodlands following Evelyn's advice, facilitating the aristocratic pursuit of hunting, and fostering a great surge in demand for trees and shrubs, native and exotic. In reality, of course, collecting new plants and reshaping extensive landscapes went on in parallel. Lord Bute (1713–1792), a distinguished amateur botanist, tutor to the Prince of Wales (the future George III) and his brother Edward, and adviser to their mother, Princess Augusta, at Kew, introduced exotics and rare local plants from the downland around his seaside house at Highcliffe, near Christchurch in Hampshire. Brown was consulted for the landscape at Highcliffe and for Bute's principal seat at Luton Hoo in Bedfordshire. For noble families town gardens and the pleasure gardens near the country house gave scope for collections of the latest introductions from America, while the view expanded across the ha-ha to a panorama of an idealized English landscape. With new editions of Evelyn's *Sylva* preaching the importance of tree planting and an increasing flow of nursery catalogues offering plants from a distant paradise, young men of substance set out to create a new Garden of Eden in their English parks.

5

An American Eden

PROMISES OF A SECOND GARDEN OF EDEN also featured large in promotional material encouraging settlers to the colonies. In 1732 George II granted land to James Oglethorpe to found a new colony of Georgia to settle debtors, religious refugees and others. Each settler received a 60 × 90 ft plot, a 5-acre garden and a 44-acre farm. The central city, Savannah, was built in wards, each of which had a central open space, a pattern which survived into the mid-nineteenth century.

By the mid-eighteenth century Williamsburg in Virginia and Charleston in South Carolina were important centres of botanical knowledge. Tobacco was grown along the James River in Virginia and rice and indigo around Charleston, creating enormous wealth – much of which was expended in building large mansions and planting elaborate gardens. Middleton Place in Charleston, South Carolina, was designed by George Newman, who was brought from England by Henry Middleton in 1741. With its 40 acres of gardens it employed a hundred slaves for 10 years in its construction. The gardens have since been restored by Middleton's descendants.

Farther north, in common with changes in England, taste evolved towards a more democratic landscape – a landscape of liberty. This evolution was greatly influenced by two of America's future presidents, George Washington (1732–1799) and Thomas Jefferson (1743–1826).

The American 'Farmer George', George Washington – later to do battle with the English 'Farmer George', King George III – was a keen and intelligent gardener as well as the owner of five farms along the Potomac River in Virginia. He visited Bartram in Philadelphia and a new nursery established by William Prince in Flushing, New Jersey. He owned a copy of Batty Langley's *New Principles of Gardening* of 1728, an early and remarkable book advocating the new style of garden with groves of trees penetrated by intestinal writhings of paths. Also at hand was a catalogue from Lee and Kennedy's Vineyard Nursery, one of England's most important nurseries. Washington owned Claude Lorrain landscape engravings and was thoroughly in tune with the newly fashionable ideas of the Picturesque, scenes of which were readily at hand in the wilder landscape which surrounded him.

From 1761 until his death he planned his 500-acre landscape garden as the core of his 8,000-acre Mount Vernon estate, latterly while fighting for and achieving independence for his country and becoming its first president. The summit of the highest point was levelled to create a site for the house with its veranda looking down to the river. On the other side of the house a circular drive circuited a lawn and connected with twin serpentine drives framing a large, bell-shaped green, thus neatly combining the symmetry of a French parterre with the looser freedom of the English landscape garden. On either side of the green were enclosed flower and vegetable gardens. In 1794, when president of the United States, Washington arranged for his secretary, Tobias Lear, to send him six varieties of gooseberry, red, white and black currants, two types of apple, four of pear, three of plum, three cherries, apricots and nectarines as well as almonds from London. Mount Vernon, though, was not imported wholesale from the Old World. The wildernesses and enclosing tree belts of the garden were planted largely with native trees – robinia, maple, sassafras, magnolia, dogwood, hemlock, elm and many others.

Thomas Jefferson, like Washington, was a polymath very much in tune with the Age of Enlightenment. Educated in the classics by tutors and at a local school, a talented player of the violin and cello with a keen interest in scientific agriculture and gardening, Jefferson began his 'Garden Book' in 1766, at the age of 23. In it he listed and described in meticulous detail his successes and failures with fruits, vegetables and flowers. On the death of his father in 1757 he inherited the 5,000-acre estate of Monticello, the 'little mountain'. In 1764, at 21, his inheritance was complete, and in 1768 he began work on a new house, moving into the partially completed building in 1770. The guiding light of his building works was Andrea Palladio, the model favoured by liberty-loving Whigs in England, and it was set in a naturalistic landscape expressing the liberty of free-growing trees. Here Jefferson could beat the English because the setting of his house was truly and naturally sublime.

Jefferson's interests lay in scientific farming and gardening, but his career was as a lawyer. After two years of mathematics, metaphysics and philosophy at the College of William and Mary from the age of 16, he studied law and was called to the bar in 1767. As a lawyer and landowner he was drawn into the politics of the increasingly independence-minded colonies and became a leader in their bid for freedom from a dominating and domineering Britain. He was the primary author of the Declaration of Independence and was appointed as the Virginia delegate to the Continental Congress. When victory was finally recognized by the Treaty of Versailles in 1783 and George Washington was elected as first president of the new United States, Jefferson and his friends Benjamin Franklin and John Adams were sent by Washington to Paris to negotiate trade agreements with England, France and Spain. Ironically, he revelled in the culture of a nation long subject to an autocratic monarch but one which was soon to undergo its own revolution.

In 1786 Jefferson wrote from France to John Bartram junior in Philadelphia with a long list of plants and seeds 'which I should be very glad to obtain from America for a friend here whom I wish much to oblige'.[24] While enjoying the cultural life of Paris, he was urged by John Adams to travel to London to negotiate a treaty with Portugal. Jefferson admired France but much preferred English gardens so, taking advantage of this official visit, on 1 April and with his copy of Thomas Whateley's *Observations on Modern Gardening* (1770), he began a tour of English gardens. He found Whateley of enormous benefit: 'While his descriptions, in point of style, are models of perfect elegance and classical correctness, they are as remarkable for their exactness.'[25] Perhaps part of his enthusiasm came from the fact that Whateley had earlier published a pamphlet protesting at the injustice of taxing the colonies.

Jefferson's visits included Chiswick, Hampton Court and Pope's Twickenham (all near London), Claremont and the neighbouring garden of Esher Place, Painshill and Wooburn in Surrey, Stowe – the most famous of all the gardens of that period – and neighbouring Wotton, William Shenstone's *ferme ornée* at The Leasowes near Halesowen in the West Midlands, Capability Brown's masterpiece at Blenheim in Oxfordshire, and, back in the vicinity of London, Kew. Jefferson clearly had in mind gathering information on design and maintenance expenses for his own estate at Monticello, and although he considered England far superior to all other countries in gardening his comments were not entirely flattering.

Of Chiswick, the fount of William Kent's new style of gardening for Lord Burlington, 'A garden of about six acres; – the octagon dome has an ill effect, both within and without: the garden shows still too much of art. An obelisk of very ill effect; another in the middle of a pond useless.' His account book records: 'April 2, gave servants at Chiswick 4/6 [4*s*. 6*d*. or 22½ pence].' Hampton Court was 'Old fashioned. Clipt yews grown wild.' At Twickenham the account of Pope's garden is entirely descriptive with no comment. Perhaps it was too important a monument to the English landscape garden to admit criticism.

Esher Place clearly made a favourable impression. Here William Kent had been 'Kentissimi' to his patron Henry Pelham, younger brother of the Duke of Newcastle at nearby Claremont: 'The house in a bottom near the river; on the other side the ground rises pretty much … On the left the ground descends. Clumps of trees [the result of Brown's later work at Esher Place], the clumps on each hand balance finely – a most lovely mixture of concave and convex.' At neighbouring Claremont, however, where William Kent succeeded Charles Bridgeman, 'Lord Clive's. Nothing remarkable.'

Painshill, the ill-fated garden created by Charles Hamilton, who then had to sell it to pay his debts, 'Paynshill – Mr. Hopkins … Well described by Whately [*sic*]. Grotto said to have cost £7,000 … there is too much evergreen. The dwelling-house built by Hopkins, ill-situated: he has not been there in five years. He lived there four years while building the present house. It is not finished; its architecture is incorrect. A Doric temple, beautiful.'

Stowe received a lengthy but mixed review. Perhaps his response was a purely visual one, as the Whig sentiment which the garden displayed at every turn should have recommended it to this particular visitor more than to most:

Fifteen men and eighteen boys employed in keeping the pleasure grounds. Within the walk are considerable portions separated by enclosures and used for pasture … Kent's building is called the temple of Venus. The enclosure is entirely by ha-ha. At each end of the front line there is a recess like the bastion of a fort. In one of these is the temple of Friendship, in the other the temple of Venus. They are seen the one from the other, the line of sight passing, not through the garden, but through the country parallel to the line of the garden. This has a good effect … In the approach to Stowe, you are brought a mile through a straight avenue, pointing to the Corinthian arch and to the house, till you get to the arch, then you turn short to the right. The straight approach is very ill. The Corinthian arch has a very useless appearance, inasmuch as it has no pretension to any destination. Instead of being an object from the house, it is an obstacle to a very pleasing distant prospect. The Grecian valley [one of Brown's contributions to Stowe during his time as gardener] being clear of trees, while the hill on each side is covered with them, is much deepened to appearance.

Here the servants were paid 8*s.* (40 pence).

The Leasowes, the highly influential *ferme ornée* created by the poet William Shenstone, has a salutary message. 'One hundred and fifty acres within the walk. The waters small. This is not even an ornamented farm – it is only a grazing farm with a path round it, here and there a seat of board, rarely anything better. Architecture has contributed nothing … Shenstone had but three hundred pounds a year, and ruined himself by what he did to this farm. It is said that he died of the heart-aches which his debts occasioned him.' However, 'The first and second cascades are beautiful. The landscape at number eighteen, and prospect at thirty-two [of Whateley's descriptive itinerary], are fine. The walk through the wood is umbrageous and pleasing.' Jefferson himself also spent more than he could afford on his library and gardens, and struggled with debt during the latter part of his life.

The review of Blenheim, like that of Stowe, is lengthy but again mixed:

Twenty-five hundred acres, of which two hundred is garden, one hundred and fifty water, twelve kitchen garden and the rest park. Two hundred people employed to keep it in order … About fifty of these employed in pleasure grounds. The turf is mowed once in ten days … The water here is very beautiful, and very grand [again

Brown's handiwork]. The cascade from the lake, a fine one; except this the garden has no great beauties. It is not laid out in fine lawns and woods, but the trees are scattered thinly over the ground, and every here and there small thickets of shrubs, in oval raised beds, cultivated, and flowers among the shrubs. The gravelled walks are broad – art appears too much. There are but few seats in it, and nothing of architecture more dignified. There is no one striking position in it.

On completion of his tour Jefferson called in at the Vineyard Nursery to order plants for a French friend in Tours. In 1774 Lee and Kennedy had published a 76-page catalogue of plants available at the Vineyard. John Claudius Loudon, the landscape gardener and prolific writer, described the nursery in 1822 as 'unquestionably the finest nursery in Britain, or rather the world', and Loudon was very well informed on gardening worldwide.[26]

Armed with his impressions of the most notable English gardens, on his return to Monticello Jefferson set about the improvement of his own estate with renewed vigour but with increased obstacles. In 1801 he was elected third president of the young republic, and in 1804 he was re-elected with a huge majority. President Jefferson, like Washington before him and perhaps inspired by his classical studies of Virgil and the other ancients, saw the ideal future of the country as a nation of farmers – in contrast to the crowded industrial cities of England or the narrow, mob-ridden streets of the Paris which he had hoped to see transformed from a dictatorial monarchy to an egalitarian republic. Circumstances would overpower that vision, but Jefferson instigated a national grid of 36-square-mile townships subdivided into 160-acre quarters to facilitate rapid settlement of vast tracts of farmland.

Jefferson, too, successfully lobbied Congress to fund the Corps of Discovery Expedition of Meriwether Lewis and William Clark to cross the continent. The primary objectives of the mission were to survey the Louisiana Purchase, 828,000 square miles of land forming the middle third of the continental United States bought from France for 15 million dollars, and to find and map a passage to the west coast. The mission was planned at the Philadelphia home of Bernard McMahon, the son of an Irish nurseryman who had come to America in 1796 to start his own business as a nurseryman and seedsman. The Corps succeeded in their mission, making many scientific observations in the process and bringing back many new plants, most of which the president passed on to Bartram and McMahon to propagate and distribute. In 1806 McMahon published *The American Gardener's Calendar*, an influential book for the next 50 years with its advice on good taste and a catalogue of 3,700 plants, half of them from America.

While shaping a new nation, Jefferson found time in 1802 to ask John Bartram junior to send seeds to the Agricultural Society of Paris. In 1805 he added to a book order from

London Thomas Knight's *On the Culture of the Apple & Pear, Cider and Perry* of 1801. Thomas Knight was the younger brother of Richard Payne Knight, the fierce critic of Capability Brown and champion of the Picturesque. In 1807 Jefferson was awarded a gold medal by the Agricultural Society of Paris for his design of the mouldboard plough.

In July 1808, in anticipation of his impending retirement from office and with plans to devote himself to his garden, he wrote a lengthy letter to his friend William Hamilton of Philadelphia, who, like Jefferson, was an accomplished botanist and horticulturist and a friend of John Bartram. Unlike Hamilton, though, whose garden was more a collection of plants than a coherent landscape, Jefferson's botanical interests were subservient to his aesthetic ambitions. In his letter he spoke of the difficulty of adopting the English landscape garden to his Monticello estate and of his strategy for overcoming the difficulties:

Having decisively made up my mind for retirement at the end of my present term, my views and attentions are all turned homewards … The grounds which I destine to improve in the style of the English gardens are in a form very difficult to be managed. They compose the northern quadrant of a mountain of about 2/3 of its height & then spread for the upper third over its whole crown … The hill is generally too steep for direct ascent, but we make level walks successively along its side, which in its upper part encircle the hill & intersect these again by others of easy ascent in various parts. They are still chiefly in their native woods, which are majestic, and very generally a close undergrowth, which I have not suffered to be touched, knowing how much easier it is to cut away than to fill up … You are sensible that this disposition of the ground takes from me the first beauty in gardening, the variety of hill & dale, & leaves me as an awkward substitute a few hanging hollows & ridges, this subject is so unique and at the same time refractory, that to make a disposition analogous to its character wold [*sic*] require much more of the genius of the landscape painter & gardener than I pretend to.

Jefferson then refers to Hamilton's and his own visits to England:

Thither without doubt we are to go for models in this art. Their sunless climate has permitted them to adopt what is certainly a beauty of the very first order in landscape. Their canvas is of open ground, variegated with clumps of trees distributed with taste. They need no more of wood than will serve to embrace a lawn or a glade. But under the beaming, constant and almost vertical sun of Virginia, shade is our Elysium. In the absence of this no beauty of the eye can be enjoyed … The only substitute I have been able to imagine is this. Let your ground be covered with trees of the loftiest stature. Trim up their bodies as high as the constitution & form of the tree will bear, but so as their tops shall still be united & yield dense shade. A wood, so open below, will have nearly the appearance of open grounds. Then, when in the open ground you would plant a clump of trees, place a thicket of shrubs presenting a hemisphere of crown which shall distinctly show itself under the branches of the trees … The thickets may be varied too by making some of them of evergreens altogether, our red cedar made to grow in a bush, evergreen privet, pyrocanthus [*sic*], Kalmia, Scotch broom. Holly would be elegant but it does not grow in my part of the country.

Apart from the fierce glare of sunlight the Monticello estate had a superabundance of advantages:

Of prospect I have rich profusion and offering itself at every point of the compass. Mountains distinct & near, smooth & shaggy, single & in ridges, a little river hiding itself among the hills so as to show in laggons [*sic*] only, cultivated grounds under the eye and two small villages. To prevent a satiety of this is the principal difficulty. It may be successively offered, & in different portions through vistas, with the advantage of shifting the scene as you advance on your way.[27]

In 1809 Thomas Jefferson left office, as planned, to spend the rest of his life struggling with financial problems, suffering from crippling pains in his arms but working on his estates, and to establish the Central College, later University of Virginia, designing the campus, as ever, with Andrea Palladio as his guiding spirit.

6

Another revolution

T HE LATE EIGHTEENTH CENTURY saw many revolutionary changes in life and in art. The War of Independence in the colonies ran from 1775 to 1783. The French Revolution lasted from 1789 to 1799. England was spared such violent revolution, but a quieter one took place in the realm of building and gardening with the gradual reappraisal of Gothic architecture and the evolution of the Picturesque.

Through the early part of the eighteenth century, when Palladio reigned in aristocratic households, Goths and Vandals were seen as the savage tribes who brought down the Roman empire. 'Gothicism' had the same significance for many people as does 'vandalism' today, and buildings in the Gothic style were constructed in the landscape to shock, to emphasize – by contrast – the noble beauty of their Palladian counterparts. By the middle of the eighteenth century, though, as England's politics were becoming more authoritarian and oppressive in the eyes of the younger generation, the qualities of the Goths were reinterpreted as vigour, hardiness and loving liberty in contrast to the spineless servility of the Latin people. The noble republic of Rome had given way to the despotic empire, and a similar fate seemed possible in England. Sir John Vanbrugh's unsuccessful pleading with the Duchess of Marlborough to keep the remains of the ancient Woodstock Manor and the remarkable multi-turreted and battlemented Vanbrugh Castle in Greenwich which he designed for his own use were early examples of the lively and free expression of architecture in contrast to the prevailing rule of Palladio. The triangular and castellated Gothic Temple at Stowe, designed by James Gibbs in 1741 and dedicated by Lord Cobham 'to the Liberty of our Ancestors', marked a high point of anti-Tory feeling in Cobham's highly charged political landscape.

By the 1770s it became increasingly clear that Palladian buildings, based on Greek and especially Roman antiquity, were pre-Christian, pagan buildings and that the great medieval Gothic cathedrals that adorned every major European city could not be dismissed as the work of savage tribes. They were true Christian buildings with their pointed arches like hands lifted to heaven in prayer. This realization coincided with trading probes into China and India where the early adventurers saw buildings of a very high state of sophistication that were clearly not Palladian. Obviously, Palladio did not possess a monopoly of taste in building.

As these messages gradually sank home, a new generation of landed gentry inherited their fathers' estates. This generation rebelled against the stiff rules of its elders and sought

A sketch from William Gilpin's 'Observations, relative chiefly to Picturesque Beauty, made in the year 1772, on Several Parts of England, particularly the mountains and lakes of Cumberland, and Westmorland', published in 1788.

more freedom of expression. Into this scenario stepped the unlikely figure of William Gilpin (1724–1804), a schoolmaster and curate who spent his summer vacations exploring wilder parts of the British landscape and analysing the suitability of the various scenes as subjects for his sketches. Gilpin coined the term 'Picturesque' to describe those landscapes that gave scope to his pencil, and what gave scope to his pencil were roughness of texture and animation. Tumbling streams, jagged rocks, twisted trees, shaggy sheep or cattle, or perhaps stooped rustic peasants enlivened the picture and helped to differentiate roads (with cattle or carts) from rivers (with boats and cascades). Gilpin was eventually persuaded by his friends to publish his thoughts and sketches. His 'Observations' made in the 1770s – on the river Wye, on the New Forest, on Cumbria and Westmorland – were published a decade later to widespread acclaim.[28] With Europe riven by conflict, it was possible to travel in safety on English roads and to indulge in a Grand Tour of a few days or weeks at very much less expense than two or three years in Rome.

Gilpin's 'Picturesque' was applied by him only to the drawing of natural scenes, but the idea quickly took on a wider significance. If we can travel Britain in search of the

Picturesque, why could we not create such landscapes at home? In 1794 Uvedale Price (1747–1829) published an *Essay on the Picturesque* and Richard Payne Knight (1750–1824) published his long poem *The Landscape*. Both had estates in the rugged terrain of the Welsh borders. Although near neighbours, neither seemed to know of the other's efforts, and acrimony ensued as each sought to establish the priority of his ideas. Both, though, agreed that the real villain was Capability Brown, the 'genius of the bare and bald' who had destroyed the old gardens of England to replace them by vapid lawns and limpid lakes.[29] Brown had died in 1783 so was unaffected by these criticisms, but Knight and Price turned their attacks to the person they saw as Brown's successor, Humphry Repton (1752–1818).

Repton was born in Norfolk, the son of a customs official in Norwich, then an important port. After four years as a young man in Holland to study with a wealthy merchant, Repton tried to meet his father's wishes by becoming a merchant himself. He hated commerce and failed. On his parents' death he used his inheritance in 1778 to lease the manor of Sustead in Norfolk. He became a farmer and lord of the manor, but he could not earn enough to support his wife and daughters. In 1788, five years after Brown's death and with no obvious successor, Repton awoke from troubled sleep and decided to become a landscape gardener, a term which he devised and which combined his love of art and the countryside. He wrote to his many acquaintances informing them of his decision, and commissions started to pour in. He used an ingenious method of conveying his proposals, illustrating the 'before' scene in watercolour on a flap overlying the 'after' on the sheet below. As the flap was lifted, the transformation of the landscape was revealed. His written report and his overlays were bound in red Morocco leather with lettering in gold leaf. The Red Books, as they are known, were proudly displayed in their owners' libraries so that visitors could admire them and seek their own Repton landscape.

Despite a flourishing career as a landscape gardener, Repton was constantly plagued by financial difficulties. He worked as an illustrator, and when his practice declined during the war with France – funded by increasing taxes on the rich – he decided to pull together the general advice from his many Red Books to produce a volume for publication. In all he produced four books which neatly encapsulate the dramatic changes affecting society in general and gardens in particular. His first, *Sketches and Hints on Landscape Gardening*, was supposed to be published in 1792 but was delayed by pressure of work, so it did not appear until 1795 – fortunately, as it enabled Repton to counter the criticism levelled against him by Richard Payne Knight. Repton was deeply hurt by Knight's outburst. He was very much in favour of the ideas encompassed by the Picturesque and had thought of Knight as a friend. In *Sketches and Hints* he described Knight's estate at Downton Castle:

The path … branching in various directions … is occasionally varied and enriched by caves and cells, hovels and covered seats or other buildings in perfect harmony with the wild but pleasing horrors of the scene. Yet, if the same picturesque objects were introduced in the gardens of a villa near the capital or in the tame yet interesting pleasure grounds which I am frequently called upon to decorate they would be as absurd, incongruous and out of character as a Chinese temple from Vauxhall transplanted to the Vale of Downton.[30]

For Repton, the Picturesque had its place but it was not universally appropriate.

By the end of the eighteenth century, plant introductions from North and South America and early introductions from South Africa, Australia, China and India were beginning to flood into the country, but the capacity to absorb these horticultural riches in the progressively smaller landscapes of newly wealthy industrialists who looked to Repton for advice was shrinking. In *Observations on the Theory and Practice of Landscape Gardening* (1803) he wrote: 'A flower garden should be an object detached and distinct from the general scenery of the place … within this enclosure rare plants of every description should be encouraged and a provision made for soil and aspect for every different class. The flower garden, except when it is annexed to the house, should not be visible from the roads or walks about the place. It may therefore be of a character totally different from the rest of the scenery, and its decorations should be as much those of art as of nature.'[31]

Repton's solution to the problem of too many flowers was to conceal enclosed gardens within the tree clumps of the park so that 'rare plants of every description' could be cultivated in specially adapted soils and without impinging on the wider landscape.[32] He suggested rose gardens, fern gardens, American gardens (by which he meant gardens with wet, peaty soils suitable for azaleas, kalmias and other lime-hating American plants) and geometrical flower gardens. He was often verbose, sometimes tediously so, in the explanation of his ideas. He argued that, if we want our landscapes to look completely natural, we should live not in a house but in a cave or underground. As we like to live in houses, the house should meet the landscape on equal terms, using an architectural terrace attached to the house and therefore appropriately laid out as a flower garden.

The other remarkable point of his advice is that, on the terrace and in the concealed flower garden, 'its decorations should be as much those of art as of nature.'[33] Throughout the eighteenth century it had been widely accepted that all art consists of a study of nature with an implied suggestion that the nearer to nature one came, the more artistic was the achievement. Repton began to suggest that art and nature were in some way different. By 'nature' he meant the carefully dressed nature of the landscape park, but a separation had begun.

His third book was *Inquiry into the Changes of Taste in Landscape Gardening* (1806), in which he began by tracing the history of the English garden from the monastery, through the grandeur of the Elizabethan age to gardens inspired by France and Italy and finally to the 'modern' landscape garden. He then went on: 'After tracing the various past changes of taste in gardening and architecture I cannot suppress my opinion that we are on the eve of some great future change in both these arts, in consequence of our having lately become acquainted with the scenery and buildings in the interior provinces of India.'[34]

By 1806 there was regular trade with India. The East India Company received its charter from Queen Elizabeth I in 1600 and by 1757 was effectively in control of the subcontinent. Company employees spent many years amassing fortunes in trade, legal and less legal, but by the end of the eighteenth century accounts of travel in India and drawings of Indian palaces and temples – magnificent, exotic but picturesque in semi-decay – were widely circulated. Repton argued that while a Palladian house could sit comfortably on a smooth, grassy hill, something as exotic as an Indian palace demanded a more exotic setting. At Sezincote in Gloucestershire, he worked with Thomas Daniels, the most accomplished illustrator of Indian buildings, to advise Charles Cockerell, returned from trading in India, and his brother, the architect Samuel Pepys Cockerell, to create a picturesque 'Thornery', a small valley crossed by a bridge guarded by Brahmin bulls and protected by a three-headed serpent made of lead. The Prince Regent saw Sezincote on his way from Warwick to London and commissioned John Nash (who ousted Repton after initial plans were discussed) to design his fantasy palace: the Royal Pavilion overlooking the sea at Brighton.

In 1811 Repton was badly injured when his carriage overturned while he was escorting his daughters back from a ball. He never fully recovered and was increasingly confined to a wheelchair. In *Fragments on the Theory and Practice of Landscape Gardening* (1816) he explained, rather wistfully, 'Having so long dedicated the active part of my professional career to increasing the enjoyment of *rural* scenery for others, my own infirmities have lately taught me how the solace of *garden* scenery and *garden* delights may be extended a little further when the power of walking fails.'[35]

A later edition of *Fragments* shows Repton in his wheelchair being pushed through an arch of trained fruit so that he could see, smell and taste the fruit, while a gardener climbed over a raised bed of strawberries with his watering pot, the fruits hanging at wheelchair height for Repton to pick – perhaps the first example of horticultural therapy. Repton died in 1818.

7
A collector extraordinary

Throughout the latter part of the eighteenth century and into the nineteenth, Sir Joseph Banks, an immensely wealthy man devoted to natural history, appointed himself as adviser to the dowager Princess Augusta at Kew after the death of Lord Bute. Banks had accompanied Captain James Cook on his voyage to the southern hemisphere from 1768 to 1771 and funded the expedition. A second expedition was planned, but Banks's ambitions were so great that the impossibly laden ship, transformed into a floating laboratory, was so unstable that it barely made the journey from London to the mouth of the Thames. The captain refused to take the ship any farther until it was refitted, after which the disgruntled Banks contented himself with watching from the sidelines as English influence spread across the globe. In 1801 John Wedgwood, son of the great potter Josiah, wrote to the elderly William Forsyth at the Chelsea Physic Garden, suggesting the formation of a horticultural society, adding as a postscript: 'If you should see Sir Joseph Banks, will you be so good as to ask him his opinion of the plan, and learn how far we might have a chance of having his patronage of the scheme.'[36] Letters went back and forth between Wedgwood, Forsyth and Banks (who wrote, 'I approve very much the idea'),[37] but it was not until 1804 that a meeting was held in Hatchard's bookshop in Piccadilly with Wedgwood in the Chair and Forsyth, Banks, Charles Greville, Richard Salisbury, William Townsend Aiton and James Dickson in attendance and the Horticultural Society of London came into being. (In 1861, with Prince Albert as president, it gained a royal charter and became the Royal Horticultural Society.)

The Hon. Charles Francis Greville, second son of the Earl of Warwick, was, like Banks, an office-holder in the Society of Dilettanti, with an interest in precious stones in their natural state and a Fellow of the Royal Society when he was only 20. He lived much of his life in financial difficulties, but in 1790 he moved to a more substantial house in Paddington Green with a large garden in which 'the rarest and most curious plants, from various climates, were cultivated with peculiar success.'[38]

Richard Salisbury, born Richard Markham, was a keen botanist and gardener whose studies at the University of Edinburgh were funded by Anna Salisbury, a connection of his maternal grandmother, on condition that he adopted her name, which he wisely did. In 1800 he moved from his renowned garden near Leeds, in the north of England, to Mill Hill in Middlesex, the former home of Peter Collinson, the garden still containing many of Collinson's plants. Salisbury, too, was a Fellow of the Royal Society and a member of the

David Douglas endured great hardship to collect plants on the east and west coasts of America before dying in mysterious circumstances in Hawaii.

Linnaean Society. He was later to serve a very important role as the first honorary secretary to the fledgling Horticultural Society.

William Townsend Aiton was the successor to his father, William Aiton, as gardener to George III at Kew, appointed on Banks's recommendation.

James Dickson, a Scotsman who moved to London as a young man, was a founder member of the Linnaean Society in 1788, a friend of both Banks and Forsyth, and in 1804 a seedsman and nurseryman in Covent Garden. He was also an eminent botanist with a particular interest in mosses and ferns.

This motley band of plant enthusiasts invited friends to meetings at which new plants were shown and new ideas discussed. The Horticultural Society of London was established.

When Banks died in 1820 the stream of plant collectors from Kew ceased, and the Horticultural Society decided to send its own collectors but with a significant change of emphasis. Whereas Kew was intent primarily on the botanical collecting of dried herbarium specimens for scientific research, the Horticultural Society wanted live plants and seeds of garden value, with hardy plants of the greatest importance – except for orchids, of which any number would be welcomed.

John Potts was sent to China in 1821, returning to England with a large collection of plants including chrysanthemums and camellias. Later in the same year George Don went to West Africa, South America and the West Indies, returning in 1823 with a rich collection of tropical plants to furnish the hot-houses or 'stoves' of wealthy collectors. In January 1822 John Forbes was sent, at the invitation of the Admiralty, on a survey of the East African coast via Spain, Brazil and the Cape of Good Hope, but he died, aged 23, making his way up the Zambezi River. In April 1823 John Parks followed Potts to China, but increasing unrest in the country dissuaded the Society from sending a second collector to assist him. Instead, the young Scottish collector earmarked for the role was sent to the much safer territory of New England. That young Scot was David Douglas (1799–1834).

Bitterly disappointed at being sent on what was effectively a jaunt to a tame, English-speaking country instead of to China, Douglas nevertheless arrived in New York in August 1823. It was not an easy voyage. As his meticulous diary recounted, departure was delayed by a day awaiting a steam tug. There then followed three days of gales after which the ship was becalmed. Six weeks later it was off Newfoundland in thick fog, and when it finally arrived in New York a two-week quarantine was imposed for fear of smallpox. During the next four months Douglas made innumerable contacts, and visited fruit growing areas in New York, Pennsylvania and Canada where he saw apples, pears, plums, peaches and grapes growing in abundance. In September he was robbed of his money, coat and notes by his guide and had to walk five miles to his horse, having then to hire a Frenchman to take him to his lodgings as the horse understood only French. On 10 October he 'called on Stephen van Ransalleer [Rensselaer] who is the most wealthy man in the United States' with a large garden and orchards. 'He has a large space of ground occupied as pleasure or flower garden, which is a novelty in America, as little attention is paid to anything but what brings money or luxury for the table.' Rensselaer had roses from France and herbaceous plants from Germany, 'with annuals &c from London'.[39]

In October, too, Douglas was invited to a meeting of the Horticultural Society of New York and felt 'glad to see it in such a stage of perfection. Being the first effort to establish a society in America, they labour in having no other establishments to co-operate with them in their laudable exertion.'[40] Later in the month he set off at 5:30 a.m. with Thomas Hogg, a Scottish nurseryman's son recently arrived in the United States to set up his own nursery, in a hunt for the insectivorous *Sarracenia purpurea*. Torrential rain and waist-deep mud forced abandonment of their first attempts, but retreat to the woodland on higher ground yielded '*Neottia repens*' (*Goodyera pubescens*, a hardy orchid), vacciniums, *Kalmia latifolia*, *Rhus vernix* and seeds from 'immensely large' trees of *Rhododendron maximum*.

After further delays Douglas arrived back in London on 10 January 1824. The Council of the Horticultural Society hailed his expedition as a success beyond all expectations, and in July 1824 Douglas set out on a second mission, under the auspices of the Hudson's Bay Company, to explore the largely unknown north-west coast. As he left England he wrote to a friend: 'By degrees the goddess of night threw a veil over the rocky shores of Cornwall and my delightful view of happy England closed – probably for ever,' but his gloomy premonition was not to be fulfilled on this occasion.[41]

This was to be a much more arduous exercise, but it is remarkable how Douglas recorded his ordeals with such equanimity and his discoveries in such detail. Setting sail in July 1824, the *William and Ann* spent the first half of September in Rio de Janeiro before heading for cooler climes. Douglas collected and studied fish, seabirds and seaweeds as well as land plants, preserving many for science but eating many others. The ship was in the Galapagos in early January 1825, and after twelve days of continuous rain and six weeks of 'boisterous and frightful' weather and several attempts to find the entrance to the Columbia River (now the border between the states of Washington and Oregon), it reached what the captain hoped was the river in mid-April. The bad weather was not entirely without its advantages. A thunderstorm on 16 March lasted from 4 a.m. to 2 p.m., during which time the ship's sails collected five tons of water, so drinking rations were increased and the crew were able to wash their clothes. On reaching the river mouth, Douglas described the scenery as 'romantic and wild' with high mountains on each side of the river clothed with timber of immense size while lupins 6 to 8 feet tall covered the lower land. 'On stepping on the shore *Gaultheria Shallon* was the first plant I took in my hands. So pleased was I that I could scarcely see anything but it. Mr Menzies [an explorer who preceded Douglas but who introduced few plants himself] correctly observes that it grows under thick pine-forests in great luxuriance and would make a valuable addition to our gardens.'[42]

Douglas set about collecting plants and seeds with his usual vigour, sleeping in a deerskin tent, in a hut of thuya bark, under an upturned canoe or often just under the branches of a pine tree. After his second foray he listed 120 plants, including, at No. 82, 'Pinus sp; exceeds all trees in magnitude; I measured one lying on the shore of the river 39 feet in circumference and 159 feet long; the top was wanting, but at the extreme length 2½ in diameter, so I judge that it would be in all about 190 feet high if not more ... This species, although I have not yet seen the cones, I take to be *P. taxifolia*.'[43] Douglas's 'Pinus taxifolia' was corrected by the editors of his journal to *Pseudotsuga Douglasii*. Botanists later renamed the tree *Pseudotsuga menziesii* after Archibald Menzies, but its common name remains today the Douglas fir.

Throughout his journeys he inflicted a punishing regime on himself. After three days reduced to crawling and hunger, he managed to kill two partridges, 'placed them in a kettle to boil but fell asleep until morning revealed supper in ashes & 3 holes in kettle bottom'.[44] In May 1826, after an uncomfortable night of rain:

As I could not sleep I rose at two o'clock and with some difficulty dried my blanket and a spare shirt, in which I placed my paper containing the few plants collected ... Felt a severe pain between my shoulders, which I thought might arise from the cold in swimming and lying in wet clothes. Therefore, as I had no medicine to take, I set out a little before 4 A.M. on foot, driving the horses before me, thinking that perspiring would remove it, which it partly did. On arriving at my first night's encampment at midday I stopped a short time to look for the currant in perfection which I saw on my way out just coming into blossom, and fortunately found it in a fine state.[45]

When the Horticultural Society eventually received Douglas's currant, the pink-flowered *Ribes sanguineum*, they declared that this one plant alone would have justified all his efforts.

In June 1826, 'Having had very little sleep since I left Kettle Falls I thought of indulging six or seven hours at least, so I laid myself down early on the floor of the Indian Hall, but was shortly afterwards roused from my slumber by an indescribable herd of fleas, and had to sleep out among the bushes; the annoyance of two species of ants, one very large, black ¾ of an inch long, and a small red one, rendered it worse, so this night I did not sleep, and gladly hailed the returning day.'[46] A week later,

> 4 A.M. start along the rocky shore of Columbia, after taking a little breakfast, the same as my supper last night [boiled horse flesh and small rodents] I proceeded. Long before twelve o'clock I felt fatigued, as I could not get so much as a mouthful of water. My eyes began to trouble me much, the wind blowing the sand, and the sun's reflection from it is of much detriment to me. My eyes so inflamed and painful that I can scarcely see distinctly an object ten yards distant. Gathered a few more seeds of *Phlox speciosa*.[47]

Douglas was repeatedly troubled with his eyes, on one occasion receiving no relief until they bled to reduce the pressure. He was soaked by rain and river, baked in scorching sun, lost his possessions when his canoe overturned in rapids, and had to walk barefoot through the painfully spiky stubble of grassland recently burned by Native Americans to encourage new vegetation. Finally, though, on 28 August 1827 at sunrise he saw sun glinting on the tin roof of the York Factory with the Hudson's Bay Company's ship from England riding in the bay. He was greeted by his old friend Mr McTavish with gifts of 'a new suit of clothing, linen, &c., ready to put on'.[48] Douglas calculated that he had walked 2,105 miles in 1825, 3,932 miles in 1826 and 995 miles in 1827, a total of 7,032 miles. He finally arrived home to find himself a national hero.

Although Douglas was famed and feted by society, he was unable to cope with his new surroundings. John Murray initially undertook to publish his journal, but it was deemed to be too botanical yet with insufficient botanical knowledge. Publication had to wait 80 years. The famous explorer languished on a gardener's pay and with no obvious role, better able to cope with the hazards of nature than with the demands of civilized society. Finally, Joseph Sabine, secretary of the Horticultural Society and Douglas's revered boss and mentor, arranged for him to take part in a survey of the Columbia River organized by W. R. Hay, the English representative on a boundary conference. Armed with an array of instruments and with an offer of transport and accommodation from the Hudson's Bay

Company through its chain of trading posts, Douglas left England again in October 1829, for the last time.

He was held up in Monterey on the coast of northern California waiting for a travel permit, but with permit issued, he went on to discover seven of the 17 West Coast pine species, the coastal redwood and Monterey cypress. His seed of the cypress was lost, so it was left to Karl Hartweg, a German botanist employed by the Horticultural Society, to introduce it to England in 1848. It was this hardy conifer, tolerant of wind and salt, that enabled gardeners on the west coast of Britain to create such sheltered gardens from Tresco in the Scilly Isles off the Cornwall coast to Inverewe in northern Scotland. Douglas also discovered the giant redwood and was awestruck to measure a fallen tree at 300 feet. He collected seeds but these were lost in a canoeing accident, so again it was left to Hartweg to introduce it to England.

In August 1832 he boarded a tiny ship to Hawaii in the hope of finding a north-bound ship. News reached him that Joseph Sabine had been dismissed by the Horticultural Society so Douglas resigned his own position. In October he returned to Fort Vancouver but found it now too civilized so, after a bitter winter, he visited the new trading post at Fort Nisqually, turned back down the Fraser River to Vancouver and, in August 1833, embarked once more for Hawaii, spending Christmas in Honolulu. After climbing and calculating the elevations of several of the highest mountains in the islands, he returned to Hawaii and called on Edward Gurney, an English expatriate and former convict who showed him the system of fences and pits he had constructed and dug around a local water hole to trap cattle. On 12 July 1834 Douglas left Gurney and was later discovered in one of Gurney's pits, trampled to death by a young bull which had also fallen into the trap. Whether his death was murder or suicide – it could hardly have been an accident – remains a mystery, but it brought to an end at the age of 35 the life of probably the most significant introducer of plants from America to England that there has ever been.

However, Douglas was not the first to awaken interest among English gardeners in the riches of the New World. The Menzies whom Douglas referred to on several occasions in his journal was Archibald Menzies (1754–1842), who studied at the Royal Botanic Garden in Edinburgh and then medicine at the University of Edinburgh. In 1790 he was appointed naturalist on the voyage by Captain George Vancouver to explore the Pacific Ocean. The ship sailed first to Cape Town, then to Australia, New Zealand, Tahiti and China before reaching the coast of North America, sailing into what is now Washington State in 1792 and exploring the coast from Nootka Sound in the north to California and the Hawaiian Islands. When the ship's surgeon became ill, Menzies took over his role, medicine and botany being closely related disciplines. In 1794 Menzies and two colleagues climbed

Mauna Loa, the largest, though not quite the highest, of the five volcanoes which form the island of Hawaii, 40 years before David Douglas. The only plant which Menzies is known to have brought back to England is the monkey puzzle, *Araucaria araucana*, that archetypal plant of Victorian gardens. He claimed to have been presented with its nutty seeds at a dinner in Chile. He hid a few in his pocket, germinated them on board ship and brought the young plants back to Kew, but this first introduction did not populate Victorian gardens. He did, though, make notes on many plants and was commemorated in *Menziesia*, a heather-like shrub now called *Daboecia*. He also remains honoured in the Douglas fir, now correctly named *Pseudotsuga menziesii*, and in the beautiful cinnamon-barked madrone, the California strawberry tree, *Arbutus menziesii*.

Another plant collector in the shadow of Douglas is Thomas Nuttall (1786–1859). Born in Yorkshire, Nuttall moved to Liverpool when he was 14, on the death of his father, to become an apprentice printer. He travelled to America in 1808 and there met Benjamin Barton, Professor of Natural History and Botany at the University of Pennsylvania. Barton persuaded him to take up botany, and he travelled to the Great Lakes in 1810, then up the Missouri River on an expedition financed by John Jacob Astor in 1811. Nuttall crossed the route taken by the explorers Lewis and Clark on their 1804–6 expedition to the Pacific coast ordered by Thomas Jefferson, but he introduced many plants new to science. During the War of 1812 he returned to England but came back to America in 1815. In 1818 he published his *Genera of American Plants*. From 1825 to 1834 he was curator of Harvard's botanic garden, the precursor of the Arnold Arboretum, then he travelled west again, through Kansas, Wyoming and Utah, retracing Douglas's steps along the Columbia River and to Hawaii. From south-west Oregon he introduced *Cornus nuttallii*, the beautiful Pacific dogwood which flowers so much more freely in England than does *C. florida*, the flowering dogwood of the eastern states. From 1836 to 1841 he joined the Academy of Natural Sciences in Philadelphia, but returned to England to take up residence at Nutgrove Hall in Lancashire, a property left to him by an uncle.

The most notable collector following in Douglas's footsteps was William Lobb (1809–1864). William and his brother Thomas (1820–1894) were two of the 23 plant collectors sent to various parts of the world by James Veitch and Son, by far the most important English nursery of the late nineteenth and early twentieth centuries. Thomas made repeated visits to South East Asia between 1843 and 1860, but William, the first of the Veitch collectors, travelled to South America, especially to Chile, in 1840–44 and 1845–8. He sent 3,000 seeds of the monkey puzzle back to Veitch, and it was this introduction that made this spiky little tree a signature tree of Victorian gardens.

In 1849, the year of the California Gold Rush, William Lobb travelled to Oregon and California, from where he sent seeds of many of the trees first sent back by Douglas, including commercial quantities of the giant redwood. John Lindley, secretary of the Horticultural Society, proposed the name *Wellingtonia* for the tree, arguing that the *Wellingtonia* stood head and shoulders above other trees, as did the Duke of Wellington above ordinary mortals. This met with outrage from American botanists who proposed the name *Washingtonia*, but that name was already spoken for, so a compromise was reached. The giant redwood became *Sequoia* (now *Sequoiadendron*) *giganteum*, named after a Native American tribe. The giant redwood, still widely known in England as Wellingtonia, continues to mark many vicarage and other nineteenth-century rural gardens, standing well above all other trees on the English skyline. There is also a Wellingtonia avenue on the Duke of Wellington's estate at Stratfield Saye between Reading in Berkshire and Basingstoke in Hampshire, and a much longer Wellingtonia avenue at nearby Finchampstead Ridges, just west of Wellington College.

There were other lesser collectors and many more individual dispatches of seeds and plants from people working on the West Coast to friends and family in England, but David Douglas remains the outstanding figure in enriching English gardens with American plants. His introductions ranged from colourful annuals such as the California poppy *Eschscholzia californica*, *Phacelia tanacetifolia* with its curling 'horns' of blue flowers loved by bees, and his own *Limnanthes douglasii*, the fragrant 'poached egg' plant with yellow-centred white flowers, to giants such as the noble fir *Abies procera*, Sitka spruce (*Picea sitchensis*, beloved of English foresters) and *Pinus coulteri* with its impressive cones 12–14 inches in length. In between were lupins, 18 species of penstemon, the handsome evergreen *Garrya elliptica* named after Nicholas Garry, deputy governor of the Hudson's Bay Company, who had supported Douglas in his travels, and a host of other flowering plants, including of course *Ribes sanguineum*, the flowering currant, which the Horticultural Society considered was in itself justification for his long expeditions.

8

The Gardenesque

I n England at the close of the eighteenth century fierce arguments had raged about the definition and desirability of the beautiful, with its smoothly rounded hills and rounded clumps of rounded trees, the sublime, with its vastness of scale inspiring lofty thoughts, and the picturesque, with its studied irregularities of tumbling rocks, twisted trees and shaggy cattle. As the nineteenth century advanced, these debates became increasingly irrelevant. In 1801 the population of England was just under 10 million; by 1850 it had more than doubled, and by 1901 it had nearly doubled again to 40 million. As the Industrial Revolution gained momentum small villages swelled into towns; towns became sprawling cities, swallowing up surrounding villages, and new roads were lined with new houses. Substantial suburban residences were built on the west side of the towns for the fortunate managerial and professional classes, while closely packed back-to-back houses with no sanitation on the east side, under clouds of polluted air borne by the westerly winds, appeared for the lower classes who served as fodder for the industrial machine which was England. In such circumstances niceties of definition between sublime, beautiful and picturesque were meaningless.

The way forward for a nation of modestly sized suburban gardens was signalled by a Scotsman, John Claudius Loudon (1783–1843). Loudon was born near Edinburgh but moved south to England early in the nineteenth century. It was not unusual for Scots gardeners to migrate southwards from what was a relatively poor country to a land of wealth and employment opportunity, but Loudon's motive was different. Having attended lectures in agriculture and botany at the University of Edinburgh, he travelled south with the intention of teaching the English how to farm properly. His first publication was a pamphlet on the planting of London squares, suggesting the use of deciduous trees and shrubs, and especially the London plane (sycamore in American) to replace the soot-laden evergreens which struggled to survive.

Loudon was enormously hard-working, going one night each week without sleep to study languages. He travelled extensively, always on the cheaper outside of the coach, which built up severe problems with his health, leading ultimately to the amputation of one arm by a quack doctor and to near paralysis of the other with rheumatism. He wrote five encyclopaedias, his *Encyclopaedia of Gardening* of 1822 extending to 1,600 pages of very small print. He was initially critical of Repton, but later came to respect him and

Fountain, flowers and shrubberies from J. C. Loudon's *The Villa Garden* of 1850.

edited Repton's collected works as the intended first but, because of his early death, only monograph of key publications in garden history. The Loudon edition of Repton's works was much more widely available to the nineteenth-century reader than were the original books. He edited his own *Gardener's Magazine* from 1826 until his death, but his most important contribution was to address himself to the new suburban gardener.

Loudon realized that philosophical arguments about the relative merits of the sublime, the beautiful and the picturesque had become irrelevant. In their place he proposed a new style, the 'Gardenesque', which he described as 'the production of that kind of scenery which is best calculated to display the individual beauty of trees, shrubs and plants in a state of culture; the smoothness and greenness of lawns; and the smooth surface, curved directions, dryness and firmness of gravel walks'.[49] In his *Suburban Gardener and Villa Companion* of 1838 he advised, 'As a garden is a work of art and a scene of cultivation, every plant or tree placed in it should be so placed as never to be mistaken for a plant placed there by nature or accident or as to prevent the practices of cultivation being applied to it.'[50] This sentence, one of his shorter in a book whose full title occupied a whole page in a variety of fonts, combines two ideas. 'As a garden is a work of art' it should not be mistaken for nature. This took Repton's suggestion that the design of the (concealed) flower garden could be as much that of art as of nature to its ultimate conclusion. Second, he advised that the placement of plants should allow 'the practices of cultivation being applied to [them]'. Instead of rounded 'beautiful' clumps or irregular 'picturesque' tangles, plants were to stand as individuals, each in its own neat circle of cultivated soil.

His book gave advice on the planning and planting of gardens of different 'rates' or property-tax bands. 'First-rate' gardens might have 10 acres or more, second rate 2 to 10 acres, third rate 1 or 2 acres, and fourth rate 1 perch (5½ yards square or 160th of an acre) to 1 acre. A fourth-rate garden would be attached to a terraced (row) house, with a tiny patch at the front where only a path to the front door, a flower bed in the 'ancient or geometric style' and a narrow border of perennials would fit, with a long, narrow, brick-walled enclosure at the back.[51] For this Loudon recommended climbers on the walls, with lists of new or well-established or cheap species for north, south, east and west-facing walls, and a central panel of grass dotted with interesting trees and shrubs. In one sample garden his recommendations, for a lawn of a few square yards only, included red oak, liriodendron and a few dozen more. It did not matter that these would ultimately become large forest trees. They were exciting new introductions from America, they had large handsome leaves as young specimens, and by the time they outgrew their situation there would be even newer and more exciting plants to replace them.

Although Loudon was still writing about 'a work of art and a scene', his words could easily be misinterpreted by an uneducated gardener wanting to impress his employer or by the newly rich employer wanting to impress society. The message they took from Loudon's writing was that to make an artistic garden the planting should look unnatural and the plants should be widely spaced as individuals so that the circles of bare ground in which they stood could be regularly hoed. That was not what Loudon intended, but it was what happened in innumerable new suburban gardens, further enriched by Chinese bridges, statues of Roman emperors, wire baskets and other accoutrements advertised in the new magazines and soon to be available anywhere thanks to the rapidly expanding railway network. Many gardens of the mid-nineteenth century were marvels of design and content, but the collective reputation from which the Victorian garden has suffered until recent years, deprived of its large garden staff and with long-lived evergreen survivors of the original planting struggling under decades of dust and soot, has led to a dismissal of Loudon and the gardens he represents.

Although much of Loudon's writing addressed the private garden, his practice was directed much more at the public landscape, in particular at public parks and cemeteries. His earliest publication had been on the planting of the semi-public London squares. In 1839 he was asked by Joseph Strutt, a wealthy industrialist and former mayor of Derby, to design a park which would be freely open to its citizens. Loudon's plan for the long and narrow site created a series of mounds to separate serpentine walks through the park while the mounds were planted with a wide array of trees and shrubs, all labelled so that visitors could educate themselves while enjoying respite from the noise and pollution of the city around them.

During the nineteenth century the population exploded, but life expectancy for the majority was short. The traditional burial grounds around parish churches were overwhelmed. Decaying bodies buried below the water table polluted water sources and released foul, black liquids into the church. Gravediggers and the mutes who accompanied the more elaborate funerals were overcome by fumes. In an attempt to deal with the problem, new cemeteries were planned on the outskirts of towns, and Loudon played a major role in the design of these new landscapes, seeing in them opportunities to create arboreta which would educate the living as well as provide a dignified resting place for the departed. *On the Laying Out, Planting, and Managing of Cemeteries and on the Improvement of Churchyards*, published in 1843, the year of his own death, was an early example of the Victorian obsession with death and with the need to cope with the vastly increased numbers of the dead. With typical thoroughness, he recommended a proprietary box which would hold the soil excavated from the grave and then release it by removing the sides without spilling soil over the surrounding lawn. He also had diagrams showing deep foundations for headstones designed to keep them vertical in perpetuity. No slovenly sloping for this eminently tidy gentleman.

Ironically, Loudon met his death, at the age of 60, after working in terrible weather conditions on Southampton Old Cemetery. It has been generally thought that he contracted a chill, but his friend the philanthropist Edwin Chadwick, who was with him, recorded that Loudon suffered a blast of foul air as he entered a mausoleum, and he attributed his friend's death to that foul air. Six years after Queen Victoria's accession to the throne, Loudon died with appropriately Victorian melodrama, dictating the last chapter of his book on self-improvement for young gardeners to his much younger wife, Jane.

Loudon's place in the horticultural world was taken by his younger rival Joseph Paxton (1803–1865). Born the seventh son of a farmer – not an auspicious beginning – Paxton was admitted to the Horticultural Society's recently acquired garden at Chiswick on a new trainee programme, having lied about his age to gain entry. On completion of his two-year course he was appointed as under-gardener in the arboretum. The Chiswick garden was leased from the Duke of Devonshire, who had his private door from Chiswick House into the garden, and Paxton caught the attention of the duke. When in 1826 the duke needed a head gardener for his Chatsworth estate in Derbyshire, he offered the post to Paxton. At 23, Joseph Paxton became head gardener in one of England's greatest gardens, albeit one which had languished in neglect for many years. His arrival at Chatsworth, noted in his diary, is utterly characteristic of his energetic, industrious and productive life:

> I left London by the Comet coach for Chesterfield, and arrived at Chatsworth at half past 4 o'clock in the morning of the 9th of May, 1826. As no person was to be seen at that early hour I got over the greenhouse gates by the old covered way, explored the pleasure ground, and looked around the outside of the house. I then went down to the kitchen garden, scaled the outside wall, and saw the whole of the place, set the men to work there at 6 o'clock, then returned to Chatsworth, got Thomas Weldon [his deputy] to play me the waterworks, and afterwards went to breakfast with poor dear Mrs Gregory [the housekeeper] and her niece, the latter fell in love with me, and I with her, and thus completed my first morning's work at Chatsworth before 9 o'clock.[52]

Paxton married the niece, Sarah Brown, and she played an important role in managing her husband's affairs at home while he travelled with the duke to Russia, to Europe and frequently to London, and later to meetings connected to his own interests in railways, public parks and the design of mansions such as Mentmore in Buckinghamshire (1852–4) for Baron Mayer de Rothschild and Château de Ferrières (1855–9), 16 miles east of Paris, for Mayer's brother James.

Chatsworth had substantial remains of a seventeenth-century French-inspired garden set in an eighteenth-century Capability Brown landscape, but it had fallen into disrepair. Paxton brought the garden back to life and inspired the duke to take a new interest in his estate. Clipped Portugal laurels were planted in tubs to simulate the oranges of more southern climes. At the duke's request Paxton sent one of the Chatsworth gardeners, John Gibson, to India to bring back *Amherstia nobilis*, a tree of famed beauty not then grown in England. The duke was appointed to the Council of the Horticultural Society in 1837, and he was president from 1838 until his death in 1858.

His employer's role as president of the Horticultural Society brought many advantages. In 1829 newly introduced seedlings of 'Douglas's pines' (Douglas fir) came from London in Paxton's top hat. By 1845 they were 35 feet tall. In 1835 an arboretum was established, its cost more than recouped by the sale of timber cleared from the site, and in 1836 work began on the Great Conservatory, in which Paxton adapted Loudon's ridge and furrow principle (described in the next chapter) to a curvilinear glasshouse, making it a light but

Joseph Paxton's daughter Annie on a leaf of the giant waterlily, *Victoria amazonica*.

immensely strong structure heated by coal brought on an underground railway. The Great Conservatory became one of the wonders of the age. Fifty thousand visitors came to see it each year. A small plant of the giant waterlily, *Victoria regia* (now *V. amazonica*), was sent from Kew. Paxton designed a glasshouse with no internal supports, spanning a pool heated by underwater pipes and with a small paddle wheel to simulate the flow of the Amazon. The Chatsworth giant waterlily flowered before the plants at Kew, and the first flower was sent to Queen Victoria, who was inconveniently holidaying at Osborne House on the Isle of Wight. Paxton also brought thousands of tons of stone to what had been a bare, grassy hillside to construct the Strid, a gigantic rock garden, and he created the Emperor Fountain, the tallest in Europe, planned for a visit of the Russian tsar in 1843. Sadly, the tsar had to cut short his visit to England and returned to Russia from London.

Paxton could not compete with Loudon's vast literary output but, like Loudon, he published two magazines, the *Horticultural Register and General Magazine* from 1831 to

1835 and the *Magazine of Botany and Register of Flowering Plants* from 1835 to 1849. These rivalled Loudon's *Gardener's Magazine*, which suffered a significant drop in circulation although Loudon continued to publish it until his death in 1843. Not surprisingly, Loudon's first report on Chatsworth was far from favourable, but on a later visit he was more generous and the two men became friends. Also like Loudon, Paxton became caught up in philanthropic attempts to improve the lives of those at the bottom of the social pyramid, playing a key role in the development of public parks. In 1831 his magazine carried two articles on subscription gardens, suggesting that middle class people who could not afford a substantial estate for themselves might group together and subscribe to the creation and upkeep of a garden to which they would have access. In 1832 the Sheffield Botanical and Horticultural Society took up the suggestion and created a garden which still continues to give pleasure to its visitors in the twenty-first century.

9

An American treatise

◡‿◡

FOR NEARLY TWO CENTURIES 'the colonies' had been an outlying piece of Britain with state governors and other officials appointed by the Crown. A trickle of immigrants from England to America established family links, albeit initially difficult and tenuous, across the Atlantic. The younger Tradescant's crossing and recrossing of the Atlantic, Catesby's visit to his sister and the exchanges of plants between Bartram and Collinson – horticulturally significant events – represent a small fraction of an interchange which took place throughout this early history. As transatlantic shipping increased in speed and reliability, and international conventions more or less eliminated the threat of piracy, communications increased exponentially and 'the colonies' and 'the mother country' evolved in parallel. In the events leading up to the War of Independence many influential English people were appalled at the actions of their government, acting for George III, in looking upon the colonies as a source of finance. When the separation finally occurred, with the Treaty of Versailles in 1783 and the subsequent battles over boundary disputes in the War of 1812, the new United States emerged as an English-speaking country with many of its institutions continuing to reflect an English inheritance – albeit with a strong republican ethic.

Many of the people that Douglas met on his visits to the United States were Fellows (as members were called) of the Horticultural Society of London. The most distinguished of them were also Fellows of the Royal Society. In 1829 the Massachusetts Horticultural Society was established. One of its first activities was to establish, on high ground overlooking the city, an arboretum-cum-cemetery, Mount Auburn. The initiative came from Henry Dearborn (1783–1851), a distinguished amateur botanist, and Jacob Bigelow (1787–1879), a Harvard physician. As with Loudon, Chadwick and others in England, Bigelow was deeply concerned about the unhealthy conditions of traditional burial grounds in overcrowded churchyards. Inspired by the Père Lachaise Cemetery in Paris and with the guidance of Henry Dearborn, Mount Auburn was laid out on wooded hills four miles from Boston, on the Watertown/ Cambridge borders, with winding drives among the trees. It served as a peaceful resting place for the dead and a tranquil place of contemplation for the living. The name Mount Auburn was taken from Oliver Goldsmith's poem 'The Deserted Village' of 1770, in which 'Sweet Auburn' referred to an idyllic but vanished rural landscape, its impoverished inhabitants victims of the Enclosures. The new American Mount Auburn was very influential, providing the inspiration for Laurel Hill Cemetery in Philadelphia (1836), Mount Hope in Rochester,

New York, Green-Wood in Brooklyn and Green Mount in Baltimore (all in 1838), and many others in succeeding decades. It paralleled English efforts such as Loudon's Derby Arboretum and his efforts to improve the lives of the poor by creating cemeteries which would provide leafy retreats and expose them to the natural world.

Queen Victoria's reign in England (1837–1901) was one of the most extraordinary periods in world history. The near-doubling of the UK population during her reign was more than matched by population growth in the USA, where a population of 16 million in 1838 increased nearly five-fold to 76 million by 1900, due in large part to massive waves of immigration from Ireland in the wake of the potato famine in the mid-nineteenth century and from Eastern Europe as a result of political unrest later in the century.

Between 1845 and 1853, following the vast Louisiana Purchase from the French in 1803, a second set of land acquisitions by negotiation, conquest and purchase created a contiguous United States. By 1890 the country was more populous than any European country except Russia. After the 1890 Census the Superintendent of the Census observed that, for the first time in American history, a single frontier line (with fewer than two people per square mile) was no longer visible on his map. The frontier, in this statistical sense, had come to an end. However, to quote the editors of the *Times Atlas of World History*, 'as an experience, myth and symbol, the frontier continues to dominate American thought even today [1978]. The movement, progress, energy, expectation, confidence, prosperity and hope which it engendered still remain central to American culture. The unique experience of built-in empire makes it especially difficult for Americans to understand the conditions of other less fortunate people, and for others to understand America as well.'[53]

In England Robert Stephenson's steam locomotive, the Rocket, powered the first scheduled rail service on the Liverpool–Manchester Railway in 1830. A web of railway lines soon criss-crossed the country and then extended throughout Europe. American industry matched that of England. The Baltimore and Ohio Railroad also began its first scheduled services in 1830, the Mohawk and Hudson in 1831, and the Saratoga and Schenectady in 1832. A network of services linked most cities in the North and Midwest by 1860, and on 10 May 1869 the combined efforts of the Union Pacific and Central Pacific Railroads, backed by government funds, linked the east and west coasts. After 1865 the steel plough and barbed wire subdued the Great Plains, and waves of immigrants settled the seemingly limitless expanses of the Midwest.

On both sides of the Atlantic the railways consumed and transported huge quantities of coal, iron and steel, feeding the Industrial Revolution and generating – for those investing in, directing and managing the railways and other industrial ventures – large fortunes. Those fortunes were spent on magnificent houses and large, elaborate gardens, of which

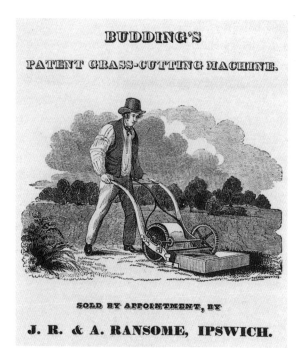

the largest and most elaborate was the 120,000-acre Vanderbilt estate of Biltmore in Asheville, North Carolina, designed by Frederick Law Olmsted.

The atmosphere of innovation which fuelled the Industrial Revolution and thus stimulated the creation of elaborate gardens also provided materials for the new gardens. Edwin Budding's lawnmower was patented in 1830. It allowed the gardener to manoeuvre around more complicated flower parterres than was possible with the scythe, and had the further advantage of allowing the gardener to mow later in the day, when the grass was dry, rather than at dawn before the dew (which made the grass blades stiff and heavy for the scythe) had evaporated. The lawnmower quickly took hold on both sides of the Atlantic. An advertisement and trade card by J. L. Reed & Bro., dealers in general hardware, farming implements &c., of Canajoharie, New York, showed a horse-drawn mower with a high-stepping horse pulling an elegantly scrolled cylinder mower on which sat a well-dressed gentleman, presumably a gardener, on rolling parkland in front of a three-storey mansion. Another by the Coldwell Lawn Mower Company of Newburgh, New York, obviously specialists rather than general hardware merchants, proclaimed: 'We make lawn mowers of all kinds STEAM, HORSE and HAND POWER.' Their 'Coldwell Steam Lawn Mower and

The lawnmower revolutionized gardening on both sides of the Atlantic.

OPPOSITE Edwin Budding's mower, patented in 1830, was manufactured by J. R. & A. Ransome from 1832.

ABOVE Horse-drawn mower (top) with last year's (left) and this year's (right) fashions in boots to stop the horse's hooves spoiling the lawn.

Roller Combined' had half a ton or more of boiler, cutting cylinders, gears and chains with the gardener sitting high aloft in a suit and trilby hat, while another by the Chadbourne and Coldwell Manufacturing Company showed a smartly dressed young girl and boy pushing their 'Excelsior' lawnmowers with the adults of the family playing croquet in the distance.[54] Thomas Coldwell was born in 1838 in Staleybridge, Lancashire, but moved to America at an early age and, by the time of his death in 1905, was the longest established manufacturer of lawnmowers in America.

In 1870 the first influx of American-manufactured mowers arrived in England. Designed to cut American bluegrass lawns rather than the fine-leaved fescues and bents of England, they were lighter and cheaper than English machines. In 1878 a young English businessman, John Post Lawrence, visited the Chicago World's Fair and was introduced to the makers of the 'Pennsylvania Lawn Mower', Lloyd, Supplee & Walton. On his return to England Lawrence set up Lloyd, Lawrence & Company to import the American mower. Lloyd's mowers still hold the record for the machine longest in production.

In 1832 Lucas Chance's cylinder glass replaced the traditional bubble glass. Instead of cutting small panes of more or less flat glass from a large spherical bubble, Chance blew the glass into a mould to produce a sausage shape, removed both ends, sliced the hollow cylinder from end to end, and spread out the glass while still soft into a much larger and flatter sheet. In England a punitive glass tax was repealed in 1845, and over the next 20 years the cost of glass fell to a fifth of its pre-1845 level.

J. C. Loudon experimented with many aspects of glasshouse design, developing slender iron glazing bars for his curvilinear houses and suggesting, but not developing, a ridge-and-furrow glazing system to improve morning and evening light transmission while also strengthening the structure. It was left to Joseph Paxton to develop Loudon's ridge and furrow for his Great Conservatory at Chatsworth in 1836–40. Cast iron coal-fired boilers sending hot water through cast iron pipes in trenches covered by decorative cast iron grilles created a controlled and humid environment in which orchids and other tender plants brought from all corners of the world by steam-powered iron ships could be cultivated.

New wealth, new gardens and new plants stimulated the rapid expansion of the nursery trade, generalists and specialists alike, on both sides of the Atlantic, but the newly rich and newly landed businessmen needed advice on how to establish themselves as men of taste. In England much of that advice filtered down from the *ancien régime* as gardeners moved from lowly positions on great estates to higher positions in more modest establishments, or moved from private service to establish nurseries supplying plans as well as plants. Advice came, too, from the writings and examples of Repton, Loudon, Paxton and an increasing host of proprietors of magazines on botany, horticulture and landscape.

BELOW A portrait, attributed to Thomas Critz, of John Tradescant the younger, *c*.1650.
RIGHT A drawing from *Curtis's Botanical Magazine* of *Tradescantia virginiana*, one of many plants introduced to English gardens by Tradescant the elder.

LEFT AND ABOVE *Robinia pseudoacacia*, the black locust or false acacia, introduced by John Tradescant the younger in 1634.

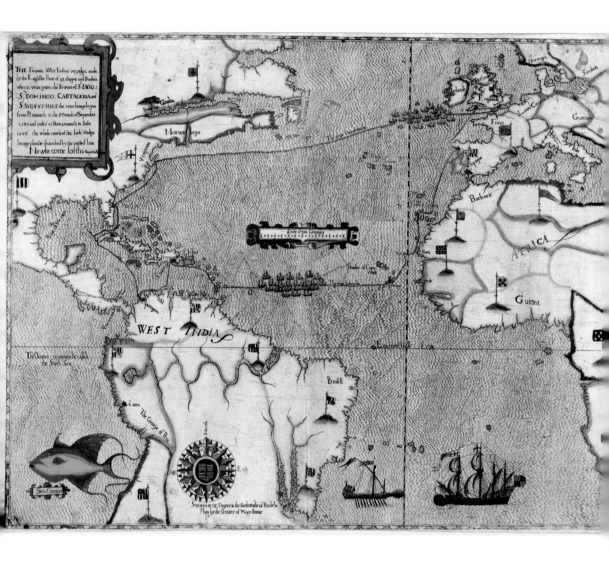

ABOVE Baptista Boazio's 1589 map illustrating
Sir Francis Drake's West Indies Voyage 1585–6.

RIGHT Williamsburg: capital of Virginia
from 1699 and restored from the late 1920s
by W. A. R. Goodwin with financial support
from J. D. Rockefeller.

IV

George Washington's Mount
Vernon, where he translated ideas
from the English landscape garden
to the more dramatic conditions
of the Potomac Valley.

OPPOSITE, ABOVE *Farmer George:
Washington at Mount Vernon*,
a lithograph after the painting by
J. B. Stearns, 1853.
OPPOSITE, BELOW *The Portico at
Mount Vernon*, watercolour and
pen and ink, 1796.
ABOVE Mount Vernon: showing
the front of the house.
LEFT Mount Vernon: the back
of the house and the garden,
described as neatly combining the
symmetry of a French parterre
with the looser freedom of the
English landscape garden.

ABOVE Stowe, Buckinghamshire. The Temple of Ancient Virtue (top) and The Temple of British Worthies (bottom). Thomas Jefferson wrote a lengthy if mixed review of England's most famous garden, but seems not to have appreciated its political message.

ABOVE 'An obelisk of very ill effect; another in the middle of a pond useless', recorded Jefferson of William Kent's garden at Chiswick.

BELOW Jefferson's Monticello, inspired by Andrea Palladio, absorbed much of his intellectual energy from 1786 until his death in 1826 – even during the period, from 1801 to 1809, when he served as President of the United States.

LEFT, ABOVE AND BELOW
David Douglas's *Pinus taxifolia*, now *Pseudotsuga menziesii*, was one of the many giant conifers he sent to the Horticultural Society in London.

RIGHT, ABOVE AND BELOW
Tresco, Scilly Isles. *Cupressus macrocarpa*, from the windswept shores of the Monterey Peninsula in California, provided shelter belts for exotic plantings in a chain of British west coast gardens.

ABOVE Edwin Budding's lawnmower, patented in 1830, stimulated a multitude of copies and refinements on both sides of the Atlantic. A trade card from the Philadelphia Mower Company shows a pedestrian mower operated by a young boy in the foreground and a horse-drawn mower near the house.

RIGHT, ABOVE AND BELOW Mount Auburn, an arboretum-cum-cemetery on high ground overlooking Boston, Massachusetts, was the brainchild of the amateur botanist Henry Dearborn and the Harvard physician Jacob Bigelow.

Plan of Central Park, New York, 1863. The park, in the centre of the often barren, rocky Manhattan Island, was designed by Frederick Law Olmsted and Calvert Vaux.

In the twenty-first century Central Park provides an oasis of calm in the heart of one of the world's greatest cities.

XIV

OPPOSITE English-born
Henry Shaw's Tower House
garden created the nucleus
of Missouri Botanic Garden,
a garden in which botanical
science and horticultural
excellence combined.

RIGHT *Davidia involucrata*,
the dove tree or handkerchief
tree, was the quest of the
first of Robert Fortune's
Chinese expeditions, forging
a partnership between the
Veitch Nurseries in England
and the Arnold Arboretum in
the United States.

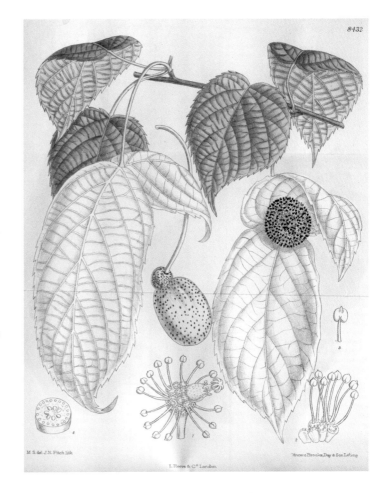

John Singer Sargent painted Olmsted in 1895 when his subject was becoming very frail. Olmsted's son John, of similar build, donned his father's clothes to allow the portrait to be completed.

In America there were nurserymen and landscape contractors, too, and the wealthiest people could always import gardeners from England, France or Germany. The cornerstone of advice, though, came from Andrew Jackson Downing (1815–1852). Downing was born in Newburgh, New York, into a family of successful nurserymen in the Hudson Valley, that beautiful terrain on the shores of the Hudson River which provided an ideal situation for building and planting by the rich. He joined his brother Charles in running the nursery after their father's death, enhancing its reputation nationally as the 'Botanical Gardens and Nurseries' of Newburgh.[55]

While still in his teens Downing wrote on aesthetics and botany and by 1839, in his early twenties, was a respected figure in the horticultural community. After three years of writing he published his most important work, *A Treatise on the Theory and Practice of Landscape Gardening adapted to North America*, in 1841. In its title and content the *Treatise* borrowed freely and openly from Repton and Loudon in England, but his advice was 'adapted to North America', where Downing thought it was necessary to mediate between taming what he saw as the 'howling wilderness' of nature and ameliorating the 'wilderness of bricks' of cities. For Downing the garden was a democratic art, accessible to all, to be found in the humblest window box or the largest estate, and while it was 'needful in civilized life for men to live in cities', it was not 'needful for them to live utterly divorced from all pleasant and healthful intercourse with gardens and green fields'.[56] The *Treatise* was hugely successful, requiring a second edition in 1844, a fifth in 1850 and a tenth in 1921, long after his death.

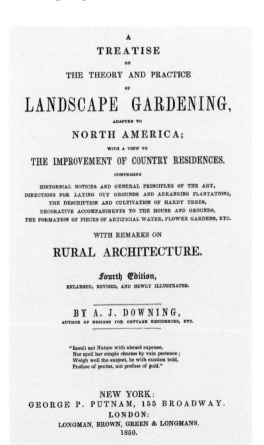

A

TREATISE

ON

THE THEORY AND PRACTICE

OF

LANDSCAPE GARDENING,

ADAPTED TO

NORTH AMERICA;

WITH A VIEW TO

THE IMPROVEMENT OF COUNTRY RESIDENCES.

COMPRISING

HISTORICAL NOTICES AND GENERAL PRINCIPLES OF THE ART,
DIRECTIONS FOR LAYING OUT GROUNDS AND ARRANGING PLANTATIONS,
THE DESCRIPTION AND CULTIVATION OF HARDY TREES,
DECORATIVE ACCOMPANIMENTS TO THE HOUSE AND GROUNDS,
THE FORMATION OF PIECES OF ARTIFICIAL WATER, FLOWER GARDENS, ETC.

WITH REMARKS ON

RURAL ARCHITECTURE.

Fourth Edition,

ENLARGED, REVISED, AND NEWLY ILLUSTRATED.

BY A. J. DOWNING,

AUTHOR OF DESIGNS FOR COTTAGE RESIDENCES, ETC.

"Insult not Nature with absurd expense,
Nor spoil her simple charms by vain pretence ;
Weigh well the subject, be with caution bold,
Profuse of genius, not profuse of gold."

NEW YORK:
GEORGE P. PUTNAM, 155 BROADWAY.
LONDON:
LONGMAN, BROWN, GREEN & LONGMANS.
1850.

Andrew Jackson Downing's *Treatise on the Theory and Practice of Landscape Gardening adapted to North America*, first published in 1841.

After the first edition there followed in rapid succession his editing of the first American edition of John Lindley's *Theory of Horticulture* in collaboration with Asa Gray, Harvard's leading botanist, *Cottage Residences* in 1842, an American edition of Jane Loudon's *Gardening for Ladies* in 1843, and in 1845 his *Fruit and Fruit Trees of North America*, which brought him international acclaim. The year 1846 saw his first issue as editor of *The Horticulturist*, a monthly magazine of architecture and landscape gardening, and finally, in 1850, *The Architecture of Country Houses*. In addition to this prolific literary output, Downing consulted on architecture and landscape gardening up and down the East Coast. In 1850 he sold his interest in the nursery and travelled to England, where he was delighted to find that his reputation had preceded him. He was fêted and welcomed wherever he went. One reason for his visit was to look for an architect with whom he could collaborate, having failed to persuade a leading American architect, Alexander Jackson Davis, to join him. At the Architectural Association in London he was impressed by the watercolour paintings made on a tour of Europe by the young architect Calvert Vaux (1824–1895). He arranged to meet him, and within a week Vaux had settled his affairs in London to join Downing in New York.

Downing had a firmly held belief in the importance of the landscape as a means of elevating national taste. In an 1848 editorial in his *Horticulturist* magazine he proposed the creation of a public park for New York City. Tragically, though, he died in 1852, at the age of 36, before the proposal took shape. He was travelling back from advising on the landscape of Washington, DC when the boiler on the steamship on which he was travelling exploded and the ship sank. However, he had already made another major contribution to the shaping of the American landscape by introducing his partner, Calvert Vaux, to the young Frederick Law Olmsted (1822–1903).

For the majority of the inhabitants of the new, sprawling industrial cities, there were no orchid houses or flower-filled parterres to delight them but lives – often short lives – of unremitting toil in appalling squalor. There were many philanthropic efforts on both sides of the Atlantic to improve working and living conditions for the poor. The most influential and durable improvements echoed the ideals of Washington, Jefferson, Penn and their contemporaries, and of later writers like Downing: a pervasive sense that connection to the land mattered in a civilized society. From the 1790s onwards, in the West End of London and Bath in England and Edinburgh in Scotland, speculative developments of elegant terraced houses around green squares to which the keyholders of the houses had access demonstrated the benefits of shared ownership of green spaces, an idea adopted in the 1840s in Boston's Louisburg Square and the elegant streets around it on Beacon Hill. Joseph Paxton's 1831 articles in his *Horticultural Register* on subscription gardens extended the idea of shared ownership to edge of town gardens, leading to the creation of the Sheffield Botanical and Horticultural Society's garden in 1833, but none of these ideals and ideas reached the bottom of the human pile in overcrowded and polluted cities.

In the same year as the Sheffield garden, Edwin Chadwick published his report from the Select Committee on Public Walks. Chadwick argued that the provision of public green space would profit the nation by taking people away from the gin palaces and gambling dens so that they would be fitter for work and more productive in their labours. Similar arguments that the abolition of slavery would have economic benefits were used some 30 years later by Frederick Law Olmsted.

In 1840 the Derby Arboretum, designed by Loudon for Joseph Strutt, was given to the city. In 1844 in Manchester, Mark Phillips raised subscriptions to create three public parks. As a result of Chadwick's report, the government passed an Act enabling local authorities to levy a penny rate (a property tax) on its citizens to acquire land and to lay out public parks. In 1842 work on Birkenhead Park began, the first truly public park: paid for by its citizens and open to everyone. Birkenhead Park was designed by Joseph Paxton on a marshy wasteland, in an area where malaria was still prevalent, on the edge of the elegant new town of Birkenhead in the Wirral near Liverpool. The initial cost estimate was £9,000, but several local politicians had (quite innocently, of course) bought parcels of the malarial marsh and were reluctant to part with their land without substantial redress, so costs rose. The final cost was £70,000, but the park paid for itself sevenfold before it opened in 1847.

Paxton's design was in essence a giant London square. He dug into the marsh to create two sinuous lakes, over which paths crossed and recrossed on covered bridges to bring visitors into frequent close visual contact with the water. Spoil from the lakes was used to create undulating tree-planted mounds separating the inner pedestrian path system from the larger-scale exterior around which a carriage drive wound its way across open meadows and through shady groves. The key element of the park, though, was that Paxton 'peeled off' the outer fringe of the land, now highly attractive and desirable property, to sell for the erection of individual and terraced houses. Not only did this sale pay for the park seven times over, but the property taxes from the substantial houses around it continued to benefit the town thereafter. The gain was twofold: gentlefolk in their carriages could peep over the park fence at elegant houses, framed as modern temples in the landscape, while the residents of those houses could look out across the park on to mile-long vistas of lawn and forest trees. This spectacular example of benefiting the poor while making a profit was a powerful influence in an era of industrial growth. Most English towns had a 'Victoria Park' or its equivalent long before the end of the century.

Birkenhead Park, though, had a much wider influence. In 1850 it was visited by a young American farmer, Frederick Law Olmsted. Olmsted was born in Hartford, Connecticut, in

1822, the eighth generation of the
family since 1636. His education
was left in the hands of clergymen
tutors, but he shared his father's
saddle on annual 'tours in search of
the picturesque'.[57] The rural scenery
and his father's admiration of it left
lasting impressions. In 1840, at 18,
he moved to New York as a clerk
in a dry-goods importers, but like
Repton in England 70 years earlier,
he was not excited by trade. In 1843
he left and found employment on a
ship sailing to Canton. His health
was never very strong, but his life
aboard ship reduced him to little
more than a skeleton such that his father failed to recognize him on his return. He then
became a farming apprentice and in 1847 – again like Repton 70 years before – acquired his
first farm near New Haven, Connecticut, moving the following year to Staten Island, New
York, where he farmed until 1855. There he founded an Agricultural Improvement Society
and imported one of the first English machines for making drainage tiles. In 1850 he left
the farm for a six-month tour of Europe, the first part of which he recorded in his *Walks
and Talks of an American Farmer in England* (1852). He landed in Liverpool and walked the
200-odd miles all the way to London, commenting on the landscape, the ecology (although
the word 'ecology' had not yet been coined) and the people.

The English landscape made a deep impression on him. From childhood rides with
his father he loved quiet scenery to be appreciated and absorbed more or less silently in
contemplation, never leading to sudden excitement. For him the landscape should exhibit
mystery, bounty and peace, engendering psychological benefits. He described his first view
of England as 'green, dripping, glistening, gorgeous'. His impression of the Isle of Wight,

off the south coast of England, was of 'dark, rugged, picturesque ravines … sublime rock masses, and soft, warm, inviting dells and dingles … strange, fascinating enrichment of half-tropical foliage, so deep, graceful and luxuriant, as I never saw before anywhere in the world'.[58] Memories of this 'half-tropical' landscape returned to him much later when he was appointed landscape architect for the 1893 Columbian Exhibition in Chicago.

After visiting Eaton Hall in Cheshire, the palatial home of the Marquess of Westminster, with its Capability Brown park overlaid near the house in 1820 with terraces by William Andrew Nesfield, he wrote: 'Probably there is no object of art that Americans of cultivated taste more generally long to see in Europe, than an English park. What artist so noble … as he, who with far-reaching conception of beauty and designing power, sketches the outlines, writes the colours and directs the shadows of a picture so great that Nature shall be employed upon it for generations before the work he has arranged for her shall realize his intentions.'[59] This is, perhaps, the most concise expression of Olmsted's belief in the importance of the profession to which his life was being directed and which he later, somewhat reluctantly, gave the name 'landscape architecture'. He was, though, still a republican and not disinclined to tilt at one of the richest men in England. 'Eaton Hall and Park is *one* of the seats of the Marquis of Westminster, a very wealthy nobleman, who has lately been named "Lord High Chamberlain to her Majesty," a kind of state-housekeeper or steward, I take it – an office which Punch [a satirical magazine] and a common report of a niggardly disposition in his private affairs, deems him particularly well fitted for.'[60]

Olmsted's understanding of the visual and ecological aspects of the landscape was profound, but it was matched by his interest in and sympathy for his fellow beings. His *Walks and Talks* began in Liverpool in the docks, where it was impossible to miss the bedraggled figures of prostitutes plying their trade. Olmsted considered the plight of these poor women and the circumstances which drove them to this dangerous situation. Later he commented on the desperate lives of agricultural labourers in their cramped hovels as he journeyed south through rural England. Soon after landing, though, he crossed the Mersey to explore the new town of Birkenhead. He stopped at a baker's shop to buy breakfast, and the baker, recognising a foreign visitor, asked him if he had seen 'our park'. With directions from the baker Olmsted found the park and in his journal commented with admiration on its design and construction. While there it started to rain, and he took shelter on one of the covered bridges which had been incorporated into the design for this wet part of a wet country. He was surrounded by other people taking shelter: gentlemen and ladies in their finery mingled with poor women selling milk to earn a few pennies while children clung around their skirts. Having seen the baker's pride in *his* park, and the mix of all layers of society in the shelter, Olmsted wrote: 'In democratic America there was nothing to be thought of as comparable with this People's Garden.'[61] Like Downing, Olmsted sought to foster gentility and 'taste', 'that mixture of aesthetic values, cleanliness, and sense of propriety that not only marked the gentry but served as an important means of moving society from a state of barbarism to one of civilisation'.[62] Birkenhead showed how this might be achieved.

Olmsted's journal casts an interesting light on the nineteenth-century relationship between England and America. He recorded after a visit to Chester:

> Some months later than this we were at a supper party, after some old English ballads and songs had been sung, when one of the company apologized for it, saying, 'We forget our American friends. It is selfish for us to sing only these national songs ...' Have you nothing American, now?' 'Excuse me, sir,' I replied, 'those are our national songs as much as yours. You forget that we are all countrymen of Shakespeare, and Robin Hood, and Richard the Lion-Hearted ... We have as much pride in Old England, gentlemen, as any of you. We claim the right to make ourselves *at home* on that ground with you.' And the whole table rose, shaking our hands with an enthusiasm that only patriotic pride will excuse among Englishmen.[63]

From 1852 to 1854 Olmsted travelled to the southern states for the *New York Daily Times*, resulting in his three-volume *Journey to the Southern Slave States*. Like his *Walks and Talks* it was a remarkable mix of social, ecological and aesthetic observation. In 1855 he moved to New York City as editor of *Putnam's Monthly Magazine*, under the auspices of which he returned to Europe in 1856 for eight months. He was dismayed by the 'pollution' of the formerly green public parks by gaudy exotic bedding plants. In 1857 *Putnam's* failed and Olmsted found new employment as Superintendent of Central Park in New York. Since Downing's editorial of 1848, the proposal for a park had become a political football. Right-wing politicians saw America as a proud frontier nation of independent spirits not to be weakened by communistic talk of public works. Others saw public institutions – museums, galleries and parks – as the necessary indicators of a mature and civilized society. In 1853 the state legislature had passed a law setting aside a 750-acre site in the middle of Manhattan, then on the northern edge of New York City, for the nation's first major landscaped public park. In 1854 the Democrat Fernando Wood was elected mayor, and the idea became a reality. The project continued to be plagued by corruption and political manoeuvring, problems described bitterly and in some detail in Olmsted's *The Spoils of the Park*, but in 1857–8 a competition was held to appoint a designer.[64] Olmsted and Calvert Vaux submitted an anonymous design entitled

'Greensward', and it was chosen as the winner over 32 other entries. Olmsted became the superintendent implementing his own design.

From 1858 to 1861 he worked with Calvert Vaux on the construction of Central Park, but on the outbreak of the Civil War he was appointed executive director of the US Sanitary Commission, the forerunner of the Red Cross. From 1863 to 1865 he became administrator of the Mariposa mines, 44,000 acres west of California's spectacular Yosemite Valley, and in 1864, when the government ceded Yosemite Valley to the State of California for public use, he was appointed chairman of the Management Commission.

His former partner Calvert Vaux had stayed in New York, reconnecting with Central Park. When the park officially opened in 1863, more than 4 million people visited in the first year. By the early 1870s that number had risen to 10 million each year. Vaux had also been appointed to design Prospect Park in Brooklyn. At Vaux's request Olmsted returned to New York to share in the work. He set up his landscape architectural practice and for the next 30 years established a profession which sought to improve and civilize American society. His practice ranged across the United States.

In 1868 he designed Riverside in Chicago, a 1,600-acre suburban development remarkable for its elegantly curved streets in the land of the grid, and for its use of small patches and strands of green space to set the individual houses into a green matrix. In 1871 he produced plans for South Park in Chicago, a scheme enlarged and revitalized when, in 1890, he was appointed landscape architect for the 1893 Columbian Exposition.

From 1875 into the 1890s the firm worked on one of their most ambitious projects, Boston's 'Emerald Necklace', turning low-lying, often swampy wastes into a string of parks linking Franklin Park, the Muddy River and Back Bay Fens to the city centre. While in Boston (Olmsted moved to Brookline and opened an office there) he was asked by Charles Sprague Sargent, cousin of the artist John Singer Sargent and director of Harvard's Arnold Arboretum, to advise on the layout of the new arboretum. Olmsted disliked botanical gardens and arboreta for their inevitable gardenesque scattering of plants, but he was eventually persuaded to design the curving paths and drives which remain a feature of the arboretum.

Most of Olmsted's work was for public or corporate clients, but in 1888 he was asked by George W. Vanderbilt to advise on his 120,000-acre estate of Biltmore in Asheville, North Carolina. Vanderbilt's fortune was estimated to be worth 13 million dollars, and he was an avid collector of books and art. Olmsted persuaded him to plan a modest (by Vanderbilt standards) park and gardens near the house, and to devote the rest of the estate to systematic forestry as an investment and example to others. A young Gifford Pinchot, trained in forestry in Europe, was appointed overseer of an 80,000-acre National

Forest with an arboretum to facilitate the study of dendrology, forestry and the art of landscape improvement.

Olmsted's 1890 appointment as landscape architect for the 1893 Columbian Exposition on the Lake Michigan shore in Chicago was regarded as pivotal to the success of the exposition, earning him a gold medal from the American Institute of Architects. Although the Exposition was predominantly an architectural scheme with numerous pavilions in the cumbersome Beaux Arts style, with its heavy ornamentation based very loosely on French Renaissance architecture, Olmsted wanted to create a counterpoint with a central island and the lakeshore richly planted like a tropical forest: memories of the Isle of Wight. A hundred thousand willows were planted. Seventy-five railroad cars of aquatics were dredged from nearby rivers; 140,000 other aquatic plants and 285,000 ferns and herbaceous perennials were used to create the 'jungle'.

With his stepson John, his son Frederick Law junior, and a string of young apprentices, Olmsted designed housing developments, university campuses, parks and park systems across the United States. By 1895, though, his memory was failing and he was becoming increasingly frail. When John Singer Sargent was commissioned to paint his portrait, the artist used Olmsted's 25-year-old son, of very similar build to his father, suitably dressed, as stand-in for most of the sittings, with Olmsted senior sitting only for the head.

Olmsted died in 1903, but not before transforming Humphry Repton's 'landscape gardening' into the larger and more socially directed profession of landscape architecture and more or less single-handedly training the first young generation of landscape architects. England and Birkenhead Park provided key inspirations in shaping his career, but these favours would be returned to England in full measure in the twentieth century.

10

Arts and Crafts

O LMSTED'S EFFORTS to enhance the well-being of the young American nation were matched in England by a growing concern about the evils of the Industrial Revolution. Joseph Paxton's building to house the 1851 Great Exhibition in London's Hyde Park, dubbed the 'Crystal Palace' by *Punch* magazine, was a triumph of ingenious engineering, but its contents raised deep concerns by those aware of the enormous social cost represented by the exhibits. A giant machine for converting rolls of paper into envelopes – embedded in a frame of cast iron classical columns, topped by peacocks, dragons, eagles and other symbols of who-knows-what – was not only ugly in itself but represented the product of lives spent in misery in the factories and mines, children losing limbs as they toiled to clean the machinery while it was still operating, foul air and polluted rivers.

Leading the campaign for a better life for all was the artist and writer John Ruskin (1819–1900). Ruskin believed that art, life and nature were inseparable. People deprived of art and of contact with nature were less than human. Ruskin had personal reason to be displeased by the Great Exhibition. The Commissioners for the Royal Parks had insisted, against public clamours, that the building be removed from Hyde Park when the exhibition closed. Paxton bought his glasshouse, dismantled and re-erected it, with some rather bulbous additions, at Sydenham, south of the capital. The new Crystal Palace was to be a place of entertainment and education for the common man. It had its own railway station. It had firework displays and concerts. It had a landscape setting with a spine of Italianate fountains and cascades, grey and cold under an English sky, and a fringe of naturalistic landscape with meandering walks and sinuous lakes, on the shores of which 'roamed' life-sized models of dinosaurs. The Ruskins (John lived with his parents) had moved out to Denmark Hill, Camberwell, to escape the spread of London in 1842, only to find their rural peace shattered 20 years later as hordes of common people streamed past their doors on the way to the Crystal Palace.

As a prolific writer, lecturer and, from 1869, as Slade Professor of Fine Art at Oxford University, Ruskin had a very wide following. The most important of those followers was William Morris (1834–1896). Even more than Ruskin he was a man of many parts. A home-taught and precocious reader, Morris later recorded quite dispassionately, 'My father died in 1847, a few months before I went to Marlborough [School]; but as he had engaged in a fortunate mining speculation before his death, we were left very well off, rich in fact.'[65] The irony that miners of arsenic were toiling underground in the Cornish mines that provided his wealth, suffering painful and early deaths, seemed to have escaped his notice as he wrote and campaigned on the need to improve the lot of the working man by education.

As a student at Oxford he moved from theology to poetry and history, immersing himself in medieval romance, and was drawn into the Pre-Raphaelite circle of Dante Gabriel Rossetti, Edward Burne-Jones and their artist friends, firebrands who poured scorn on the elaborate art of recent times and looked back to what they saw as the simple, pure art of the medieval age before Raphael. After graduating in 1856 he joined the office of G. E. Street, a leading architect of country houses, for nine months, meeting another young architect, Philip Webb, before rejoining Burne-Jones in Red Lion Square, his new home in London. In 1857 Morris met, and fell in love with, Jane Burden, the daughter of an Oxford innkeeper. The unlikely couple were married in 1859, and Morris commissioned his friend Philip Webb to build them a house among the Kentish orchards in Bexley. The Red House, of warm red brick, was considered revolutionary for its simplicity in an age of architectural excess. They moved in in 1861. Morris's biographer Aymer Vallance wrote: 'The surrounding garden [of Red House] divided into many squares, hedged by sweetbriar or wild rose, each enclosure with its own particular show of flowers; on this side a green alley with a bowling green, on that orchard walks amid gnarled old fruit trees … The building had been planned with such care that hardly a tree in the orchard had to be cut down; apples fell in at the windows as they stood open on hot autumn nights.'[66]

Life in the Red House was delightful, an extension of student life in Oxford with young friends talking and drinking long into the night to solve the world's problems, but it proved difficult to find furniture to suit this revolutionary new house. The answer, of course, was to do it yourself. In 1861 Morris, Marshall, Faulkner & Co. was established in London's Bloomsbury with Morris, the engineer and amateur painter Peter Paul Marshall, Ford Madox Brown, Rossetti, Burne-Jones, Webb and the mathematician Charles Faulkner to keep the accounts; they offered a wide range of furniture, fabrics, wallpapers, stained glass and other products of their combined craftsmanship to a discerning public. The firm exhibited at the London International Exhibition of 1862.

In 1865 the Morrises left the Red House to move back to London, where he became much involved with adult education, mainly the education of working men, in the East End, preaching the delights of the creative life of the guild worker of ages past. In 1871 he leased Kelmscott Manor, near Lechlade in the Cotswolds, with Rossetti. In the Cotswolds he found a life combining art and craft and life still more or less intact. A medieval inheritance of wealth from the wool trade in a region of rolling hills and workable, honey-coloured limestone had populated the area with many small towns and villages in which labourers' cottages jostled with the richly carved houses of wealthy merchants. By the late nineteenth century changes in world trade – with industrial England selling its wares worldwide in exchange for wheat from Canada, lamb from New Zealand, and beef from Argentina brought in on refrigerated steamships – had left the Cotswolds as an impoverished and crumbling backwater, but the charm of the old buildings in their bucolic settings proved irresistible to Morris.

By 1874 the newly restructured Morris & Co. was producing stained glass, tiles, wallpapers, woven and printed fabrics, carpets, tapestry and furniture. From 1881 Morris acquired Merton Abbey in Surrey, where he revived ancient techniques using natural dyes instead of the new and crude synthetic dyes. His daughter May took charge of embroidery work. In 1888 Morris joined the newly formed Art Workers' Guild, becoming its president in 1891. Also in 1888 the Arts and Crafts Exhibition Society, an offshoot of the guild, held its first Arts and Crafts Exhibition, giving its name to a movement which had been evolving for a variety of reasons for more than 30 years.

In his later years Morris became increasingly frail in body, though never in mind. His last public speech was in January 1889, to second a motion of a society devoted to checking 'the Abuses of Public Advertising', arguing: 'It is a national interest to protect rural scenery from unnecessary disfigurement.'[67] His doctors recommended a sea cruise to Norway, but this failed to restore him. Suffering from diabetes and with congestion of the lungs, he was too weak to travel to Kelmscott and died in London on 3 October 1896. The official cause of death was recorded as pneumonia, but a medical friend declared: 'The disease is simply being William Morris and having done more work than most ten men.'[68] He was taken by train from London to Lechlade station, and then in a plain oak coffin carried on a hay cart from the station to Kelmscott Church, where he is buried.

The ethos and practices of Arts and Crafts designers in England struck sympathetic chords throughout America, especially in architecture and interior design. Ruskin and Morris were very widely read and the products of Morris's workshops eagerly sought. The magazine *House Beautiful*, published in Chicago from 1896, had many examples of English design, and the Chicago Arts and Crafts Society was formed in 1897 with the architect Frank Lloyd Wright as a charter member. The East Coast artist/craftsman Gustav Stickley, widely considered to be the American William Morris, met Charles Voysey and Charles Robert Ashbee in their English studios in 1898 before launching his widely read magazine, *The Craftsman*, in 1901. He went on to establish a utopian community at Craftsman Farms in New Jersey in 1908, living in stately poverty in a log cabin until the community closed in 1915.

California had special attractions for the mobile American population because of its mountains, the ocean, clean air and favourable climate. Its attraction to wealthy Americans seeking summer homes made it a particularly attractive environment for architects of ability, and the traditions of Spanish Colonial architecture, well adapted to the climate of southern California, blended with Arts and Crafts architecture in which house and garden were conceived as a single entity.

The wide range of landscapes and climates of America made it difficult to adopt or adapt the English garden, but the spirit of the movement spread from coast to coast. In those parts of America where the weather permitted, the English garden had enormous influence, especially through the writings and practice of its two giants of the late nineteenth- and early twentieth-century garden, Gertrude Jekyll and William Robinson, themselves deeply influenced by Ruskin and Morris.

Gertrude Jekyll (1843–1932) was born in London, the daughter of a soldier father with a keen interest in gadgetry and explosives and a charming mother, a devoted homemaker and talented musician who took lessons from Felix Mendelssohn. When Gertrude was five, the Jekyll family moved to Bramley House, near Guildford in Surrey. Young Gertrude was a strong character, 'sailing' in an old wine cask on the lake in the garden, making dens and surfacing the path leading to her own garden plot with cinders, knowing that this would deter her father, who hated the crunching noise. At 18 she enrolled at the Kensington School of Art and Design, a remarkable event for a young lady when nude statues had to have their vital parts covered to prevent blushes. At Kensington she had lectures and classes in painting. There were lectures on colour theory and colour perception of the human eye, building on the 1854 translation into English of Michel Eugène Chevreul's *Principles of Harmony and Contrast of Colours*. She had lectures from John Ruskin, who admired her draughtsmanship and introduced her to the works of J. M. W. Turner. She spent many hours in the National Gallery, where Ruskin had directed the hanging of many Turner paintings.

In London she had many friends: Mary Newton, for example, whose husband was keeper of antiquities at the British Museum, and Leoni Blumenthal, whose mansion in Hyde Park Gate offered splendid relief to student life. She travelled to the eastern Mediterranean with the Newtons and spent summers at the Blumenthals' chalet, built in 1869 overlooking Lake Geneva in France, with party games, musical recitals and long mountain walks among carpets of wild flowers. She designed a special pickaxe for prising alpine plants from rock crevices and had it made by a local blacksmith.

Gertrude Jekyll had a wide range of interests involving design and making, art and craft: wood carving, silver work, embroidery, shell pictures, the young art and craft of photography and, at least from the age of five, gardening. She painted for much of her life, but recognising that she would never be an outstanding painter and always suffering from painful short-sightedness, she turned gradually to gardening as the main outlet for her creativity. In 1868 the family moved to Wargrave in Berkshire, a move which she hated only because it was not Surrey, but on the death of her father in 1876 she moved with her mother back to Surrey, to Munstead, a tiny hamlet near Godalming, into a new house built on the heath, Munstead House. Here she developed the garden, and from here she continued to enjoy social life in London, Switzerland, France and Italy. From 1881 she produced a steady stream of articles and sent specimens of interesting plants to *The Garden*, a magazine founded in 1870 by William Robinson, with whom she developed a life-long friendship.

In 1883 the initials 'O.S.' began to appear in her diary. She had acquired 11 acres of land on the 'other side' of Munstead Lane in which to develop her own garden, recognising that she could not live for ever with her mother, who in old age was less and less able to cope with her daughter's steady stream of gardening and artistic friends. The garden 'on the other side' developed in much the same way as had that at Munstead House, a cluster of rectangular gardens merging gradually into the natural scenery of the heath.

In 1889 Jekyll was invited to tea by Harry Mangles, a neighbour and pioneer rhododendron grower. Mangles was having some cottages built on his estate and had commissioned a young architect, Edwin Lutyens, to design them. Jekyll and Lutyens met at tea. Lutyens recalled a 'bunch of cloaked propriety' with a feathered hat which bobbed as she talked.[69] (It was the fashion for those bobbing feathers that spurred Emily Williamson and a small group of fellow activists in Didsbury, near Manchester, to form 'The Plumage League' in 1889. Later they joined forces with another protest group against women's fashions, 'The Fur and Feather League' in Surrey, to form the Society for the Protection of Birds, England's first conservation society. That society received its Royal Charter in 1904 and as the RSPB now has more than a million members.) Lutyens, at 22, was slim and understandably nervous in contrast to the large, confident figure of Gertrude Jekyll, whom he later referred to as 'Aunt Bumps'. They did not speak much but, when about to depart, Jekyll invited the young architect to tea. Thus began a friendship which spanned the 43 years until her death. They rode together in her pony cart – a hazardous occupation for Lutyens given her poor sight – exploring nearby villages and discussing the subtle adaptations of roof pitch, window span and other details that had evolved in each village over centuries by craftsmen builders.

In 1891 Gertrude Jekyll commissioned Lutyens to build 'The Hut', a simple building with one room upstairs and one down, in which she could work on her own side of the lane in inclement weather, store the materials of her many activities, and camp out for a day or two if necessary. When her mother died, Jekyll's eldest brother, Herbert, inherited the family home and she needed a proper home of her own. Lutyens was commissioned to build

Munstead Wood. Work started in 1895 and she moved in in 1897, the year in which she was one of the 60 recipients of the Royal Horticultural Society's Victoria Medal of Honour, minted to celebrate the queen's Diamond Jubilee. Despite their friendship the relationship of architect and client was not always an easy one. On one occasion, when Lutyens wanted an expensive modification to the plan, Jekyll exploded, 'My house is to be built for me to live in and to love; it is not to be built as an exposition of architectonic inutility!' She reflected later that 'I learnt from the architect's crushed and somewhat frightened demeanour, that long words certainly have their use, if only as engines of warfare of the nature of the battering-ram.'[70] In general, though, the relationship was one of mutual admiration. Jekyll was always in awe of architectural skills and of Lutyens's abilities in particular. In return she discussed his many commissions with him and, in the words of Lutyens's collaborator, the architect Herbert Baker, taught him the poetry of making a home rather than a house.[71] Lutyens fitted this new home into its established garden setting with consummate skill.

Between 1881 and 1896 Jekyll wrote more than 200 articles, some short notes, others longer, mainly for William Robinson's *The Garden* and his later, more successful *Gardening Illustrated*, but also occasionally for the *Journal of the Royal Horticultural Society*, the long-established *Gardeners' Chronicle* and other periodicals. In 1896–7 she wrote a series of 16 'Notes from Garden and Woodland' for the *Guardian* newspaper. These were collected in her first book, *Wood and Garden* (1899), followed in rapid succession by *Home and Garden* (1900), *Lilies for English Gardens* and *Wall and Water Gardens* (both 1901), *Roses for English Gardens* (1902) and a dozen other titles over the next 20 years. Many of her books – 'notes and thoughts practical and critical of a working amateur'[72] – were immediately successful on both sides of the Atlantic and went through many editions. Frank Lloyd Wright advised that her *Home and Garden* should be in every library.

In 1908 came *Colour in the Flower Garden*, first rehearsed as a chapter in William Robinson's *English Flower Garden* (1883) and reprinted in 1914 as *Colour Schemes for the Flower Garden*. Her many books were based on her 50 years of 'artistic gardening'. They were full of practical hints – how to divide, stake and cultivate plants, which plants to grow where – but they had a deeper vein of philosophy which appealed to her readers as much as Ruskin's and Morris's ideals on the need for everyone to have a creative life. For Gertrude Jekyll there was a need to strive for perfection knowing that perfection would never be achieved and a duty to use one's talents to the full in gratitude for the gift of those talents from a benevolent Creator.

The meeting at teatime between Gertrude Jekyll and Edwin Lutyens in 1889 was a moment of serendipity which resulted in the creation of wonderful gardens and the dissemination of a philosophy of gardening which was eagerly absorbed in England,

America and Australia – throughout the English-speaking world – and in much of Europe. Twelve years later came another meeting, between Jekyll's neighbour Edward Hudson and Lutyens, which would have a similar impact on architecture. Edward Hudson was head of the Hudson and Kearns Publishing House. He saw the English countryside around him changing rapidly as a result of the suburban railways and the beginnings of the motor age and decided to publish a new weekly magazine capturing the best of traditional life in the country. *Country Life* began in 1897 and is still widely read on both sides of the Atlantic.

Hudson asked Jekyll to be its first editor. She declined because of age, inexperience and the pressures of other work, but in 1901 she introduced Edward Hudson the publisher to Edwin Lutyens the architect. They were both essentially overgrown schoolboys and struck up an immediate friendship. Lutyens designed two houses for Hudson and remodelled the ancient Lindisfarne Castle on Holy Island off the coast of Northumberland for him. Many of Lutyens's later houses were written up in *Country Life*, bringing his work to a wealthy and discerning potential clientele. Lutyens's career was given a massive and well-deserved boost, and he went on to become England's leading architect, considered by some second only to Sir Christopher Wren 200 years before. Typically, when Lutyens became infatuated with the mathematically determined classical architecture, what he called 'the high game', and moved away from his earlier vernacular style, he dubbed his new style 'Wrenaissance'.[73]

Of his first house for Edward Hudson, the Deanery in Sonning, Berkshire, Lutyens's biographer Christopher Hussey wrote: 'The Deanery Garden, at once formal and irregular, settled that controversy of which Sir Reginald Blomfield and William Robinson were for long the protagonists, between formal and naturalist garden design. Miss Jekyll's planting wedded Lutyens' geometry in a balanced union of both principles.'[74] Their marriage of architecture and gardening provided a – perhaps the – major source of inspiration for gardens throughout the twentieth century in England and elsewhere, especially America. In *The Simple Home* (1904), the poet Charles Augustus Keeler wrote: 'My own preference for a garden for the simple home is a compromise between the natural and formal types – a compromise in which the carefully studied plan is concealed by a touch of careless grace.'[75]

In the later editions of her books Jekyll pleaded to be left in peace to work in her garden. 'If only I knew who were the genuine applicants, I would still make exceptions. You can have no idea how much I have suffered from Americans, Germans and journalists.'[76] She did, though, continue to receive American visitors. Henry F. du Pont visited Munstead Wood more than once, and Jekyll's books inspired the planting of his garden at Winterthur in Wilmington, Delaware. He even attempted her practice of planting clematis behind delphiniums so that the clematis could be trained over the cut-down stems of the delphiniums when they had finished flowering.

Grace Groesbeck was the first American to commission a garden plan from Jekyll, in 1914, for her new house in Perintown, Ohio. In October 1914 Mrs Groesbeck wrote:

My dear Miss Jekyll,

Your letter of Oct. 31st received, Mr. Groesbeck and I have come to the conclusion that your idea of the position of the house is best and will ask you to go ahead with your original plan of placing it at the head of the main valley.

In regard to the other buildings, we had thought of putting them in some other place with the exception of the pump house suggested in one of your previous letters. We plan to have gate posts at the foot of the hill where [the] road enters and had thought of having a gardener's cottage at or near the entrance but I want you to understand that we do not wish to thrust our ideas upon you but have you feel perfectly free to work out the plan in any way you think best as of course your ideas are infinitely better and we have perfect confidence in whatever you decide is best.[77]

The resulting plans, on 24 sheets, were for a strongly architectural more or less Italianate garden descending from the house in a series of terraces to the Ohio River. Detailed planting plans were made for the terrace on which the house sat, but the slopes were left for someone with a local knowledge of what plants would grow in the region, perhaps Grace Groesbeck herself, to decide: 'Groups of the wilder Rambling roses with wild trees and bushes', 'bushes and trees of wild character' and for the wide prospect down to the river, 'Rough grass and bushes (if any) such as brambles, etc.'[78] Despite the Groesbecks' confidence in her, Jekyll's plans proved unworkable once the contractors came to build. The sandy ground was unstable, the house had to be relocated and, after much delay, it seems probable that Mrs Groesbeck gained the confidence to design her own garden.

The second American garden, begun in 1925 when Jekyll was 82, was for Helen and Stanley Resor in Greenwich, Connecticut. The Resors knew the editor of *Homes and Gardens*, who knew Edward Hudson, the editor of *Country Life*. Hudson wrote to Jekyll of the Resors' intended visit to England. They were 'quite charming people and I should be glad to hear if you would mind their coming down to see you.'[79] They were indeed charming, and after the visit Helen Resor wrote to Jekyll, 'Mr. Resor and I consider our afternoon with you the happiest time that we experienced in the seven weeks we were abroad and we have told many people that the outstanding personality among the hundreds of people we met was Miss Gertrude Jekyll.'[80]

As the Resors travelled widely in the summers they had no need for colourful flower borders, and they requested *no grass*. Instead, Jekyll designed a wild garden with boldly curving paths among groups of shrubs with spring flowers, autumn colour and/or evergreen foliage. There were long drifts of azaleas and rhododendrons, cotinus and pieris, junipers and dogwoods among pines, firs and hemlocks. Although the plan is sophisticated in its elegantly controlled curvature, Jekyll advised: 'The outer paths should have no formal edging; in fact it would be best if the path was merely cleaned so that one could see where it is intended to be with any low plants coming to the edge, but nothing hard or clearly defined.'[81]

Her third American garden was again quite different in character. It was designed at the behest of Annie Burr Jennings, the wealthy and public-spirited daughter of the co-founder, with J. D. Rockefeller, of Standard Oil. Annie Jennings visited Jekyll, during a trip to England with her brother and his wife in 1926, to discuss a project in Woodbury, Connecticut: an 'old-fashioned' garden for the Old Glebe House, part of which dated from 1690 and in which the first American Episcopalian bishop, Thomas Seabury, was elected in 1783. From earlier correspondence with Mrs Francis King, Jekyll had been made aware of the lack of a cottage gardening tradition in America. For Glebe House she designed a simple garden in which there would be 'that delightful combination of dignity, modesty and restfulness'.[82]

Members of the Seabury Society at the Old Glebe House in Connecticut, before the creation of Gertrude Jekyll's garden.

Jekyll's influence continues to be felt. When my book *The Gardens of Gertrude Jekyll* was published in 1992 with a chapter on her American gardens, the reference to the Groesbeck garden near Cincinnati was seen by a master gardener in Virginia who had a landscape contracting friend in Cincinnati. That friend, Chris Tetrault, did some research, identified the site of the garden (the remains of which had become the Wildwood Christian Education Center), and organized a symposium to which Judith Tankard and other distinguished American garden historians gave papers, as did I before flying on to San Francisco where I was able to see the real Reef Point collection of Jekyll's drawings, having worked for several years with microfilm copies.

In 2001 I was asked by Scott Matthews, who had also read my book, to comment on his American landscape architect's plans for a garden to complement the house he was building in the hills above Santa Barbara. Scott Matthews is a great enthusiast for the work of Edwin Lutyens, and he was building his own 'Lutyens' house on a section of a former ranch. Having made some suggestions of my own, I was invited to see the garden in 2003, and returned in 2009 to see the lived-in house settling into a flourishing young (Munstead) wood of trees suited to the climate of southern California. The stereotypical view of Gertrude Jekyll sees her as the inventor of herbaceous borders full of delicate perennials, so the idea of a Jekyll garden in this hot, dry part of the world seems ridiculous. However, that view is far from accurate. She loved grey-leaved plants and other denizens of the Mediterranean, and she was, after all, reputed to be the first person to flower *Carpentaria californica* in England. Her spirit lives on.

A close contemporary of Gertrude Jekyll, and far more famous than she in his own day, was William Robinson (1838–1935). Although a good friend of Jekyll in the last 50 years of their lives, he was dismissive of the paper plans, architects' designs and colour schemes with which she was so familiar, the visual aspects of the Arts and Crafts movement. Instead, he was deeply influenced by the social ideas of John Ruskin and William Morris.

Robinson was born in southern Ireland, then part of the United Kingdom. Although by far the most famous gardener of his day, he managed, consciously or perhaps subconsciously, to conceal much of the detail of his early life. He did reveal that he started his career in gardening at the age of 10, as a garden boy on the Marquess of Waterford's estate at Curraghmore. This was one of the most notable landscape parks in Ireland, and at the time of Robinson's employment it was being developed with an expansive formal garden in the French style by the Scottish landscape gardener James Fraser. From Curraghmore Robinson moved to Ballykilkavan in Queen's County, to work for the Revd Sir Hunt Henry Johnson-Walsh, vicar of Stradbally, where he was promoted to foreman. Robinson was obviously an ambitious young man, and in 1861, with a letter of recommendation from

David Moore, the curator of Dublin's Royal (now National) Botanic Garden at Glasnevin, he sailed from Dublin and made his way to London.

David Moore's letter of introduction was to fellow Scot Robert Marnock, designer and curator of the Royal Botanic Society's garden in the inner circle of Regent's Park, then on the northern outskirts of London. Marnock had made his reputation as designer, and then curator, of the Sheffield Botanical and Horticultural Society's garden. He won the competition for the design of the London garden held soon after the Society's establishment in 1839 and, on the recommendation of J. C. Loudon, was appointed curator. Although primarily a botanic garden serving the needs of students of medicine, botany and art in the capital, it also hosted elaborate horticultural shows and served as the venue for the Society's social gatherings.

Robinson was appointed as foreman of the herbaceous plant collection, and his responsibilities were soon extended to include the education department, so he was able to control the ravages wrought by undisciplined students on the collections in his care. He was never less than forthright. He declared a glasshouse in his territory a ridiculous wreck, totally unfit for purpose, and he asked for its replacement, or at least its demolition so that the ground could be put to better use. Neither was he impressed by the plants in his care. He began exploring the countryside around London 'from the orchid-flecked meadows of Buckinghamshire to the undercliffs of Essex' to supplement the collections,[83] and in 1863 obtained a grant of 15 pounds from Marnock to undertake a month-long tour of other botanic gardens, visiting gardens in Hull, York, Edinburgh, Glasgow, Belfast, Dublin, Liverpool and Manchester. He arrived back in London in September laden with plants and with offers of many more in due season.

Nothing is known of Robinson's early education. Like many other young gardeners he was probably taught by his head gardener and self-taught, but he wrote with great fluency and obviously read widely because his later writings are laced with quotations from a very broad range of classical and contemporary authors. Accounts of his first major tour were published in the *Gardeners' Chronicle*, a magazine founded in 1841 by John Lindley, secretary of the Horticultural Society, and the most important of the many horticultural magazines of the time. His accounts highlight many facets of horticulture and landscape gardening which became the themes of later enthusiasms and campaigns, and these first ventures into journalism brought him into contact with other leading gardeners on whose experiences he would call in later years.

In May 1866 Robinson was elected a Fellow of the Linnean Society, his nomination sponsored by Charles Darwin, David Moore, James Veitch of the Veitch Nurseries dynasty, and seven other distinguished botanists and horticulturists. In a letter to Robinson discussing parallel experiments in cross-pollination of plants Darwin added a postscript, 'I was plsd to see your Election to the Linnean Soc.'[84] Two months later Robinson resigned from the garden 'to devote myself to the study of our Great Gardens and of the literature of Horticulture for a year or two',[85] an aim strongly reminiscent of Humphry Repton's 'retirement' to Hare Street in Romford, Essex, to prepare himself for his new career as a landscape gardener. Robinson had been preparing for a visit to France, an ambition stimulated by his reading of old French gardening books in the Royal Botanic Society's library.

In February 1867, after an intensive French course, Robinson travelled to Paris to report for the *Gardeners' Chronicle* and *The Field* on progress of the great horticultural exhibition being mounted by the city throughout the spring, summer and autumn. In March, while the exhibition was still being prepared, he visited Le Jardin Fleuriste de la Ville de Paris, the main nursery for the city. The scale of operations, the combination of mass production and ornamental display of foliage plants, and the ingenuity of using the limestone caverns created by excavation of building materials for Napoleon's rebuilding of Paris to store canna roots over winter all impressed the young writer. He commented, though, that a single ball at the Hotel de Ville [City Hall] cost more than 30,000 livres [pounds] 'while the poor Jardin des Plantes gets from the State not more than one-third of that sum to exist upon for a whole year'.[86] As always, the gardeners lost out.

In his third letter he commented on the pathetic sight of faded everlasting flowers on the graves of the poor and fulminated against the ghastly burial wreaths – his first mention of the cemeteries to which he would later devote so much attention. In June he

> called in at the Cemetery of Mont Parnasse on my way to M. Chantin's nursery. Saw them making a new drive, *the bottom being made of broken headstones, many of them bearing the date of 1860 and thereabouts.* These had been placed on ground not paid for in perpetuity, and were consequently grubbed up when, as I before described, they wanted to fill the trenches a second time. I have read and admired Lyell's illustration that all flesh is grass … but I never knew what a poor, transient, weedy kind of Grass is the flesh of the Lord's creation till I came here.[87]

A small illustration in Robinson's later book on cemeteries, *God's Acre Beautiful* (1880), shows a crowded mass of headstones and other memorials in the Montparnasse cemetery.

In April the first exhibition opened. Robinson was not impressed with the exhibits, except for that of England's Veitch Nurseries, and the second was not much better, so he turned his attention to the parks and other public places of Napoleon's splendid refashioning of the city. In the Parc des Buttes Chaumont he met Charles Edouard Alphand, the engineer responsible in large part for Napoleon's transformation of Paris under Baron Haussmann, and saw 'the boldest attempt at what they call the picturesque style that I have ever seen'. After five hours in the Bois de Boulogne he decided it was 'infinitely better than any of our London parks'.[88]

By late April the exhibitions were getting into their stride. Robinson was at last impressed. 'The world has seen some great shows of this kind, but this is the first in which horticulture has been given a significant, even a leading, role.' This late April exhibition brought together the finest collection ever of conifers and 'for new conifers Veitch have beaten all comers'.[89] Many, perhaps most, of these plants were of North American origin with the dozens of cultivars of Lawson's Cypress, a species so uniform in its native land, beginning to express themselves in their different foliage colours and forms. Two other finds particularly impressed him. *Gunnera manicata*, the giant rhubarb-like plant from South America, he later recommended in his book on *The Subtropical Garden* as a plant which looked subtropical but was hardy in the gardens of southern England. The cut-leaved sumac (*Rhus typhina* 'Laciniata') he raved about for its finely divided foliage, finer than any fern, and only growing to 9 inches tall. He was unaware that the sumac might eventually grow to 9 feet tall and sucker to colonize large areas of the garden. How easy it is to be impressed by the tiny new offerings of the nurseryman!

Robinson's stay in Paris, and later travels further south, resulted in two books: *Gleanings from French Gardens* in 1868 and the much larger *Parks, Promenades and Gardens of Paris* in 1869. In them the twin themes which shaped the rest of his career – plants and people – are clearly discernible. He had a great interest in plants. In 1870 came his *Alpine Flowers of English Gardens* extolling the delights of plants from the mountains, and *The Subtropical Garden*, in which he illustrated the (especially French) use of plants with exotic foliage. Also in 1870 came his highly influential book *The Wild Garden*, in which he encouraged the use of those plants from the temperate parts of the world that were too vigorous to be used in borders and beds near the house. Instead, they would embellish the meadows, hedgerows and woods of his readers' large country estates. In 1871 he followed this with his more prosaic *Hardy Flowers*. His one aversion was with the bedding system, then reaching the pinnacle (or depths?) of its development in the flower parterres of the great gardens and in public parks. Robinson drew unmistakable analogies between the bedding system and the evils of the Industrial Revolution. Drawing on Ruskin's comments on the evils of a society which tore children from their homes, forced them to work in mines and factories in appalling conditions, and threw them on the scrap heap when unable to work, Robinson painted a picture of plants torn from their native homes, propagated in steamy hothouses, planted by the thousand in geometrical beds where they lost any individuality, and thrown on the compost heap when they had outlived their brief useful lives.

His other interest was in people, especially the poor. In the parks, tree-lined boulevards and squares of Paris he saw places where even poor people could enjoy the benefits of nature. Parks were an indicator of a civilized society. In his admiration of the intensive practices of market gardening, mushroom and fruit growing that he saw in France (much to the annoyance of older English growers who were slighted by the comparisons), he argued that if the English adopted these techniques, food would be cheaper and the poor better fed. He was outraged, too, at the inequalities which followed people even into the grave, with the poor being interred in makeshift trenches while the rich had ugly temples in their attempts to buy immortality. 'Let us hope', he wrote in *Gleanings*, 'that whatever else may be "taken from the French", we may never imitate them in their cemetery management.'[90] He was an outspoken advocate of cremation instead of burial, and his *God's Acre Beautiful*, with its appalling descriptions of conditions in England's overcrowded cemeteries, makes disturbing reading.

He sought to help the middle classes too. In his *Subtropical Garden* he had a chapter on plants which looked subtropical but were hardy, including that giant *Gunnera manicata* which had excited him when he first saw it in the Paris exhibition, so that middle class enthusiasts who could not afford extensive ranges of heated glasshouses might still indulge in exciting subtropical gardening.

In the action-packed year of 1870, with five books published and more on the way, he travelled to America. He crossed the Atlantic in the three-year-old liner *Russia*, the fastest of the Cunard fleet, perhaps with ambitions to publish a *Gleanings from American Gardens*. If so he was sadly disappointed. After travelling a thousand miles in America, he wrote, 'as regards horticulture, [I] have found as much interest and novelty as a student of snakes could collect during a like period in the land of St. Patrick. Around the houses generally there is about as much garden as on the parched wooden roof.'[91]

There were other compensations, though. In New York there were buildings 10 storeys high! He was, however, appalled by living conditions in the city, relieved only by the parks then being created by Olmsted and Vaux. He met Olmsted in Prospect Park and the two became friends; Olmsted later visited Robinson in England and sent him plants. On a visit to Niagara Falls he thought the scenery so beautiful that it should be made a national park (two years before Yellowstone was designated as the world's first national park). In Cambridge, Massachusetts, he met America's leading botanist, Asa Gray. With letters of introduction from Gray he travelled to Chicago, where he noted with pleasure that the popcorn industry had increased by 6,000 per cent in a year, then on to California to meet Albert Kellogg, an expert on the flora of the Sierra Nevada Mountains, and Henry Bolander, the state botanist of California.

'Mountain Woods of California' from William Robinson's *Alpine Flowers*.

The journey from coast to coast, only a year after the completion of the transcontinental railroad, made an indelible impression on the 32-year-old Robinson. Although there were no gardens to excite him, he saw many beautiful wild plants, including *Sarracenia purpurea*, which had evaded David Douglas and Thomas Hogg in the black swamps in 1823; America's white water lily, *Nymphaea odorata*, with its fragrant white stars shining in the black peaty New England lakes; and *Darlingtonia californica*, the California pitcher plant, of which he brought quantities back to England. He was overwhelmed by the richness of the flora he saw as the train climbed into and through the Sierra Nevada. The western slopes of the mountains were 'densely populated with noble pines and glossy evergreens – an ocean of huge land waves over which the spirit of tree-life has passed, creating giants. The autumn days I spent among these trees were among the happiest man could desire.'[92] A small engraving of the trees was included in a later edition of *Alpine Flowers for Gardens* (no longer *for English Gardens* as he thought that might limit its overseas sales), and a very similar sentence appeared much later in his life when he stood in his own plantations of North American conifers on his Gravetye estate in Sussex, which he bought in 1885. In California, too, he noted the new vineyards which were springing up, commenting that they offered the prospect of more gold than did the mines: 'We shall hear much more of Californian wines.'[93]

Robinson travelled back to the East Coast via Salt Lake City through seemingly endless desert: 'Dust, dreariness and alkali … nothing better than starved wormwood … represents the vegetable kingdom in the plains of the desert region.'[94] In contrast, Salt Lake City itself was a city of gardens, except on the main street where 'the demon of trade … destroyed all the little gardens … piled store after store … precisely as he has done in the gentle thoroughfare known as the Marylebone Road, London NW.'[95]

On his homeward journey Robinson took back herbarium specimens from Bolander in California to Asa Gray at Harvard and boxes of apples from Gray to Joseph Hooker at Kew, together with American tools and samples of tinned vegetables and fruits for his own use. Lily bulbs went to G. F. Wilson for his gardens in Weybridge and Wisley in Surrey, the latter to become the home of the Royal Horticultural Society in 1903. In 1872 the Veitch Nurseries were awarded a First Class Certificate at a Royal Horticultural Society show for a penstemon brought back by Robinson.

In July 1865, five years before his American expedition, Robinson had confided in Dean Reynolds Hole, a keen rosarian (later first president of the Royal National Rose Society) and fellow contributor to *Gardeners' Chronicle*, his ambition to publish his own gardening periodical, and Hole suggested that he should call the new publication *The Garden*. Sailing back on Cunard's *RMS China*, he decided that the time had come to fulfil his ambition. The first issue of *The Garden* appeared in November 1871 and the first half-yearly volume, dedicated to the memory of J. C. Loudon, in June 1872. *The Garden* remained a focus and clearing house of ideas about gardening in general, and naturalistic gardening in particular, for more than 50 years. Its scope was extraordinary. There were articles on new parks in America, a good digging fork which he had discovered there, and an article, citing Samuel Parsons from the *American Agriculturist*, in which Robinson recommended replacing all the pitched roofs in London with flat roofs containing greenhouses to stimulate food production and healthy living. *The Garden* was read by the horticultural elite in England, Europe and America.

A brief account of his American travels was added to the next edition of *Alpine Flowers*, while later editions of his small but influential *Wild Garden* make frequent references to plants seen from the train or found in the mountains of America. The tall autumnal asters, goldenrods and rudbeckias of the American grasslands, so different from the English concept of a flowery meadow, made a deep and lasting impression on him.

In addition to his writing and editing of *The Garden* and his new editions of several of his earlier works, Robinson's publishing activities continued to increase. In 1879 he launched *Gardening Illustrated for Town and Country*, a less expensive magazine than *The Garden*, which was immediately successful. In 1883 came his magnum opus, *The English Flower*

Garden, again hugely successful, going through 15 editions in his lifetime. Throughout these years Robinson had no garden of his own, living over his offices in Covent Garden. In 1885, at the age of 47, he bought Gravetye Manor in Sussex, a 14-bedroom Elizabethan manor house with 360 acres of land. Ernest George, the distinguished architect of country houses, remodelled the house. He also designed the high wall which supported Robinson's new terraced garden west of the house and the summer house at the end of the terrace where Robinson did much of his writing. At last, Robinson was a man of property and able to practise what he had so long preached to others. As well as his writing, publishing and now gardening, he was called on to advise other people on their gardens, some of which had American connections.

In 1893 Robinson was consulted on the gardens of North Mymms Park in Hertfordshire. The house was enlarged by Ernest George for Walter Burns and his wife, the sister of the immensely wealthy American banker (John) Pierpont Morgan. The new west elevation of the house overlooked a rose garden in which the many square beds were edged with pinks and 'every inch was used for the purpose of flower growing,' very much in the character of Robinson's rose garden at Gravetye. Also like Gravetye, North Mymms had a pergola, praised in *Country Life* for the practical touches and handsome proportions showing 'the influence of such a trained mind as that of Mr Robinson', and a large pool for aquatic plants including, of course, 'Nymphaeas', another Robinson favourite.[96] In 1899 Mary Burns, the daughter of Mr and Mrs Burns of North Mymms, married Lewis Harcourt (later Viscount Harcourt), and in 1904 the young couple moved into the Harcourt family home at Nuneham Courtenay near Oxford, where, probably inspired by his mother-in-law's passion for gardening and with advice from William Robinson, he added 'terraced Rose gardens, the Nymphaea garden, the herbaceous garden, the sundial garden and the swamp garden' praised in a 1908 *Gardeners' Chronicle* description, and a long dry wall for alpine plants.[97] He also added a gallery to the house to hang pictures from his 'friend', in fact his wife's uncle, Pierpont Morgan. Clearly, as in many other Edwardian country homes, American money was being used to hold together this historic English estate.

11

An American invasion

R OBINSON's *Wild Garden* has had an impact on gardening far beyond its small size. It
continues to be read into the twenty-first century in various new editions emphasising
the ecological aspect of wildflower planting and the visual delights of 'prairie planting',
which will be discussed in chapter 16. However, it was also responsible, quite accidentally,
for fostering another very important aspect of Anglo-American gardening.

In 1881 Robinson decided to publish a second edition of *The Wild Garden*. In the
introduction he wrote:

> Getting this edition ready for the press, I had a look at the first … In the first edition
> there was one woodcut, and now, as the book showed signs of life, there was some
> doubt as to get [*sic*] drawings worthy of the theme. In a picture show in London I
> happened to see a sketch in oils of an English meadow in flower in June. A bold thing
> to attempt, but I liked it so well I sought the author in town, and we went in quest
> of lost flowers … Alfred Parsons [the artist] had a true eye for flowers in the open,
> and his many drawings I had the pleasure of engraving in the way we thought best
> for the time.

Alfred Parsons (1847–1920), the son of a Somerset doctor who was an expert on alpine
plants, began his career as a post-office clerk but quickly abandoned that to study at the
School of Art in Kensington before setting up his studio in Marylebone Road. After the
London exhibition he met Robinson and produced dozens of illustrations for the new
edition of *The Wild Garden*. In the first edition, with its one woodcut, the tone was of
planting meadows and hedgerows and woods with the contents of the vast plains of the
temperate world, which might resonate with the landed gentry but had very little obvious
relevance to a wider audience. Parsons's charming illustrations – a rose clambering over an
old thorn tree, a clump of snowdrops springing from a bank, or saxifrage, pinks and ferns
on a cottage garden wall – made it clear that the ideas of the wild garden might be carried
out in the corner of any modest suburban garden where perhaps an overgrown lilac or two
needed to be made more of.

Parsons continued to work for Robinson, and he spent many weeks at Gravetye Manor,
together with other artist friends with whom he lived and worked, painting Gravetye and

nearby gardens. Edwin Abbey and Francis (Frank) Millet, with whom Parsons shared a house and studio in London, worked as illustrators for *Harper's Magazine* in New York, and Parsons was later invited to contribute to the magazine. In 1885 Abbey and Millet, and the latter's wife, Lily, moved to the village of Broadway in the Cotswolds. Initially, Parsons joined them in renting a house before he moved permanently from London in the 1890s and bought his own house in 1903. Luggershill was a hillside property from which he could look across to Broadway Tower, a landmark that William Morris had visited and written about in glowing terms some 20 years earlier.

Parsons worked increasingly designing gardens as well as capturing them on canvas. His first was for Frank and Lily Millet at Russell House. It was here, in an almost bare yard before the garden was made, that another garden was 'contrived' with pots of roses and lilies so that an American visitor, John Singer Sargent, could create the lantern-lit backdrop for Polly and Dolly Barnard, daughters of another American illustrator, Frank Barnard, in his painting *Carnation, Lily, Lily, Rose*. Millet also bought the adjacent fourteenth-century Abbot's Grange for use as his studio. Parsons helped to combine the two gardens, and he illustrated them in his 'Broadway Garden' paintings.

He designed a garden at Court Farm in Broadway for the American Mary Anderson, a renowned Shakespearian actress who was married to the English Antonio de Navarro. Mary Anderson de Navarro described how 'there was nothing but a riot of rough, nettle-grown, uneven ground, some old outhouses, barns and rows of pigsties; no paths – disorder and ugliness everywhere. I knew nothing of gardens and felt bewildered. Fortunately for us, our old friend Alfred Parsons R.A. was living in Broadway at that time, and his hobby and recreation was the planning and planting of gardens.'98 The de Navarros then bought the adjacent Bell Farm, an old building which had been admired by William Morris. They linked the two buildings and Parsons unified the garden. The pond became a swimming pool, and the garden was furnished with a rose pergola, hazel coppices, orchards and formal rows of limes. It is amusing to think of Mary Anderson moving from the theatres of Broadway in New York to the very different life of Broadway in the Cotswolds.

Alfred Parsons also designed the garden of Lamb House in Rye, East Sussex, when another notable American, Henry James, moved there in 1897. In 1891 Parsons had exhibited a series of 'Gardens and Orchards' at the Fine Art Society with an introduction to the exhibition by Henry James: 'Parsons is an artist who knows exactly how Americans would like England to appear,' capturing 'that peculiarly English look of the open-air room … [that] nook quality, the air of a land and life so infinitely sub-divided that they produce a thousand pleasant privacies'.99 In a very similar vein he wrote of Parsons in Broadway, 'Was it there that Mr. Parsons learned so well how Americans would like England to appear?

…The England of his pencil … is exactly the England that the American imagination, restricted to itself, constructs from the poets, the novelists, from all the delightful testimony it inherits.'[100] It was Henry James's 1889 article for *Harper's Magazine*, 'Our artists in Europe', that ended the rural if run-down calm of the Cotswolds. Parsons's atmospheric illustrations combined with Henry James's seductive prose to attract many American Anglophiles to the area. One of the most significant of these was Lawrence Waterbury Johnston (1871–1958).

In many ways Johnston was the archetype of the American abroad. Born in Paris of American parents, he was educated at Trinity College, Cambridge, gaining a second-class degree in history. He took British citizenship in 1900, fought in the Boer War and was wounded twice in the First World War. He was a friend of Mary Anderson and in 1907, with his mother, bought Hidcote Manor, near Chipping Campden, less than 10 miles from Broadway, with 300 acres of farmland, a hamlet of seven cottages and the seventeenth-century manor house with its walled garden. Johnston had an interest in architecture and a much stronger interest in gardening. With the help of Thomas Mawson's *Art and Craft of Garden Making*, Gertrude Jekyll's *Wood and Garden* and *Home and Garden*, and other books borrowed from the Royal Horticultural Society's library in London, he began to shape the area around his golden Cotswold stone house.

The only tree of note in the old walled garden was a Cedar of Lebanon, flat topped as its new growth was regularly shaved off by the wind sweeping across the hilltop site. Johnson laid out the old garden as a cluster of compartments, a long, narrow strip along the outer wall to capitalize on the little stream which ran from the village pond, a raised square for the cedar, wide borders around the other walls, and quartered plots in the centre. His ambitions quickly outran the limited space of the walled garden. A long vista extended up the slope through a circular garden of lilacs, along double borders of red and orange flowers and coppery foliage, and up a short flight of steps to twin gazebos. The vista continued between hornbeam hedges on stilts and through a wrought iron gate to a grassy space, a ha-ha and a spectacular view of the countryside with the Malvern Hills in the distance.

The twin gazebos were not identical twins. The one on the right as one walked up the slope had some of Johnston's old Delft tiles. On the left, the door revealed another door and a long view down the slope and up to another country view. At the low point in the vista the path crossed a bridge under which the little stream which first made its appearance in the old garden reappeared to flow through the Upper and Lower Stream Gardens, a shallow valley made to seem much more significant by low planting along the stream and taller, partly evergreen planting above the banks. Levels were carefully calculated so that, from above, the bridge and stream were invisible, a 'mini-ha-ha' over which the vista continued apparently uninterrupted. This juxtaposition of the many formal enclosures and the complete informality of the stream gardens was, and remains, one of the delights of Hidcote.

On to the cross formed by the two long axes were gathered a series of other rectangular gardens: a fuchsia garden, a bathing pool garden, a pillar garden of slim yew columns rising between massed peonies, alstroemerias and other flowers. Central to the cluster of garden compartments was Mrs Winthrop's Garden, named after Johnston's mother and planted with golden foliage and yellow flowers enlivened in the best Jekyll tradition by small patches of blue flowers, all creating a feeling of sunshine even on a dull English day. From the centre of this brick-paved garden one looked down on to a seemingly endless ocean of flowers criss-crossed by invisible paths. Many of the compartments were surrounded by Johnston's 'tapestry hedges', mixed plantings of box, holly, yew, green and purple beech. A wide theatre lawn provided a breathing space in contrast to the eventfulness of the other compartments and separated the main flower gardens from tennis courts, vegetables and an orchard. Hidcote became a charming mix of English cottage garden and French sophistication with its pleached hornbeams and pillars of yew.

Lawrence Johnston became more English than the English, never seen without his dachshund dogs for company and demanding tea from his butler at 4 p.m. sharp. In 1922 he went on a plant hunting expedition to the Alps with the renowned plantsman E. A. Bowles and in 1927 to South Africa with Collingwood 'Cherry' Ingram, Reginald Cory (who later left a considerable fortune to the Cambridge Botanic Garden), and the young George Taylor, later director of the Royal Botanic Gardens at Kew. His journey to the plant-rich Chinese province of Yunnan with George Forrest, an even more successful collector than Wilson, was not a success. Although Johnston had a very good eye for superior plants, he was more interested in gardens than in plants from a botanical perspective, and his morose companion complained that Johnston spent too much time socialising in clubs and playing tennis. He became ill and returned home early.

In the early 1920s Mrs Winthrop began to suffer from dementia, and her son found a place for her in a sanatorium in the south of France. In 1924 he decided, like many other wealthy Americans and English, to take refuge from the English winter on the border of France and Italy on the Mediterranean coast. He bought the villa Serre de la Madone

OPPOSITE, ABOVE The fuchsia garden at Hidcote Manor, Gloucestershire, with twin peacock topiary pieces characteristic of the era.
OPPOSITE, BELOW Lawrence Johnston with his head gardener and dogs in Mrs Winthrop's Garden at Hidcote.

in Menton, an area which had been known since 1859 to have a particularly favourable climate for sufferers of tuberculosis and other disorders. Here he developed another famous garden, growing plants which would not survive an English winter. Initially, he spent the summers in England and the winters in France, but as the English tax system began to squeeze, his visits to England were rationed to three months each year to escape the heavy taxation.

On the outbreak of war in 1939 he was repatriated to England, where he stayed until 1945. By 1948 his memory was beginning to fail, and he worried about the future of his gardens. His friend Lady Colefax, a great supporter of the National Trust, suggested that he leave his English garden to the Trust subject to a life tenancy. The scheme was agreed, and Johnston resumed his pattern of three months in England and nine months in France each year until he died in 1958.

Most Americans settling in England came for the Henry James 'nookiness' inspired by Gertrude Jekyll and Alfred Parsons, but one American in particular broke that mould: William Waldorf Astor (1848–1919). Astor was the great-grandson of Johann Jakob (later John Jacob) Astor (1763–1848), who was born in Walldorf in Germany but moved to England at 16, then to the United States in 1783 or 1784, soon after the end of the War of Independence. J. J. Astor became a fur trader with huge success, but left the trade in 1830 to invest in real estate in New York. He became the first multimillionaire in the United States and was a great philanthropist. This tradition of wealth and philanthropy permeated the Astor psyche.

William Waldorf Astor's father, also John Jacob, continued the tradition of financier philanthropist, but his public humanitarian activities were not echoed in his own household. William Waldorf was educated by governesses and private tutors in Germany and Italy with little family warmth. He returned to America to study law at Columbia University and was called to the bar in 1875; he then practised law while helping to manage his father's financial and real estate holdings. He entered the New York State Assembly and Senate but twice failed to win a seat in Congress. On the death of his father in 1890, he became the richest man in the United States. The following year, as a result of a family feud, he moved to England with his wife and five children, and in 1893 he bought Cliveden, high above the Thames near Maidenhead in Berkshire.

Cliveden was far removed from any semblance to a cosy English cottage. The first house was built by George Villiers, 2nd Duke of Buckingham, in 1666, soon after his return from France with Charles II. In 1679 John Evelyn visited and described 'Cliefden that stupendious natural Rock, Wood & Prospect … on the platforme is a circular view to the utmost verge of the Horizon'.[101] The eighteenth-century landscape at Cliveden was largely by Charles Bridgeman, a complex network of vistas criss-crossing the steep slopes and including a small amphitheatre in which Thomas Arne's 'Rule Britannia' was first performed. Capability Brown also worked on the adjacent estates of Cliveden and Taplow Court. His contribution to Cliveden is uncertain, but the gardens and woods took on an increasingly informal appearance typical of his work. The house burned down in 1795, leaving only the terraces which had supported it. A new house was built in 1824, but this too burned down in 1849 soon after its purchase by the Duke of Sutherland.

In 1850–51 the duke commissioned Sir Charles Barry, the leading architect of palatial Italianate country houses (and of the Palace of Westminster), to build the third house to stand on the old terrace. The great parterre below the house was designed by John Fleming, head gardener at Cliveden from 1852 to 1855, and Fleming embellished much of the rest of the garden with his elaborate bedding schemes, including a long, narrow ribbon border which ran around the eighteenth-century holm oaks (or holly oaks, *Quercus ilex*), forming bows in the more open spaces. Queen Victoria was a frequent visitor to Cliveden, travelling on the royal train from Windsor to Taplow and then by carriage along the private Green Drive through the Cliveden estate to the house. In 1893, when the Astor family arrived, Cliveden was a magnificent house on a magnificent site, elaborately planted with late Victorian splendour.

Astor continued the tradition for the next 10 years. The statue of the Duke of Sutherland at the turning point of the drive was moved to an outer part of the garden where it could be seen from, and looked towards, the house. In its place Astor commissioned the giant Shell Fountain of Siena marble, carved by Rome-born Anglo-American sculptor Thomas Waldo Story. The terraces below the house were redefined by actual Italian balustrades from the Villa Borghese in Rome. Statues from the balustrade were considered by the Roman authorities as 'art' and could not be exported, but the same designation did not apply to the balustrade itself. At the far end of the parterre the circle of the former riding ring was given greater prominence with a statue of Pluto and Proserpine. Leftover pieces of the balustrade were used to edge a steep path up from the river towards the duke's statue, on the way to which a huge slice of giant redwood trunk on jacks served as a picnic table and reminder of America. To the north of the grounds a small pool in the meadow used as a golf course was enlarged to encompass an island on which sat a Chinese pavilion first shown in Paris at the 1867 Exposition Universelle and then bought in 1900 by Astor at the sale of the Marquess of Hereford's Bagatelle villa outside Paris. Various other statues and garden features, mainly of Italian origin, embellished the garden.

In 1899 Astor became a British citizen, a year before Lawrence Johnston of Hidcote Manor. He bought the *Pall Mall Gazette* and, in 1911, *The Observer*, one of the most important national newspapers. In 1903 he moved from the 'new-old' of Sir Charles Barry's Cliveden to the really old Hever Castle in Kent, giving Cliveden to his eldest son, Waldorf, and his wife on their marriage in 1906.

Hever Castle dates from 1270. In 1462 it was acquired by Geoffrey Bullen (or Boleyn), who built a Tudor manor house within the walls. It was the one-time home of Anne Boleyn, the unfortunate second wife of Henry VIII and mother of Elizabeth I, so steeped in history. By 1900 Hever had suffered centuries of decline and was in a romantically ruined condition. Astor restored the castle to a condition suitable for twentieth-century living and added a new 'Tudor' village, designed by Frank Pearson, to accommodate his many visitors and staff. Pearson and one of England's leading garden contracting firms, Joseph Cheal & Son, created the spectacular Italian Garden with its Pompeian wall, pergolas, rose garden, fernery and other features to provide a setting for Astor's large collection of Italian sculptures and oil jars among luxuriant planting. The walled gardens ended with splashing pools populated by marble nymphs by J. S. Frith overlooking a 32-acre lake which took 800 men two years to dig. Cheal specialized in topiary so many topiary specimens adorned the lawns surrounding the castle, and a suitably medieval maze of yew hedges was planted in 1904, a reminder of the maze at Cliveden created in 1894 (and recently recreated, though not in exactly the same position).

Like his predecessors, William Waldorf Astor continued to donate to a wide range of charities. He was created Baron, then Viscount, Astor for his war efforts in particular, but he faced unpleasant press campaigns about rich Americans buying their way into the aristocracy. This drove him into self-imposed exile, and he died suddenly of heart failure in his Brighton home at the age of 71.

William's son Waldorf (1879–1952) was born in New York City but travelled and lived in Europe until the family settled in England. He attended Eton and New College, Oxford, being academically undistinguished but excelling in fencing and polo, so already qualified as an English gentleman. In 1905 he was crossing the Atlantic to England when he met the divorcee Nancy Witcher Langhorne (1879–1964). A rapid courtship followed and they were married in 1906. It was a close marriage with a shared interest in social reform. Waldorf, Member of Parliament for Plymouth in Cornwall from 1910, had many parliamentary posts in his friend Lloyd George's government. On his father's death in 1919 he inherited the title of Viscount. He tried unsuccessfully to relinquish the title but failed, and so had to leave his seat in the House of Commons and move to the House of Lords. Nancy Astor fought and won her husband's Plymouth seat and became the first woman to sit in the Commons. She remained an MP until persuaded to step down in 1945. Both husband and wife undertook much charitable work and were involved in international relations, including attempts to come to terms with Hitler's Germany, casting a cloud on 'the Cliveden set'. The house was a focus of political activity and discussion, not always amicable. Nancy Astor and Winston Churchill, both strong characters, had many now famous exchanges:

WC: Having a woman in Parliament is like having one intrude on me in my
      bathroom.
NA: You're not handsome enough to have such fears.

WC: What disguise should I wear to a masquerade ball?
NA: Why don't you come sober, Prime Minister?

NA: If you were my husband, I'd poison your tea.
WC: Madam, if you were my wife, I'd drink it.[102]

In the garden things were rather more peaceful. Even in the 1850s the head gardener John Fleming had noted that the shade and drip from the evergreen oaks (*Quercus ilex*, or 'Ilex') hampered his attempts to create a continuous ribbon of colour around the Ilex Grove. By the early twentieth century the oaks had grown and the fashion for bedding had waned: the Ilex Grove became a calm area of dark trees and pale green lawn. The box-hedged borders of the Long Garden were redesigned and filled with billowing herbaceous borders by Norah Lindsay, one of the doyennes of the English garden.

Norah Lindsay (1873–1948) was a charming, beautiful, clever and witty woman but ultimately a tragic figure. Born in India where her uncle was Governor General, she came to England with her family in 1875. At 22, she married Henry (Harry) Lindsay, a tall, handsome officer of 29 in the Gordon Highlanders. On their marriage a relative of Lindsay, Lord Wantage, gave them Sutton Courtenay Manor, a delightful muddle of Norman, Tudor and Georgian buildings bordering the Thames. A sparkling hostess, Norah made the Manor the centre of a lively social scene for young people from Oxford and for other friends. She developed the garden to match the social scene, described in *Country Life* as 'without grandeur but not without formality'. Her 'Persian' garden had a grape arbour overlooking a sea of herbaceous perennials punctuated by narrow conifers. Beyond this there were orchards and walks through wildflower-strewn meadows to the river for boating and swimming. This all sounds like the beginning of a Hollywood film, but the couple were always short of money. Harry could never quite adjust to the routines of married life, and the two gradually drifted apart. In 1905 Norah leased out the Manor and moved to London into 'a kennel, a cupboard just for myself and a maid'.[103] Even an impoverished lady could not exist without a maid.

In 1919 Harry returned home from the war, so Norah took herself off with some friends and drove from New York to California in a convertible, visiting gardens. She had already started to share her knowledge of gardens with friends. In 1921 her brother Nigel wrote from Canada to his other sister, Madeleine: 'I'm glad Norah is making money. She should go to America where they will cheerfully pay her £500 as a fee. You have no idea how rich they are in the States.'[104] In 1924, at 51, Norah decided to turn her interest in gardening into a career, and she spent much of the rest of her life in a semi-nomadic existence, moving from house to house belonging to friends and clients, getting up at dawn to speak to gardeners, working late into the night on plans, and being summoned here and there across the country.

At Cliveden she was engaged by Nancy Astor on a retainer of £100 per annum. From 1928 to 1933 she worked for Ronald and Nancy Tree, American expatriates (see chapter 18), at Kelmarsh in Northamptonshire, again on a £100 retainer, which meant that she had to attend to their needs whenever they arose. In November 1930 she had to leave Hidcote, where she was staying with her friend Lawrence Johnston, to travel to Kelmarsh because Nancy Tree, Nancy Astor's niece, needed her advice. Later she also worked for the Trees at Ditchley Park in Oxfordshire, planning a magnolia walk and a garden of white-flowered cherries and embellishing the woods with camellias. She managed to hold on to Sutton Courtenay and to garden there in moments of peace. In 1929 she was visited by 90 members of the Garden Club of America accompanied by a hundred English hostesses in a week of visits including Cliveden, Sutton Courtenay, Hidcote and Sir Philip Sassoon's remarkable garden at Port Lympne in Kent, all of which showed the hand of Norah Lindsay.

At Cliveden other changes were also taking place. A hospital was built on the edge of the estate in the First World War. William Waldorf Astor's Italian Garden, an elliptical space dug into the western slope below the house, was converted into a cemetery for those who died in the hospital; the secluded atmosphere, the broken columns, antique busts and trails of ivy created a tranquil and melancholy scene. In 1959 Waldorf Astor commissioned Geoffrey (later Sir Geoffrey) Jellicoe, one of England's most distinguished landscape architects, to design a new rose garden in the woods a short distance from the house. The clearing – initially a circular rose garden in the 1850s, then a bowling green, then a tennis court – was redesigned as an informal, meandering line of brick and grass paths, rose beds and lawns. Sitting on a terrace near the rose garden long after Astor's death, Sir Geoffrey explained how the meandering line of the plan represented Astor's sensitive and uncertain response to life, but it was also inspired by the paintings of Paul Klee. Jellicoe owned Klee's

1932 painting of *The Fruit*, which has unmistakable similarities with his rose garden plan. A statue of Apollo stood in the centre of the garden, so Jellicoe rescued a dryad, a shy wood nymph of Greek mythology befriended by Apollo's twin sister Artemis, from the basement of the house to follow him for ever; the paths were punctuated by arches 'of vaguely human form' which Jellicoe later admitted were not entirely successful but which remain today.[105]

In 1942 Astor gave Cliveden to the National Trust, but he continued to live there until his death 10 years later. He expressed a wish that the estate continue to be used to foster understanding between English-speaking peoples. It was entirely appropriate, therefore, that in 1969 Cliveden became the English home of Stanford University. National Trust visitors saw games of American football being played on the great parterre until Stanford moved to the livelier environs and closer academic community of Oxford.

Another remarkable Anglo-American castle owner was Olive Wilson Filmer, later Lady Baillie, of Leeds Castle in Kent, adding to a long history of transatlantic connections. The Culpeper family, who owned the medieval castle in the seventeenth century, had divided loyalties in the English Civil War. Sir Cheney Culpeper was a Parliamentarian and the castle escaped damage during the war. His brother John, later first Lord Culpeper, was a Royalist, and in 1660 was granted five million acres of land in Virginia as a reward for helping the king, as Prince of Wales, escape to France. In 1680 Lord Culpeper left the castle and sailed to become Governor of Virginia. On his death it was inherited by Catherine, Lady Fairfax, wife of Thomas, 5th Lord Fairfax, and on her death by her son, another Thomas, 6th Lord Fairfax. In 1747 this Thomas left for Virginia to manage the family estates, leaving the castle to his brother Robert. In 1793 sale of the Virginia estates released large sums of money which were used to repair and remodel the building, adding a new 'Tudor' castle completed in 1823. Decline then set in until it was rescued by Olive Wilson Filmer in 1926.

Lady Baillie was born in 1899 as Olive Cecilia Paget in New York, the elder daughter of Almeric Paget, later Lord Queensborough, and his wealthy American wife, Pauline Whitney. In 1916 Olive and her sister inherited large fortunes on the death of their mother. In 1919, at the age of 20, Olive married the Hon. Charles Winn. They had two daughters, but the marriage was dissolved in 1925. She then married Arthur Wilson Filmer in 1925 and bought Leeds Castle the following year. With her fortune, she modernized it, adding bathrooms, central heating and other conveniences, and enriched its setting. The picturesque castle, sitting in a wide moat and extensive park and overlooking the Kent countryside, did not need extensive gardens, but Olive's restored and modernized castle, the scene of many social gatherings, remains as one of the most beautiful garden ornaments ever built. Her second marriage ended in divorce in 1931. She remarried in the same year, to Sir Adrian Baillie, and had one son, Gawaine, but divorced for a third time in 1944 and died in 1974.

Perhaps the saddest example of the 'trade' by which wealthy American parents provided a dowry for their daughters in exchange for an aristocratic title. was at Blenheim, where Consuelo Vanderbilt was introduced to Charles Spencer Churchill, 9th Duke of Marlborough. The matchmaker was Lady Paget, born Mary 'Millie' Stevens, a minor heiress turned major but poor English hostess. Consuelo had been groomed since early childhood to make a good match. She had a steel rod down her spine to ensure good deportment and was punished with a riding whip whenever she strayed from 'correct' behaviour. She gave up her secret fiancé and Churchill gave up the woman he loved, but he gained a 2.5 million dollar dowry. This enabled him to make repairs to the great house and to bring it into the twentieth century, and to create splendid new gardens. The grass forecourt was replaced by a paved yard. The French garden architect Achille Duchêne was commissioned to design the water parterre and Italian Garden on terraces descending from the house to Capability Brown's lake. The 5th Duke's Rock Garden below Brown's cascade was greatly enlarged, and half a million trees were planted in the park between 1895 and 1919. Money may be necessary to build spectacular gardens, but it cannot ensure marital happiness: the couple separated after only 11 years.

12

A love triangle: America, England
and the Mediterranean

B Y THE LATE NINETEENTH CENTURY America had wealth and power. The one thing that Americans lacked was a long history. For the second and third generations of industrial tycoons, wealthy and able to leave much of the management of their empires to professionals, the temptations of life in England – with its long history, its charming if often derelict villages and its lower cost of living – had a powerful appeal. The main disadvantage, again neatly summed up by Henry James, was the climate. He attributed the English love of colourful flowers to 'the unanimous protest against the greyness of some of the conditions', not only of its skies but of its cities.[106] Climate was no problem, though, if one could escape the rigours of an English winter for Italy or the south of France. Thus began a love triangle between America, England and the Mediterranean, an affair in which women played a particularly important role.

Now remembered primarily as a novelist, Edith Wharton was the most important figure in that affair. Born Edith Newbold Jones in New York City in 1862, she was the youngest member of a family which, because of its very long history in America, was part of New York's 'aristocracy'. Her parents and two much older brothers were pillars of polite society. At the age of four, at the end of the Civil War, Edith moved with her parents to Italy, France, Germany and finally back to Italy. Here in Florence she met other young children of expatriate families and played among the statues and fountains of Renaissance villas. At 10 she returned to New York, which she found ugly and boring, but she spent the summer months at Pencraig in fashionable Newport, Rhode Island. She was an avid reader but was forbidden by her mother to read novels for fear that they might corrupt her young mind. Instead, she plundered her father's library and found John Ruskin. His 'wonderful cloudy pages gave me back the image of the beautiful Europe I had lost, and fed me with visions of Italy for which I had never ceased to pine'.[107]

In 1881, because of her father's failing health, the family returned again to Europe, this time to Cannes. Here, when her father's health permitted, he and Edith took Ruskin's *Stones of Venice* and *Mornings in Florence* on trips as guidebooks. Ruskin 'awoke in me the habit of precise visual observation' and showed her how to respond to beauty in all its expressions.[108] When her father died in 1882, the family returned to America, and in 1885

Edith married Edward Wharton, a man 13 years her senior but with a sunny disposition and a wanderlust to match her own. They travelled every year for three or four months in Italy, usually via France.

In 1893 the Whartons moved to Land's End, a house on the Rhode Island cliffs which Edith built and furnished with the help of a young Boston architect, Ogden Codman. The two shared an admiration for the architectural simplicity of Italy in contrast to the suffocating excesses of the Beaux Arts school in France. During the 1890s Edith Wharton teetered on the edge of a nervous breakdown because of the difficulty she found in launching a writing career, but her recovery was aided by advice that she might consider writing fact rather than fiction. In 1897, in collaboration with Codman, she published *The Decoration of Houses*, drawing on her own experience at Land's End and on her extensive travels to villas and châteaux in Europe. Its success restored her faith in herself. In 1902 the Whartons moved again, from Land's End to The Mount in Lenox, Massachusetts, a house inspired by Belton House, near Grantham in Lincolnshire (then thought to have been designed by Christopher Wren but now attributed to William Winde or Roger Platt). With its stately home, formal gardens and historic deer park, Belton is often considered to be the perfect example of an English country house estate. On seeing the Whartons' house and garden the Austrian ambassador declared, 'Ah, Mrs Wharton, when I look about me I don't know if I am in England or Italy.'[109]

In 1903 Edith was asked by the *Century Magazine* to write a series of articles to accompany Maxfield Parrish's evocative paintings of Italian villas of 'moonlight and nightingale' fantasy. The magazine was expecting florid prose to match the paintings, and the editor was disappointed with her brisk, factual descriptions. However, the collected essays were published in 1904. *Italian Villas and their Gardens* inspired many – including the country house architect and garden designer Inigo Triggs, the architect turned landscape architect Geoffrey Jellicoe with his friend Jock Shepherd and, in a very different vein, Sir George Sitwell of Renishaw Hall in Derbyshire, recuperating in Italy from a nervous breakdown – to publish their own books to satisfy a growing English demand. Lawrence Johnston of Hidcote and Serre de la Madone was an early reader of and a frequent visitor to Mrs Wharton when she was in Italy.

Edward Wharton began to suffer mental problems, and the couple were divorced in 1913. Edith moved to Paris where she managed to survive the war years because of her American connections in high places, gaining huge admiration for her tireless work to help French women. After the war she moved to Saint-Brice, outside Paris, and then to Sainte-Claire overlooking the Mediterranean at Hyères. She suffered a heart attack in June 1937 and died two months later.

Edith Wharton's writings, both fact and fiction, were deeply infused with a love of Europe, and of Italy in particular. This resonated among the Anglophile and English population who travelled to Italy for holidays or for longer stays to absorb the culture and enjoy the climate. Many bought villas or, across the border, châteaux, and made gardens which were a fusion of Italian craftsmanship and English/American plantsmanship.

The French-born English writer Violet Paget, who wrote under the pseudonym Vernon Lee, was an early arrival in Italy, moving to Villa Palmerino at Maiano near Florence in 1889. It was to her especially that Edith Wharton turned for help in her writing. Many later arrivals were helped to create or remodel villas and gardens by two English architects, Cecil Pinsent and Harold Peto. Both had a great love of gardens and sensitivity to the unity of house and garden so evident in the villas of the Italian Renaissance. When Peto eventually returned to England and made his own garden at Iford Manor near Bradford-on-Avon in Wiltshire, he wrote: 'old buildings or fragments of masonry carry one's mind back to the past in a way that a garden of flowers only cannot do. Gardens that are too stony are equally unsatisfactory; it is the combination of the two in just proportion that is the most satisfactory.'[110] Pinsent worked for the American art historian Bernard Berenson on his villa I Tatti at Settignano near Florence and at Villa Le Balze for the American philosopher Charles Strong. Peto designed Villa Sylvia on Cap Ferrat, near Nice, for Ralph Curtis, an expatriate Bostonian painter, pupil of John Singer Sargent and close friend of Henry James. His work on Cap Ferrat was so prolific that the peninsula was dubbed Peto Point. He also designed Villa Maryland on Cap St Jean for Mrs Arthur Wilson, wife of a shipping magnate from Hull in north-east England.

This powerful evocation of refined architecture and luxuriant planting filtered back across the Atlantic to inspire the creators of American gardens and especially the women who, by now, were taking centre stage as garden makers.

13

Women in the garden

⟨⟩

ONE OF THE MAJOR DIFFERENCES between the United States and England in relation to gardens in the early twentieth century was in the role of women. With rare but notable exceptions such as the Duchess of Beaufort at Badminton in Gloucestershire, the self-effacing Jane Loudon transcribing her husband's wisdom for what she saw as her mentally inferior sex, Louisa Lawrence of Drayton Green and later Ealing Park, who brought dismay to the Duke of Devonshire when she flowered *Amherstia nobilis* before him, English horticulture was a male domain until the late nineteenth century, when Gertrude Jekyll took centre stage, in the flower garden at least. In 1897 when the Royal Horticultural Society awarded its first 60 Victoria Medals of Honour to commemorate the queen's Diamond Jubilee, only two of the recipients were women: Gertrude Jekyll and Ellen Willmott, who had famous gardens at Warley Place in Essex, Tresserve in the south of France and Boccanegra on the Italian Riviera (and whom Jekyll considered to be England's greatest female gardener). Well into the twentieth century serious gardening was the province of the man of the house. Radio and later television presenters of gardening programmes were, without exception, men. Women undoubtedly gardened and were often, like Daisy Lloyd at Great Dixter, the main conductors of the flower garden, but their efforts were largely kept below the horticultural parapet. Despite the world renown of women such as Gertrude Jekyll, Penelope Hobhouse, Rosemary Verey and Beth Chatto in the twentieth century, the 200-year-old RHS waited until 2010 to appoint Elizabeth Banks as its first female president, serving until 2013. In America women played a significant professional role in gardens, and American women at home and abroad played key roles both individually and collectively in the making of gardens and in the wider environmental sphere.

Three women in particular, Beatrix Farrand (1872–1959), Ellen Biddle Shipman (1869–1950) and Rose Standish Nichols (1872–1960), made significant contributions to the newly defined profession of landscape architecture, although the overwhelming majority of their work was in designing gardens for female clients. Architecture, 'hard' landscape and public works were still the province of men, and as Beatrix Farrand noted, it was impossible to make a career as a female landscape architect without family wealth and connections to launch and sometimes sustain that career.

When the American Society of Landscape Architects was formed in 1899 Beatrix Farrand was the only woman member among ten men. Women were not admitted to the landscape courses then available at Harvard, MIT and the University of Pennsylvania. In 1901 the

Lowthorpe School of Landscape Architecture and Horticulture was established in Groton, Massachusetts, and in 1910 the Pennsylvania School of Horticulture followed. Both catered exclusively for women, but both focused almost exclusively on horticultural aspects of garden design. In 1915 the Cambridge School of Architecture and Landscape Design for Women opened its doors, with Henry Frost as its male principal. This focused on design and construction. The Great Depression severely reduced the demand for private garden design, forcing the Cambridge school to close in 1942, but possibly because of a fall in male student applications, the long-established Harvard course finally admitted women students.

Beatrix Farrand was born Beatrix Cadwalader Jones in New York into what she claimed was the fifth generation of garden lovers. The family spent summers on their Reef Point estate in Maine, where Beatrix enjoyed studying the beautiful scenery and native plants around her. At 20 she was introduced to Charles Sprague Sargent, Professor of Horticulture at Harvard and the first director of Harvard's Arnold Arboretum. She lived with the Sargents for a year at their home in Brookline, Massachusetts, near neighbours of the Olmsted office, studying botany and land planning, then enrolled at the Columbia School of Mines to study the technical aspects of drafting, surveying and engineering. As a niece of Edith Wharton and life-long friend of Henry James, Beatrix Jones had many connections. She travelled with her aunt to Italy and England and, like most Americans with an interest in gardens, was greatly influenced by Gertrude Jekyll, her garden and her writings, and by William Robinson's magazine *The Garden*. She met them both in England, and later collected Jekyll's books as they began to appear in 1899. She also found much to inspire her in Thomas Mawson's *Art and Craft of Garden Making* (1900) with its balance of dignified architectural compartments set in naturalistic surroundings. In 1895 she began designing gardens for her Bar Harbor neighbours in Maine, rapidly establishing a successful career. At Edith Wharton's home in Lenox, Massachusetts, Wharton herself designed the main garden, but for her vegetable garden she turned for advice to her niece.

In 1913 Beatrix married Max Farrand, a distinguished historian at Yale and Stanford. When her husband moved to California in 1928 to become director of the Huntingdon Botanical Library, Beatrix moved with him, but she found it difficult to establish herself professionally in the very different climate of California with its existing cluster of successful garden designers. She did design the native plant garden in the Santa Barbara Botanic Garden, and much later produced designs for the California Institute of Technology in Pasadena and Occidental College in Los Angeles, but her ties remained with the East Coast and she commuted regularly to plan and supervise her work there. With her aunt's and her mother's social connections she obtained commissions from the wives of Woodrow Wilson, J. D. Rockefeller, Theodore Roosevelt, J. Pierpont Morgan and other luminaries.

Dumbarton Oaks in Washington, DC, with gardens designed by Beatrix Farrand for Mildred and Robert Woods Bliss.

Because of her sound technical training allied to her international travels, Beatrix Farrand was capable of much more than the design of pretty flower borders. Terraces, steps, pools and garden buildings – requisite components of the Anglo-Italian gardens of the period – all came within her abilities. Her work, though, was not a dry professional process of drawings, contracts and contractors, although she was thoroughly professional and competent in her work. Rather it was an often prolonged conversation between client and consultant, determining what was best for the site and for the family.

Her most significant and durable work was at Dumbarton Oaks in Washington, DC, where she worked from 1921 to 1947 for Mildred Bliss. In 1920 Robert Woods Bliss, a retired diplomat, and his wife, both from wealthy backgrounds and with a shared interest in the arts, bought Dumbarton Oaks in Georgetown with 53 acres of land. They asked Farrand to advise on the garden, and she returned to Dumbarton Oaks many times during the rest of her life, evolving a series of interconnected formal gardens within a naturalistic setting. Her *Plant Book for Dumbarton Oaks*, with detailed management advice for the garden, was written in 1941 when she was 70.

Another long-term association developed with Willard and Dorothy Straight at Old Westbury, Long Island, from 1914 to 1932. Willard was a partner in the bank of J. P. Morgan, and his wife, the former Dorothy Payne Whitney, was a wealthy and much-travelled heiress. They met in 1909, married in Switzerland in 1911, and undertook a six-month-long honeymoon and world tour before returning to the United States. Farrand's office produced 120 drawings for the garden at Old Westbury, incorporating full-moon gates and other features reflecting her clients' interests in the Orient.

Willard Straight died in 1918. In 1925 his widow married the Yorkshireman Leonard Elmhirst, and the Elmhirsts moved to south-west England, buying the 1,200 acre Dartington estate with its magnificent fourteenth-century Great Hall near Totnes in Devon. Here they set up a centre for the arts and crafts reminiscent of the Cornish Art Colony in New Hampshire. Music, drama, painting, sculpture and the making of pottery, glassware and wooden products from trees on the estate were all set in the steeply rolling and wooded landscape of South Devon. Dorothy Elmhirst asked Farrand to advise on the gardens, and in only a few days on her first visit, she was able to design an appropriate setting for the Hall and its attendant buildings and to organize the steps and paths giving access to the gardens. Her understated but elegant landscape, the stone-paved court, the grand flights of steps and restrained planting with no trace of fussy gardenesque perfectly suited the culture of the place. This was Farrand's one foreign commission, but it allowed her to give back some of the ideas she had absorbed on her earlier visits to England.

Through her private garden clients she also became involved in public works: the Morgan Library in New York for J. Pierpont Morgan, site planning and planting plans for the National Cathedral in Washington, DC, the East Colonial Garden at the White House for Mrs Woodrow Wilson, and designs for the setting of buildings on the campuses of Princeton, Yale and the University of Chicago. Her private garden commission for Abby Aldrich Rockefeller at Seal Harbor, Maine, led to her advising John D. Rockefeller junior on the road network for Acadia National Park in Maine which he had funded. Lessons from Olmsted's elegantly winding roads in the Arnold Arboretum and on the huge Biltmore estate in North Carolina were put to good use.

When Farrand's husband died in 1947 she moved back to Maine, and to Reef Point, intending to establish a centre for the study of garden design. However, her plans were thwarted by a wildfire which swept through the property in 1955 and by the refusal of the local authorities to grant her a favourable tax status. She therefore sold the estate and bequeathed her library to the School of Environmental Design at the University of California, Berkeley.

Among the material bequeathed to Berkeley were the papers of Gertrude Jekyll sold at auction in 1940 by her nephew and heir, Francis Jekyll, to raise money for the Red

Cross. The papers disappeared but appeared again in the offices of the Massachusetts Horticultural Society in 1948, when they were bought by Beatrix Farrand. Some 30 years later, in 1979, Mavis Batey, secretary and then president of the Garden History Society, was giving a course in garden history at Worcester College in Oxford for students and alumni of Berkeley. After a visit to a Lutyens/Jekyll garden where the owner expressed the difficulty she was finding in restoring the garden because of a lack of original plans, Batey commented to a Berkeley vice-chancellor visiting the group that one had to travel to California to do research on Jekyll's gardens. He undertook to send microfilm copies of the Jekyll plans to the Garden History Society, and these are lodged in the English Heritage (now Historic England) library in Swindon, Wiltshire – a wonderful example of the serendipitous nature of gardens and garden history and of transatlantic friendship.

Ellen Biddle Shipman was born in Philadelphia but moved to Texas, Arizona and finally to New Jersey as her father was an army officer. She began sketching gardens at an early age, but her tentative steps to develop a career in this direction by entry to Radcliffe College at Harvard lasted only a year as she fell in love with the playwright Louis Shipman. They married, left Harvard and moved to New Hampshire to be near the Cornish Art Colony, where Ellen met the architect Charles Platt. Platt was impressed by her drawings, and she was tutored by him. When, in 1910, her marriage ended in divorce, she decided to pursue a career in garden design and developed a nationwide portfolio of gardens, working almost exclusively for female clients. Women found in her gardens – firmly structured but overflowing with flowers – familiarity and comfort when life was otherwise too chaotic.

Least known of the trio but in some ways the most interesting was Rose Standish Nichols, who was born in Boston, Massachusetts, and spent her summers in the Cornish Art Colony, where she met Charles Platt and Ellen Shipman. Nichols had a life-long interest in gardens, fostered by studies at the Massachusetts Institute of Technology in Cambridge and the École des Beaux Arts in Paris, but she had much wider interests as a peace activist and promoter of equality for women. She befriended Queen Sofia of Greece and discussed peace with the king, and later inveigled herself into President Wilson's peace conference in 1919 as the only woman present. She was also a formidable society hostess, summoning a wide range of people to her Sunday teas on Boston Hill. Although she had travelled and studied widely and was eminently capable in her career, she worked without assistants and usually on ephemeral labour-intensive flower gardens, so little remains of her legacy. She wrote three books: *English Pleasure Gardens* (1902), *Spanish and Portuguese Gardens* (1924) and *Italian Pleasure Gardens* (1928). She worked mainly on planting plans in collaboration with Charles Platt and other male architects such as Howard van Doren Shaw, Platt's Midwest equivalent, who had studied at Yale and MIT and undertaken an extensive tour of Europe (excluding France, as he did not approve of French classicist architecture) before setting up in practice in Michigan in 1895. Rose's sister Margaret married Arthur Shurcliff, the landscape architect consulted by John D. Rockefeller in 1928 for the restoration of Colonial Williamsburg.

All three women knew that, despite training in architecture and engineering, their work would usually be confined to the 'pretty stuff', so to a large extent they relied on collaboration with men. Charles Platt (1861–1933) served that function in many instances. Born in New York City, he studied as a landscape painter in New York and Paris. His travels in Italy in 1892 resulted in the influential *Italian Gardens* (1894). Unlike Edith Wharton's more historical treatment 10 years later, Platt concentrated on the gardens he saw rather than on their origins and evolution; to him they were simply beautiful compositions in which villa and garden were inseparable. He was much influenced by Reginald Blomfield, author of *The Formal Garden in England*, and by Gertrude Jekyll, and he chose to work whenever possible on commissions involving both house and garden. However, like Jekyll's collaborator Edwin Lutyens, Platt was honest enough to realize that his knowledge of horticulture was limited. He collaborated on many of his commissions with Ellen Shipman and Rose Nichols, both of whom allied their extensive experience of planting design with an awareness of the place of plants in the overall scheme.

The influence of women in the American garden, and indeed in the wider landscape, was much more extensive than in the work of its three most notable female landscape architects. The Massachusetts Horticultural Society, founded in 1829, was modelled on the Horticultural Society of London, founded in 1804, and was for many decades a male preserve, except for its social gatherings in which the ladies provided a suitably decorative element. In 1891, though, the Garden Club of Athens, Georgia, was founded by 12 women who wanted to exchange ideas and plants in feminine company. In 1904 the Garden Club of Philadelphia was founded by Helena Ely and Henrietta Crosby. Many other clubs followed, and in 1913 the Garden Club of America was formed, only much later admitting men to its membership. The Men's Garden Club of America was not formed until 1932.

One summer hundreds of Garden Club of America members boarded a private train in New York's Grand Central Station for a three-week tour in California, visiting 56 gardens in the Santa Barbara area. However, gardening did not have the universal place in American culture that it had in England, where gatherings ranged from high society events of the Horticultural Society to village flower shows and giant gooseberry competitions by working men. Gardening ladies in America were from the upper strata of society, typically the wives of wealthy businessmen, well educated and widely travelled. Their interests went beyond the exchange of seeds and cuttings and garden visits: there were important social and political dimensions to their activities. In 1919 the Garden Club of America started campaigns against the advertising billboards that were lining the new motor roads and in favour of wildlife conservation, lending support to the Audubon Society and other organizations. In 1948 the Hillsborough Garden Club of California initiated a scholarship to bring an English student to America for a year of study and generous hospitality. That scholarship, of which more in the final chapter, mushroomed to include a portfolio of national and international scholarships in horticulture, conservation and other environmental spheres.

American women also played an important part in the garden publishing market in the early twentieth century, all paying homage to Gertrude Jekyll and to English gardens. Mrs Francis King's *Well-Considered Garden* (1915) had a foreword by Jekyll. Living in Michigan, King was one of the few women authors not based in New England. Mabel Cabot Sedgewick's *The Garden Month by Month* was published in 1907 with long lists of plants by height, season and colour. Neltje Blanchan Doubleday, wife of publisher Henry Doubleday, wrote *The American Flower Garden* in 1909. Louise Beebe Wilder followed *My Garden* in 1916 with *Adventures in my Garden and Rock Garden* in 1923. Alice Lockwood's immense historical survey, *Gardens of Colony and State*, appeared between 1931 and 1947. Marion Cran, like Gertrude Jekyll, was a prolific author but with a livelier, even risqué sense of humour which extended to the titles of her many books. *The Garden of Ignorance* (1917) and *The Garden of Experience* (1932) marked the beginning and almost the end of her output, but these were interleaved by *The Story of My Ruin* (1924), *My Lusty Pal* (1930) and *The Squabbling Garden* (1934).

The admiration of Gertrude Jekyll extended to English gardens and gardeners in general. Marion Cran noted: 'There is a new swank! Greater and more crushing at a dinner party than wearing a new rope of pearls is to say "My Kew gardener has just arrived."' [111] One of those English gardeners was George Gilles. Born in North Devon the son of a head gardener, Gilles worked for the Duke of Richmond and the Duke of Westminster before moving to Cliveden to work for the Astors. At Cliveden he was known as Mrs Astor's pet. His first employer in America was Mrs Whitelow Reid at Ophir Hall in Purchase, New York. In 1923 Marshall Field III, who had spent his childhood in England and studied at Eton and Cambridge, asked his English butler for advice on whom he should consult on his garden and he recommended Gilles. Field, and especially Mrs Field, took to Gilles, and he was given a blank sheet to do as he wanted. Gilles knew the director of the Brooklyn Botanic Garden and met Henry du Pont as a horticultural equal.

American authors were widely read by the gardening public, but it was the original fount of knowledge, Gertrude Jekyll, who wielded the greater influence. Annie Burr Jennings, the immensely wealthy daughter of one of Rockefeller's partners in Standard Oil, was, like her father, a great benefactor to her home town of Fairfield, Connecticut, funding the library and schools, donating a public beach to the community and instigating the Fairfield branch of the Audubon Society. She was also a dedicated gardener. In 1909 she demolished her old home and replaced it with a huge Colonial Revival house, 'Sunnie Holme', set in a profusion of Jekyll-inspired gardens. Her rose garden was designed by the English-born landscape engineer Herbert Kellaway and the rose specialist Harriet Foote. It was Annie Burr Jennings who commissioned Gertrude Jekyll to design the garden for Glebe House in neighbouring Woodbury (see page 82).

George Eastman, founder of the Kodak film company, became a millionaire in 1890, and his personal wealth was estimated at 8 million dollars by 1898. In 1916 Claude Bragdon, the architect of Eastman's West Garden in Rochester, New York, wrote to his wife, 'George [Eastman] was in this morning. He's found something he likes in Lutyens' book [Lawrence Weaver's *Houses and Gardens by Edwin Lutyens*] and we had quite a visit.'[112] Eastman's orangery and the details of the grass plat were modelled on Lutyens's design for Hestercombe in Somerset, so illustrations in a 1913 book materialized in New York State in 1916.

When the British Embassy in Washington, DC was designed by Lutyens in 1927, the design of the garden was entrusted to Elizabeth Sherman Hoyt Lindsay, known as Lady Lindsay, an American who had studied architecture at Columbia University and horticulture in Boston and in England before marrying Sir Ronald Lindsay in 1924. She went on to design gardens in Ohio and Long Island with lavish use of flowering trees and shrubs for spring and early summer.

Although gardening has taken enormous leaps forward in twentieth-century America and amply justifies Rosemary Verey's later assertion that America need not be ashamed of itself as a nation of garden makers, it remains the case that gardening is not a national pastime. There are probably fewer top-flight gardens among the 325 million inhabitants of the United States than there are among England's population of 65 million or so. The archetypal American home is a detached or semi-detached (duplex) house with an open lawn at the front, a shade tree by the sidewalk and a patio with small lawn for the barbecue at the back. Planting is restricted to whatever is on offer at the local supermarket. In 1931 Mrs Francis King spoke scathingly of dull and stereotyped planting: 'Plagues sweep the country … Spiraea van Houttei … clothed the land as with a blanket; now Hydrangea arborescens seems to be an obsession. [There are] masses of Crimson Rambler [roses] and now, from that even brighter and therefore more fatal subject, Paul's Scarlet Climber, when these hang in unmeaning curtains of colour [plus] the bird bath of concrete, the seat of concrete in more or less classic design.'[113] Nevertheless, those who gardened at the top end of the social scale had intellects to match their gardens, and the results were often magnificent.

14

The modern garden and a better life for all

T HE EARLY TWENTIETH CENTURY saw dramatic changes in architecture, changes raising big questions for the profession of landscape architecture, which at that time involved to a large extent the design of sophisticated private gardens. New ideas in architecture were fostered by rapid international communications. In the seventeenth century a transatlantic journey could take months, in the eighteenth century weeks, by the late nineteenth century days and into the mid-twentieth century hours. International travel and communication through professional journals and books facilitated the rapid exchange of ideas. The house and its garden evolved on both sides of the Atlantic – although initially in England, which had created such a perfect marriage of a Lutyens house and Jekyll garden, change seemed unnecessary.

By the early twentieth century the USA had achieved a position of world significance, and American architects would lead the way for older countries to follow. In 1896 the Chicago architect Louis Sullivan wrote that 'form ever follows function' as he strove to create steel-framed buildings stripped of extraneous ornament.[114] In 1910 Frank Lloyd Wright's Robie House in Chicago, paralleling traditional Japanese expressions of carefully refined simplicity, established Wright as an architect of international renown.

In Germany in 1907 the Deutscher Werkbund (German Work Federation) was formed, an integrated design school with artists, craftsmen and designers practising and teaching students from all disciplines together. Peter Behrens, an artist and bookbinder turned architect and industrial designer, was a key figure, inspiring a generation of young architects including Walter Gropius, Ludwig Mies van der Rohe and Charles Edouard Jeanneret-Gris, who adopted the more user friendly synonym Le Corbusier. Members of the Werkbund were admirers of the Arts and Crafts movement in England. Indeed, the impetus to form the Werkbund came from Hermann Muthesius after publishing his three-volume *Das Englische Haus*, in which he extolled the achievements of William Morris and his followers, but the goal of the Werkbund had one important difference. Instead of seeking a future set in a return to the medieval age of craft guilds in opposition to the machine age, Werkbund members sought to harness the machine in their attempts to improve the quality of design and of life.

Early progress was interrupted by the outbreak of war in 1914, but in 1919, in a period of massive economic and social change, the Bauhaus (building house) was established with Walter Gropius, a great admirer of Frank Lloyd Wright, as its first director. In 1925 the school moved from Weimar to Dessau, where Gropius was responsible for designing the new buildings and the residential community around it. This was a period of rapid, revolutionary change in the arts with cubist and abstract painting, atonal music and abstract sculpture. Artists such as the Swiss-born Paul Klee and the Russian Wassily Kandinsky taught at the Bauhaus. Gropius's work in Dessau crystallized the theories and practices encapsulated in Bauhaus movement.

Gropius took the idea of 'form follows function' to new levels by creating buildings of the simplest possible form, predating in practice the declaration of his fellow architect Mies van der Rohe in 1947 that 'less is more'. In 1923 Le Corbusier wrote of the domestic house as a 'machine for living'.[115] In an age when transatlantic ocean liners and aeroplanes stimulated a new synthesis of engineering and aesthetics, echoing Sullivan's admiration for the natural engineering of a bird, houses should be built as efficient and beautifully engineered places to accommodate a modern lifestyle.

This was an exciting time for architects, but what about gardens? Young landscape architecture students faced a huge dilemma. If decoration is eschewed and function is everything, what is the role of the garden? The problem was eventually solved with the help of Adolph Hitler and Joseph Stalin. Modernism is pragmatic, treating each situation according to its merits rather than by a rule book, and pragmatism is not favoured by dictatorships. Modern architecture was banned in 1932 simultaneously in Russia and in Germany, and a heavily classical style of architecture symbolising the power of the state was imposed. In 1933 Gropius and his colleagues fled to England and then on to America. Mies also emigrated to America, first to Wisconsin and then to Chicago, where he was appointed head of the Department of Architecture at the new Illinois Institute of Technology.

Gropius became Professor of Architecture at Harvard, which when he arrived was still steeped in the Beaux Arts tradition. Students spent much of their time measuring and copying classical details which they could use to build grand country houses or even to paste on to structurally modern steel-framed office buildings. Gropius stimulated a revolution among his students. The Greek columns went to the basement, and superfluous decoration was stripped away to reveal the inherent form of the building.

As a leading School of Architecture and America's only Department of Landscape Architecture, Harvard was a meeting place of East and West: Japanese culture and a modern lifestyle from California fused with modernist ideas from Chicago, the American East Coast and Europe. Architecture became abstract sculpture growing out of the landscape and ultimately, with glass replacing concrete as the main building material, dissolving into the landscape. The excitement and opportunities of young 'modern' architects increased the trauma of their landscape architecture fellow students. They wanted to be modern too, but the big question remained: what is the purpose of a garden if it is not to be decorative?

One attempt at an answer came from the Canadian-born landscape architect Christopher Tunnard (1910–1979). Born in Victoria, British Columbia, Tunnard moved to England as a young man, studying for the RHS Diploma in 1928–30 and then enrolling briefly in the Westminster School of Art. From 1932 to 1935 he worked for Percy Cane, a prolific designer of mainly modest gardens loosely in the Arts and Crafts tradition. Tunnard then left for an extensive tour of Europe, taking particular interest in examples of modern design, before setting up his own practice in London in 1936. His few known commissions were strikingly modern extensions of modern houses. In 1938 he wrote a series of articles in *Architectural Review* fiercely critical of undistinguished Arts and Crafts gardens with their crazy paving, rockeries and sundials – what he dismissed as romantic trivialisation. The collected articles were republished in the same year as a book, *Gardens in the Modern Landscape*.

A long historical introduction was followed by 'Towards a New Technique', in which he begins: 'The modern garden architect has as much to discard as had the painter, sculptor and architect of a decade or two ago. He is faced with the necessity of ridding himself of so many comforting, if worthless, technical aids in planning that very little can be left to guide him. He must therefore evolve a new technique as a basis for contemporary garden planning.'[116] Much of what followed was logical and of great assistance to those seeking new directions in gardens design.

The next section, though, 'A Garden Landscape in Transition', used as a case study of the way forward the landscape garden at Claremont in Surrey, to which Charles Bridgeman, William Kent and Capability Brown had all contributed. Claremont had been advertised for sale. Left to market forces, Tunnard argued, the estate would be subdivided and built over with endless roads lined with mock Tudor houses, accommodating a population of perhaps 800 well-off people. Tunnard's solution was to redevelop the garden with blocks of high-rise flats and terraced houses interspersed with children's playgrounds, all set in flowing parkland, to accommodate 6,000 people. (Part of the estate was indeed populated with mock Tudor houses. Claremont House and its Capability Brown landscape is now a private girls' school, while the Bridgeman/Kent part of the landscape has been restored by the National Trust as a historic garden.)

Tunnard's polemical writing was read at Harvard by Walter Gropius, who invited Tunnard to join the staff, and he taught there from 1938 to 1943. He had always seen gardens as part of a larger landscape. He became more interested in planning and moved to Yale to lecture in city planning, in the latter years of his life somewhat ironically writing on the importance of preserving historic buildings. However, many of the 'revolutionary' generation of landscape architecture students at Harvard, including Garrett Eckbo, Dan Kiley, James Rose and Lawrence Halprin, said that Tunnard had been a major influence in shaping their ideas and careers. Rose, Eckbo and Kiley were thrown out of Harvard for their uncompromising attitude to tradition.

Other answers to the landscape architects' dilemma of the modern garden began to arrive from many directions, but two people in particular solved problems of form and function: the Brazilian painter/botanist/gardener Roberto Burle Marx (1909–1994) and the California landscape architect Thomas Church (1902–1978).

Roberto Burle Marx, son of a German father and Brazilian mother, studied painting in Rio de Janeiro and then went to pursue his studies in Berlin. In a glasshouse in the Berlin Botanic Garden he saw plants of wonderful sculptural form – from Brazil. On his return to Brazil he explored the country, collected many plants and became a distinguished botanist, but his art was expressed in many ways: painting, sculpture, mosaic, stage design, jewellery and garden design among them. He was able to translate the bold interlocking forms of his paintings into the plan of a garden. Whether in the patterns of paving along the Copacabana waterfront in Rio, the varied tones of gravel on the roof garden of the Safra Bank headquarters in São Paulo or the bold swathes of purple-leaved *Iresine herbstii*, white-striped *Chlorophytum capense* and grey-leaved *Helichrysum petiolare* in the Odette Monteiro and the Kronforth gardens in Rio, the relationship between the form of his gardens and the form of his paintings is clear to see.

A solution to the question of the function of a garden emerged from the California lifestyle, especially from the work and writings of Thomas Church, a landscape architect born in Boston and trained at Berkeley and Harvard, who practised in San Francisco. Church rounded off his formal education with six months in Rome and a tour of southern Europe, studying the adaptation of houses and gardens in the Mediterranean climate so similar to that of California. In California especially, rapid development with new houses on (relatively) small plots, in a period of rising standards of living and with near-ideal climate, presented the garden designer with a clearly established menu of functions: parking for several cars, barbecues, swimming pool, sun decks and shade houses – the garden as a place for living outside.

In 1955 Church published *Gardens are for People*: the title implying that gardens are not primarily or necessarily for plants. If people want an attractive setting for outdoor life and are not interested in gardening, that's fine: there are no rules for what a garden should be. The modern garden was firmly established in the USA. In the new smaller plot there was little scope for a multitude of compartments, and with little interest in gardening among the majority of the populace there was no reason for them. The Burle-Marx/Church free-form plan was non-axial and therefore effective from all angles. Carefully planned, the one-compartment garden looked equally good from the living room or kitchen, from the

Thomas Church's El Novillero, Sonoma, California, designed for Dewey and Joan Donnell.

poolside or a seat in a shaded corner. Plants were chosen by the landscape architect for all-year interest and low maintenance. Other books such as Garrett Eckbo's *Landscape for Living* (1950) and James Rose's *Creative Gardens* (1958) also created a vision of living outdoors in a carefully sculpted garden, while the many publications of *Sunset* magazine gave practical instructions for the all-important decks and pools.

In London, the 1951 Festival of Britain on the South Bank commemorated the centenary of Paxton's Great Exhibition, and celebrated peace and the gradual emergence from post-war austerity. It was the first major public display of modern architecture and modern gardens in England, with concrete planters, pools and fountains, and bold, sculptural foliage plants such as yuccas, bergenias and hardy palms. There was a minor flurry of books on modern gardens such as Peter Shepheard's *Modern Gardens* (1953) and Susan and Geoffrey Jellicoe's *Modern Private Gardens* (1968), but all were written by architects primarily for other architects and their impact on the ordinary domestic garden was minimal. With few exceptions English gardens remained relics of Victorian gardenesque or at best simplified imitations of Gertrude

Jekyll's plantings. The one big change in the immediate post-1945 years was in the creation of New Towns, a concept developed from Victorian model villages and Edwardian garden cities which led to many thousands of working class people acquiring their own gardens. In this, as in so many aspects of improving life for ordinary people, the American Frederick Law Olmsted played an important part.

One of the major developments in the public realm in the second half of the nineteenth century had been the creation of public parks, a movement in which Joseph Paxton in England and Olmsted and his English partner Vaux in America were key figures. The park, though, for all its benefits, was an escape from the city rather than an improvement in living conditions in the city itself. In England the evolution of local government, the provision of piped water and sewerage systems, the abolition of back-to-back houses and eventually the establishment of minimum space standards in new public housing brought widespread improvements.

The latter half of the nineteenth century also saw advances beyond these statutory provisions in a scattering of model villages, largely by Quaker philanthropic industrialists. In 1851 Sir Titus Salt, a leading manufacturer of woollen cloth in Bradford, Yorkshire, moved his factory from the congested centre of the town to Saltaire, a new site on the banks of the river Aire by the railway and the Leeds and Liverpool Canal, and he developed a small village for his workers. In 1879 George and Richard Cadbury moved their chocolate-making factory from the middle of Birmingham to a new site south of the city served by the Worcester and Birmingham Canal and soon to be served by the proposed Birmingham and West Suburban Railway. They were able to receive their supplies of milk by canal and chocolate by rail from the ports of London and Southampton. In 1893 they began building Bourneville, the 'ville' or town on the little river Bourn. Bourneville also became the name of their dark chocolate bar, still produced today.

The Lever Brothers' Port Sunlight had similar origins. In 1887 the brothers began looking for a new site on which to expand their soap-making business then in Warrington, Cheshire. The 56-acre site which they bought, strategically sited between river and railway, became Port Sunlight, named after one of their leading brands, Sunlight soap. William Lever supervised the planning of the village himself, providing allotments, schools, a hospital and other public buildings. He regarded Port Sunlight as a profit-sharing enterprise, but one in which he took a very paternalistic approach to exactly how the profits were to be shared, arguing that his employees might spend the money on whisky or sweets instead of nice houses and healthy leisure facilities.

These model or ideal villages were on the outskirts of the cities in which the companies were founded. New and efficient factories formed the heart of the new community with wide, tree-lined streets, spacious houses, each with their own garden, and access to a library, schools, parks and shops – but no pubs. Like the public parks, they were ventures combining philanthropy with profit. Abandoning old industrial complexes which had expanded haphazardly and were hemmed in by their tightly packed urban surroundings for a fresh start on a low-cost greenfield site made for huge advances in efficiency. Moving employees from grim inner-city areas to decent housing in attractive surroundings made for a healthier, more loyal and more productive workforce, again improving profitability. These were few and scattered examples of philanthropy (with major benefits also for the philanthropists), but they were indicative of a wider search for better living conditions.

In 1898 Ebenezer Howard published a slim volume entitled *Tomorrow: A Peaceful Path to Real Reform*. It was hardly a catchy title. In 1902 it was republished as *Garden Cities for Tomorrow*. Howard had worked as a legal clerk in Chicago, a city which had adopted as its motto on its incorporation in 1837 'Urbs in Horto': the city in a garden. With Olmsted's Riverside community, his South Park and the reclamation of the shores of Lake Michigan in preparation for the Columbian Exposition, by Howard's day Chicago had become a garden city in fact as well as in name.

Howard's vision for his 'garden city' was encapsulated in a diagram in his book showing 'the three magnets'. The 'town magnet' has lists of the advantages and disadvantages of town life: social opportunities, places of amusement, chances of employment, high wages and well-lit streets versus closing out of nature, isolation of crowds, high rents and prices, foul air, slums and gin palaces. Similarly, the 'country magnet' has its pluses and minuses, though interestingly in 1898 and 1902 more of the latter: 'beauty of nature, woods, meadows, water, fresh air and sunshine' but 'lack of society, poor crowded housing, trespassers beware, hands out of work, long hours on low wages'. Not surprisingly, the 'town–country magnet' combined all the benefits and none of the disadvantages. In the middle of the three magnets was an iron bar labelled 'The People' with the question, 'Where will the people go?'[117]

Howard's concept of the 'town–country' or 'garden city' was a settlement of fixed size, 30,000 people. Crucially, it was surrounded by a green belt to limit its growth. The town would be divided into six villages, each of 5,000 people and having its own school and shops, so that there could be a sense of village community while benefiting from the social facilities of the large town centre. The green belt, with farms and orchards, provided food for the town. It also provided a tranquil and therapeutic environment for an orphanage, lunatic asylum and sanatorium while absorbing brick works, a glue factory and other polluting activities.

Howard and his supporters went on to put his theories into practice, in 1904 founding Letchworth, on the main road from London to the north of England, a pioneering venture supported by George Cadbury and William Lever. Letchworth grew slowly because investors were wary of a concept in which profits from the enhanced value of land would be ploughed back into improvements rather than paid as dividends, but after the chaos of the First World War, work began on a second venture, Welwyn Garden City, south of Letchworth, in 1919. Both towns have expanded in the century since their foundation, but the heart of Welwyn Garden City, in particular, remains true to Howard's ideals. The Parkway, a wide, straight street with its central green separating the two carriageways, forms the spine of the town, still with rose gardens, a fountain and herbaceous borders punctuating the lawns. The fountain marks the intersection of Parkway with Howardsgate perpendicular to it and leading to the station. From Parkway, winding roads such as Applecroft Road, Hither Baulk, Hollybush Lane, Peartree Court and Walnut Grove (the word 'street' is banished from the vocabulary) are bordered by flowering trees and hedges behind which delightful Arts and Crafts cottages nestle in their gardens. Across the railway tracks (on the main line from London along the east coast to Edinburgh) are the factories and other businesses which provide employment to the town.

These examples of towns divided into village-like communities around a cultural and commercial hub had a great influence in shaping the UK government's post-war policy of creating a ring of New Towns, around London especially, in an attempt to decant the population from overcrowded central areas into decent accommodation, allowing those inner areas to be redeveloped in more humane ways. In practice, the decanting was not able to match the sudden increase in population – the post-war baby boom – and the centres of London and other major cities continued to become more rather than less crowded, but new high-rise buildings with modern facilities replaced the narrow crowded streets of the pre-war cities. The New Towns, though, were built at low densities with wide, tree-lined streets, open-plan front gardens (modelled on American precedents) to increase the sense of space and back gardens big enough for a lawn, flower borders and, for dedicated gardeners, a vegetable patch. Howard's idea of a green belt to contain the spread of the cities also did much to prevent southern England from becoming one gigantic suburb.

The planning of England's New Towns was also shaped by American experiments with Howard's garden cities. In the planning of Radburn in New Jersey, Clarence Stein and Henry Wright developed the concept of the 35–50 acre superblock, abandoning historically evolved street patterns in which parallel rows of houses faced each other across trafficked streets in favour of grouping the houses around green spaces and organizing a network of pedestrian routes quite separate from main roads. This not only dramatically reduced the amount of expensive roads needed to service the town, but created in essence clusters of villages set in green space. In turn, England's garden cities and New Towns inspired far-sighted developers in the United States to create privately funded settlements such as Reston in Virginia and Columbia in Maryland, with such un-American ideas as row houses (terraces in England) which were not slums, clustered around communal green spaces with pedestrian paths leading to the city centre and even bus routes to minimize use of the private automobile.

England's most recent experiment with the New Town is Milton Keynes in Buckinghamshire. Started in 1967, this was and is strongly influenced by American ideas but in a very different way to the first generation of New Towns. With car ownership increasing dramatically, the city was planned around the car. It was laid out on a grid system of roads at half-kilometre (500-yard) intervals and with a roundabout (traffic circle) at every junction. The squares within the grid were occupied seemingly at random by houses, schools, light industry and offices, to avoid concentrated flows of traffic at morning and evening rush hours, an idea which has subsequently failed under the weight of modern traffic volumes. Each housing area was designed by a different architect with a profoundly different style, so there was no endless sea of identical housing as in the earlier New Towns. The delightful Englishness of Milton Keynes, though, is that the roads of the main grid are numbered, as well as named, H1, H2, H3 … and V1, V2, V3 and so on, obviously because the city was planned on the drawing board in pre-computer-aided-design days, with the H roads running horizontally across the board and V roads running vertically. However, on the ground the roads run north-west to south-east and north-east to south-west, so both sets of roads are at 45 degrees to the drawing board's 'horizontal' and 'vertical' on the map.

The model villages of the late nineteenth century and the garden cities, suburban development and New Towns of the twentieth resulted in many thousands of new gardens, miniscule by historical standards but often cherished by their new owners. In the late 1950s and 1960s living standards in England improved dramatically. Glossy magazines and the cinema portrayed a glamorous 'American' way of life. The challenges faced by a new generation of working wives meant less time for the family to devote to the garden. Car ownership and opportunities to use the car with shorter working weeks and increased holidays took people away from home and garden. It was in this context that the young garden designer John Brookes published his *Room Outside* in 1969, translating the modernist ideas of Thomas Church and Lawrence Halprin in America and the Jellicoes, Shepheard and the Swiss landscape architect Gustav Ammann in northern Europe into language understood by a wide audience. *Room Outside* was a modern book, more square in format than the conventional oblong, with a brightly coloured dust jacket and a mix of text, diagrams and photographs on each page instead of 16 pages of text followed by 4 pages of grainy grey illustrations.

The title encapsulated two new ideas. First, in an era when more and more people sought to own their own home but could not afford as much space as they would like, why not *use* the garden as an extra room – a room outside? A California lifestyle around the swimming pool was beyond reach in England, but a patio, a barbecue perhaps, and some garden furniture would extend the family living space outdoors. Brookes wrote (in a reflection of the age) of the man of the house reading his newspaper in the garden while the wife shelled the peas in preparation for dinner. And by 1969 most young people were familiar with interiors magazines illustrating kitchens and colour schemes and were thinking about interior design, but their gardens were a mess. This led to Brookes's second idea: why not *design* the garden as a room outside? Where would we like to walk in and out, through door-like openings? Where would we like to look out into our surroundings through picture-window-like openings in the garden boundary, and where do we need to hide the surroundings with walls or fences? What sort of outdoor room would we like – a cosy den, a sophisticated place for entertaining, a rough and tumble playroom? Bravely for an English readership, Brookes paid more attention in his book to paving patterns and fencing materials – the garden structure – than to its plants. The word 'patio' entered the English vocabulary, and it gradually dawned on people that it was culture rather than climate that prevented them from using their gardens. The patio was joined by the barbecue, and the modern room-outside garden arrived in England.

Room Outside was the perfect primer for the large numbers of especially young people who were proud of their house and garden but were not especially – or not at all – interested in gardening. Its message to English gardeners was greatly facilitated by another American invention, the garden centre. In post-war England would-be garden makers had to work hard to obtain plants. Apart from bedding plants sold in trays in garden shops and some department stores, most plants were grown in the open ground. The most common method of buying plants was to obtain a catalogue from companies advertising in the national press or in garden magazines, to comb through a list of botanical names, perhaps with one-line descriptions, perhaps with a gardening encyclopaedia on hand, and send off an order by post. Some months later a bundle of twigs wrapped in straw and newspaper would arrive. These would be planted in the garden, and several more months later the twigs would produce leaves and later still flowers.

In 1953 the managing director of Waterers Nurseries in Bagshot, Surrey, a long-established traditional nursery, returned from a business trip to the United States with the idea of selling plants in pots rather than bare-root in newspaper. At the Chelsea Flower Show in May that year Waterers displayed container-grown plants with labels showing their advantages, and the idea took off. In 1954 Edward Stewart, proprietor of the long-established Ferndown Nurseries in Dorset, travelled to Toronto to seek ideas to save his failing business and also discovered the garden centre. At the same time, scientists at the University of California at Davis were working on soilless potting composts based on peat and sand to solve disease problems and facilitate handling of plants grown in containers. UC soil mixes were much lighter than conventional soil-based composts and more readily standardized for the production of the uniform batches of plants needed for large-scale production. The result of Stewart's visit was the formation in 1955 of Stewarts Garden Centre in Ferndown, followed in 1961 by a second garden centre in Christchurch, which had a coffee shop as an added attraction. Notcutts of Woodbridge in Suffolk, another long-established family nursery business, opened a garden centre next to their existing nursery in 1958.

The idea of the garden centre spread rapidly throughout the industry. Growing plants in containers with controlled nutrition and irrigation required much less space than growing in the field. Nurseries moving to container production could release some of their land for the much more profitable business of house building. Having plants in containers made it possible for customers – now car-driving customers – to collect their own plants, relieving the nurseryman of delivery costs, and to select plants in leaf and in flower. Very quickly the whole industry shifted from nurseries growing and selling plants to nurseries growing plants and garden centres selling them, although many long-established firms became and remained involved in both sectors. Very quickly, too, the garden centres added 'sundries' such as pesticides and fertilizers, garden furniture and tools, then restaurants and children's play areas – anything to entice customers to stay longer and to spend more – and, of course, Christmas displays to encourage them to visit at formerly dead times of year. The A–Z arrangement of shrubs and herbaceous plants in most early garden centres was soon supplemented or replaced by colour themed displays or plants for sun and shade. The garden centre took its place among other visitor attractions, where it was easy for newcomers to garden making to find the right plant: to choose plants for their outdoor room as they might choose wallpaper for the rooms indoors.

However, just as modern, largely American-inspired, garden making was introduced into England, the whole ethos of modernism was called into question. Rachel Carson's *Silent Spring* in 1962 warned of the dangers of the profligate use of pesticides, especially DDT, which had been thought safe to mammals until its accumulation in the food chain led to the widespread death of songbirds and to a silent spring. Her book was widely read on both sides of the Atlantic. In 1961 Yuri Gagarin made the first manned space flight, and in 1969, the year in which *Room Outside* was published, Neil Armstrong made his 'giant leap for mankind' on the moon. These were fantastic technological achievements, but the images sent back from space reinforced what some people had known for a long time: that the earth and its resources were finite, a globe of blue seas and green forests – and nasty grey smudges of urban areas, looking like the diseased scabs on an apple.

Ironically, it was the rapid growth of development and rapid increase in the standard of living in England and Europe as a whole that led to a reaction by an increasingly mobile urban population against undesirable changes in what they saw as the 'natural' landscape. In England motorways criss-crossed the country; reservoirs and power lines invaded upland areas. In the lowlands farmers were ploughing up grasslands, removing hedgerows, burning stubble left after harvesting cereal crops, and spraying chemicals to kill pests, diseases and weeds in well-meaning campaigns to feed the nation.

1970 was designated European Conservation Year, which some cynics dubbed European Conversation Year because there seemed to be so much talk and so little action. In 1973 a fuel crisis as Middle Eastern oil-producing countries turned off the taps led to shortages in the shops as transport was affected. In that same year outbreaks of Dutch elm disease were recorded in Bristol, in the west of England, and Tilbury, in the east, brought in on logs imported from America where the disease had killed vast numbers of the beautiful American elm. In the years that followed, the disease spread out from the two inoculation points like the concentric rings of fungus on a diseased apple. In 1976 England experienced the great drought. After an unusually dry winter there was almost no rain in the south, and very little in the north, from April until September, when torrential rains arrived to cause localized floods. During the summer vegetable crops failed and green English lawns turned crispy brown. Quite suddenly it seemed that 'progress' and 'modernism', with motorways, industrial farming and a general sense of unease, were perhaps not quite such good ideas. As the present was filled with foreboding, perhaps the solution lay in the past.

15

After modernism: An age of conservation

O N THE GARDEN FRONT, as in architecture, the English had never been particularly keen to adopt modernism, perhaps because they had found a solution they preferred in the work of Gertrude Jekyll, Edwin Lutyens and Alfred Parsons. Faced with a prospect of environmental disaster, real or imagined, there was a growing interest in conservation: conservation of the cultural heritage of historic houses and gardens and of the natural heritage with ecological landscapes and wildlife/organic gardens.

England was rather slow in its attempts to conserve its horticultural heritage. Perhaps because it has a tradition as a nation of gardeners, with the wealthy making changes in their gardens in every generation into the twentieth century, the idea of deliberately 'preserving' or restoring gardens of previous ages took some time to take root. After all, many owners of heritage properties were more interested in pulling down unmanageably large houses and adapting their gardens to an age of expensive labour, falling incomes from the land and rising taxes.

It was America that provided the first examples of historical restoration, starting with George Washington's Mount Vernon. After Washington's death in 1799, the mansion and its estate were inherited by a series of relatives. Without the will or the means to keep the property, it fell into decay. In 1848 John Augustine Washington, George's great-grandnephew, put Mount Vernon on the market. In 1858 Ann Cunningham campaigned to save the home of the first president for the nation as a historic landmark and an educational resource. As a result of her efforts, Mount Vernon Ladies Association of the Union was formed. In 1859 purchase of the house and part of the estate was completed, and the Association took possession in 1860. Much research was carried out in repairing the mansion, its gardens and the working parts of the estate, with a succession of superintendents, most notable among them Harrison Dodge. In his 52 years as superintendent from 1885, Dodge visited England to see Georgian gardens, and he implemented many improvements to the estate which had been planned by Washington but never carried out.

The other outstanding early example of garden restoration in the United States was Colonial Williamsburg. Dr William A. R. Goodwin discovered the delights of the ageing town, essentially the first real capital of the colonies, in 1903 when he was rector of its Bruton Parish Church. When he returned to Williamsburg 20 years later, he was dismayed

An eighteenth-century engraving of key buildings in Williamsburg, Virginia, discovered by Mary Goodwin on a visit to England.

to find this key part of American history spoiled by power lines, filling stations and unsightly modern facades on old buildings. In 1924 he met J. D. Rockefeller junior and enthused him with the idea of returning Williamsburg to its original condition. In 1928 Rockefeller engaged the Boston architectural practice of Perry, Shaw and Hepburn, with Arthur Shurcliff (1870–1957) as consultant landscape architect, to undertake a historical survey of the town, much of it done by night to avoid alerting suspicious residents.

In 1929, on a visit to England, William Goodwin's wife, Mary, discovered an eighteenth-century engraving of the College of William and Mary, the Capitol and the governor's palace; and, using also Thomas Jefferson's 1779 measured plan of the palace, work began on its rebuilding. Over subsequent decades Colonial Williamsburg grew backwards in time as buildings were repaired, rebuilt and freed of later additions. Shurcliff was treading new ground in his attempts at garden restoration. He focused rather heavily on the ornamental features of the gardens and on excessive use of box for hedges and topiary rather than including the fruit and vegetable gardens which were so important to the survival of the colonists. Today the restoration and conservation efforts continue with increasingly sophisticated techniques and ever more rigorous research. The success of Colonial Williamsburg, teetering on that awkward divide between historical reconstruction and theme park with its guides dressed in period costume, has inspired a wider appreciation of the historic landmarks which bear testament to the emergence of the New World. Both Mount Vernon and Colonial Williamsburg highlight a characteristic feature of the American way of life in which one or two people seize on an idea, tap into the wealth of other philanthropic individuals and achieve often spectacular results.

In England the care of historic gardens is associated especially with the work of the National Trust, founded in 1895. As in America, it was the work of three far-sighted people who campaigned to save England's heritage in a fast-changing world, but their efforts were directed at a wide range of targets and the funding came slowly and from a multitude of small pockets. The aim of the Trust is to protect places of natural beauty or historic interest, and it did this by acquiring and managing properties in perpetuity. Acquisitions began with small vernacular buildings and with parcels of land in the Lake District and other areas of outstanding natural beauty. In the 1930s the Trust began to acquire the 'stately homes' with which it is now – largely inaccurately – associated: houses which their donor families were no longer able to keep up because of taxation and reduced incomes.

Its acquisition of gardens began by default: the gardens happened to be attached to historic houses, and the Trust continued to maintain the gardens in a traditional manner. At Barrington Court, for example, an early acquisition in 1907, Sir Philip Lyle became the tenant of the near-derelict property. He converted the stable block into a house with modern facilities and commissioned Gertrude Jekyll to design new gardens. Lady Lyle was herself a keen gardener. She modified and added to the Jekyll plans. At Stourhead, an outstanding garden attached to a fine Palladian house designed by Colen Campbell which came to the Trust in 1946, the garden ticked over until the first Gardens Adviser, Graham Stuart Thomas (1909–2003), was appointed in 1956. As a director of Sunningdale Nurseries in Berkshire, Thomas was accustomed to advising the owners of large houses on their gardens, and he began his work for the Trust by bringing the maintenance up to his standards and adapting the gardens to their new role as essentially public spaces, adding hydrangeas and *Hypericum* 'Hidcote', for example, to provide more colour after the rhododendron season had finished. At Killerton in Devon he replaced the worn-out rose garden designed by William Robinson, never a great success, with a great swathe of low-maintenance herbaceous plants and sub-shrubs: 'ground cover' planting in the sense of covering the ground with hummock-forming vegetation but far removed from the American concept of ground cover as usually single-species planting of tough and innocuous low evergreens such as vinca, ivy or pachysandra.

Ironically, in 1948 Hidcote became the first National Trust property to be acquired for its garden, rather than as an appendage to a house. Though its strapline then proclaimed the National Trust 'for places of historic interest or natural beauty', Hidcote was neither historic – being still actively developed in the 1940s – nor natural – being a carefully designed and managed assembly of largely exotic plants. However, it was revered by the gardening intelligentsia, including Vita Sackville-West at Sissinghurst, and it remains today the archetype of what people think of as an English cottage garden just as the American colony in Broadway created the most charming gathering of English village houses from the tumble-down remains of England's once great wool-producing region. In recent years the restoration of Lawrence Johnston's garden has been greatly assisted by a large donation from an anonymous American donor.

When Hidcote came to the National Trust, the setting up of the Gardens Fund which enabled the acquisition made it possible for the Trust to accept a string of other gardens – Bodnant in Wales in 1949, Nymans and Sheffield Park in Sussex in 1954, Mount Stewart in Northern Ireland in 1955, Trengwainton in Cornwall in 1961, Sissinghurst in Kent in 1967, Knightshayes in Devon in 1972 (where Thomas had worked for Sir John and Lady Heathcoat Amory before they gave it to the Trust) and Studley Royal in Yorkshire in 1980. All of these, apart from the last, were still in active development and in most the donor family remained in residence, so it was essentially 'business as usual' – except now they were open to the public.

The first deliberate attempts to restore historic gardens, as distinct from introducing 'historic' elements into then modern gardens – such as Repton's Monks' Garden at Ashridge in the early nineteenth century and the new parterres by Achille Duchêne in 1910 and 1920 at Blenheim – stemmed from the formation of the Garden History Society in 1965. In 1964 Peter Hunt published his *Shell Gardens Book* for the petroleum companies Shell-Mex and BP. Its aim was, perhaps, to encourage motorists to visit gardens in their petrol-consuming cars. Hunt found such a dearth of information in preparing his book that he decided to set up a society for the study of gardens. Initially, its few members met for lectures and visited gardens of interest, but they quickly took on a role identifying gardens at risk and lobbying for their rescue.

Westbury Court in Gloucestershire was the first notable success, a charming remnant of a seventeenth-century Dutch-inspired garden barely visible through a wrought iron screen from the Gloucester to Chepstow road on the border of England and Wales. Much had disappeared under an old people's home and a housing estate, but the county council gave the remnant of the garden to the National Trust in 1967. Canals were dredged. The little pavilion terminating the main canal was rebuilt. Hedges were planted along the canals, fruit trees on the walls and historically appropriate flower borders below the fruit trees. Erddig, on the edge of the Welsh border town of Wrexham, was a much larger project, an early eighteenth-century formal garden illustrated in great detail in an engraving by Thomas Badeslade in 1739, but completely overgrown by almost a century of sycamore (sycamore maple) invasion. The Trust acquired Erddig in 1973, cleared the trees, dredged the rectangular lake and planted new fruit trees lining the walls of the garden. It was a dramatic transformation of a garden which had been created in the early eighteenth century and little altered since, except for the inexorable advance of nature.

The formal gardens of Ham House, the former home of the Duchess of Lauderdale on the western edge of London, were restored in 1974, and the complex garden at Claremont in Surrey, an overlay of a formal Charles Bridgeman layout by William Kent, followed in 1975. These acquisitions of near-derelict gardens to be restored led to the appointment in 1974 of John Sales as National Trust Gardens Adviser to share with Graham Thomas the Trust's rapidly increasing responsibilities. The need for wise conservation of newly acquired gardens extended retrospectively to concern for the existing garden portfolio, and the team had to face the challenges of natural growth and decay as well as the overlay, in many of the gardens, of one generation's ideas over another. In his long 1777 poem *The English Garden* William Mason wrote:

> Happier far
> Are you, ye sons of CLAUDE! …
> [whose paintings stay as they were finished]
> Not so our Landscapes: though we paint like you,
> We paint with growing colours; ev'ry year,
> O'erpassing that which gives the breadth of shade
> We sought, by rude addition mars our scene.

Mason went on to command the garden maker to 'thin the crouded glades … Nor let the axe his beak, the saw its tooth refrain' in order to prevent the garden degenerating into 'an Indian wild'. [118] It became increasingly clear that garden conservation, like gardening itself, is a dynamic process.

The publication in 1978 of a 100-year plan for the historically complex garden at Stourhead in Wiltshire, with its 1720 classical garden, its magnificent 1740–70 landscape garden around the lake, its later plantings of new rhododendrons and conifers, and its 1930 garden around the ballroom added to the house for a coming-out ball, marked a milestone in garden conservation. Since then an armoury of new techniques – archaeology, air photo interpretation and even dowsing – have been employed in unearthing the past. For the major restoration of Stowe in Buckinghamshire, the most influential of all eighteenth-century landscape gardens, Mike Calnan as head of gardens and parks for the National Trust had to travel to California where the Stowe papers are in the care of the Huntingdon Library.

In 1980 the Sussex Historic Gardens Restoration Trust was formed, financed initially by a wealthy American living in the county. Hampshire followed in 1982 and other counties as well until, with the formation of the Oxfordshire Gardens Trust in 2002 and Berkshire in 2009, the coverage of the country was complete. In 1993 the Association of Gardens Trusts was established to coordinate their activities and to share information, and in July 2015 the Association and the Garden History Society merged to form the Gardens Trust, working at local and national level to identify, protect and restore historic gardens, and to reach out to schools and other bodies to make young people in particular aware of the importance of plants and gardens to their well-being.

The activities of the National Trust and the Garden History Society stimulated and were stimulated by efforts elsewhere. In 1983 the discovery of Gertrude Jekyll planting plans in the potting shed beneath the Dutch Garden at Hestercombe in Somerset inspired a restoration of the elaborate Lutyens/Jekyll garden by the Somerset Fire Brigade, then occupants of Hestercombe House. In 1975 Elmbridge District Council in Surrey compulsorily purchased the derelict eighteenth-century garden of Painshill to save it from complete destruction. As at Erddig the garden had been overgrown by the invasion of trees, but it was gradually cleared and Charles Hamilton's remarkable garden with its vineyard, follies, Turkish tent, fantastic grotto and other features slowly emerged from the forest to create a scene which Thomas Jefferson would have recognized during his visit in 1786. Further work at Hestercombe has revealed an eighteenth-century landscape garden by Coplestone Warre Bampfylde, a close friend of Henry Hoare at Stourhead, and the most recent success of its dynamic chief executive Philip White led to the setting up in 1996 of the Hestercombe Gardens Trust to establish Hestercombe as a centre for research in garden history as well as an outstanding example of eighteenth-, nineteenth- and twentieth-century gardens. In 2006 the process began of reuniting the house, no longer headquarters of the Somerset Fire Brigade, with the gardens to extend

One of many pictures by Coplestone Warre Bampfylde of his friend Henry Hoare's garden at Stourhead, providing evidence for 20th-century restoration and management of the garden.

its potential for education and for the social events which generate important funding for the project.

As the philosophies, strategies and techniques of garden conservation have become more sophisticated, those involved have had to face the question of how to conserve twentieth-century gardens in which more or less ephemeral planting schemes are key to the garden's significance. The late Christopher Lloyd's garden at Great Dixter, now owned by the Great Dixter Charitable Trust, is an important example of this challenge, which will be faced increasingly on both sides of the Atlantic as we look back into the twentieth century as part of the past.

16

A new triangle: America, England
and the northern European mainland

MOVES TO CONSERVE AND RESTORE historic gardens in the late twentieth century were matched by similar measures to conserve, restore and mimic what is generally perceived as the natural landscape. To some extent, of course, the cultural and the natural elements of gardens overlapped in the latter part of the last century, as evidenced for example by the popularity of the Great Dixter garden with its ancient orchid-rich grasslands carefully managed by Daisy and then Christopher Lloyd as part of a sophisticated garden layout.

Among professional landscape architects, ecologists and gardeners, though, interest in nature conservation had much older roots than this resurgence. While high society immersed itself in a love triangle between America, Italy and England, more serious minded conservationists developed an equivalent partnership between America, Germany, Holland and England. Many variations on the flowery mead, the Robinsonian wild garden, the prairie garden and, in the public realm, the ecological landscape evolved as the twentieth century gave way to the twenty-first.

Awareness of the workings of nature – or what are now termed ecological systems – goes back at least to ancient Greece, but the rapid development of these ideas stems especially from the publication in 1859 of Charles Darwin's *On the Origin of Species* in England, with its concept of the evolution of species, and Ernst Haeckel's coining of the word *ökologie* (study of the house/surroundings/environment), anglicized as ecology, in 1866 in Germany. These concepts helped to form a scientific understanding of the ways in which nature operates, but the aesthetic, philosophical, almost religious appreciation of the natural landscape advanced in parallel with the scientific, stimulated in large part by disenchantment with the man-made world. Henry David Thoreau's *Walden, or Life in the Woods* of 1854 summarized his thoughts reacting against the straightjackets of American politics and 'civilized' life, and found resonance in many. George Perkins Marsh's monumental *Man and Nature* of 1864 warned of the dangers of reckless environmental damage, issuing probably the first warning of the effects of forest clearance on soil erosion and climate change.

In the same way that Darwin's *On the Origin of Species* marked a milestone in understanding the natural world, William Robinson's *The Wild Garden* of 1870 signalled a new mood in the making and appreciation of gardens. A review in the *Gardeners' Chronicle* described the book as a 'blow aimed at the vulgar craving for mere colour effect, and as such has our sympathy'. The idea of the wild garden was not new in 1870. Robinson himself had described many established examples of wild gardening in his early contributions to the *Gardeners' Chronicle*, but he gave the practice a name and voiced his disdain for the industrialized practice of mid-nineteenth-century bedding schemes. In 1877 Hermann Jäger published his *Lerhbuch der Gardenkunst* (Handbook of Garden Art) in Germany with a section on naturalising flowers in woods and meadows – the aim, as with Robinson, being to emulate the freedom of nature using bulbs and non-native perennials. In 1880 George Fergusson Wilson began his experimental wild garden at Wisley in Surrey; it was admired and visited by his friend Gertrude Jekyll and later, in 1903, acquired as the core of the Royal Horticultural Society's garden. Again, Wilson's garden used mainly exotic species – lilies, hostas, primulas, azaleas and camellias pouring in from China and Japan – but the aim was to create a sense of natural freedom beneath the canopy of native oak woods.

In 1907 Willy Lange published his *Gartengestaltung der Neuzeit* (Garden Design in Modern Times), in which he suggested that plants should be arranged by their 'physiognomie': their forms evolved in response to environmental conditions. Thus, plants adapted to sun-baked areas of low rainfall, with waxy or woolly grey foliage or succulent leaves, should be grouped together, while plants with soft green leaves would form another group for wetter, shadier areas.

These eco-naturalistic ideas crossed the Atlantic in 1884 when Jens Jensen (1860–1951) emigrated with his new wife from Denmark (where he had worked on his father's farm for many years) to Florida, Iowa and finally to Chicago. In Chicago he found employment as a labourer in the West Park system. In his first park a planting of exotics had failed so, inspired by the landscape around him, he collected the more decorative native prairie species and planted an 'American Garden' in 1888. He rose to become the general superintendent of the West Park system in 1905, establishing many areas of designed but naturalistic prairie plantings. In 1920 he left the political and bureaucratic stresses of public service and went into private practice, working especially for the Ford family. On the Fair Lane estate of Clara and Henry Ford in Dearborn, Michigan, he combined his prairie plantings with echoes of eighteenth-century English landscape principles, with drives through the landscape concealing and revealing key views in carefully controlled sequences. Clara Ford had her own ideas about garden design, though, and Jensen eventually resigned from Fair Lane as Clara continued to dot the landscape with rose gardens, specimen trees and other visual impedimenta. For Eleanor and Edsel Ford he designed three gardens in Michigan and one for their summer home in Maine. In 1935, when Jensen's wife died, he moved to

Wisconsin, where he founded the Clearing Folk School near Ellison Bay to train young landscape architects in his naturalistic principles. He continued to teach at the school until he too died in 1951.

In Chicago and in Wisconsin Jensen knew of the work of architect Frank Lloyd Wright, whose sensitivity to the natural landscape paralleled his own. The community of apprentices which Wright founded at his Taliesin home and studio in Spring Green, Wisconsin, and later at Taliesin West, in Scottsdale, Arizona, responded to the dramatically different environments of the two estates.

In many ways Wright's design philosophy was echoed in the Netherlands by Mien Ruys (1904–1999). The daughter of Bonne Ruys, another friend of Gertrude Jekyll and founder, in 1888, of the Moerheim Nursery, Mien studied garden design, engineering and architecture at various times. She developed a sometimes austere, geometric and sparsely but sensitively planted style inspired by nature in the same way that the restrained Japanese garden was inspired by, but did not mimic, nature. Mien Ruys's husband, Theo Moussault, was a publisher, and in 1954 husband and wife began publishing *Onze Eigen Tuin* (Our Own Garden), which was widely influential.

Karl Foerster (1874–1970) was born in Berlin, the son of the painter Ina Foerster. Karl began as a gardener apprentice in Schwerin from 1889 to 1891. From 1892 to 1903 he studied at the Gaertnerlehranstalt Wildpark bei Potsdam (Gardening Academy) under the plant breeder and landscape architect Ludwig Winter. In 1903 he returned to revive his parents' plant nursery in Berlin-Westend, simplifying the chaotic assortment of available plants and selecting only the most beautiful, resilient and long-lived.

The first Foerster catalogue was published in 1907, and with the relocation of his nursery from Berlin to Potsdam, he transformed a 1¼-acre field into what became a world-famous garden. During the Nazi era, Foerster took the risk of employing numerous Jewish friends in his operation, and he resisted Nazi demands to propagate and sell mainly 'racially pure' native German plants. After the war, the nursery operated under tight Soviet rule and remained the only supplier of herbaceous perennials for East Germany, but Foerster's reputation and his writings were widely influential in the western world. The grass *Calamagrostis* × *acutiflora* 'Karl Foerster', with its slender columns of stems topped by upright panicles of flowers persisting long into the winter months and now to be seen in virtually every modern garden, appropriately commemorates an outstanding nurseryman and garden designer.

While Foerster struggled with political interference in East Germany, in 1948 Professor Richard Hansen became the first director of the Institut für Stauden, Gehölze und angewandte Pflanzensociologie (Institute for Perennials, Shrubs and Applied Plant

Sociology) in Weihenstephan, West Germany. With characteristic German rigour Hansen combined plant ecology, plant breeding and garden practice to generate concepts of design and management appropriate to the low-maintenance and sometimes low-skill environment of post-war public landscapes. In 1981 he published his accumulated research and experience in *Die Stauden und ihre Lebensbereiche in Gärten und Grünanlagen*, translated into English as *Perennials and their Garden Habitats* in 1993. In 1981, the year of the first edition of *Die Stauden*, the garden architect Rosemarie Weisse (1927–2002) showed just how beautifully the seemingly dry, academic topic of plant sociology could be expressed in her designs for the Westpark in Munich. Swathes of irises and other robust perennials formed carefully choreographed carpets on poor soil and in the challenging climate of south Germany.

The gardens of Lange, Ruys, Foerster and Weisse had some similarities with the flower borders of Gertrude Jekyll, albeit usually on a larger scale and avoiding any plants requiring special care. There were broad swathes, or drifts, of carefully orchestrated herbaceous perennials including many non-invasive grasses for their late autumn and winter seed heads. William Robinson's wild gardens and the prairie gardens of Jens Jensen, though, were closer to nature in essence, with flowering plants scattered individually in a matrix of grasses – mainly low meadow grasses in the Robinsonian garden but taller prairie grasses in the landscapes of Jens Jensen. They reiterated notions of the *mille fleur* tapestries of medieval times, resurrected in the paintings of the Pre-Raphaelites and the fabrics of William Morris. The idea of the 'flowery mede' in Sir Frank Crisp's *Mediaeval Gardens* (1924), picked up by Eleanor Sinclair Rohde in *The Old English Herbals* (1922), *The Old English Gardening Books* (1924), *The Old-World Pleasaunce* (1925) and *Shakespeare's Wild Flowers* (1935), also wove into the fabric of garden making with an atmosphere of simpler times. Was it perhaps mere coincidence that the charming ninth-century garden manuscript 'Hortulus' by Walahfrid Strabo was republished by the Huntingdon Botanical Library in 1966 just as efforts to recreate North American prairies and English wildflower meadows began literally to gain ground? As Jensen retired to his last, Wisconsin, home, the prairies that he so loved were rapidly vanishing under a tidal wave of agricultural intensification. The loss of the prairie, with its echoes of vast herds of buffalo and wagon trains of pioneering settlers, created an inevitable reaction. In 1965 research on prairie restoration began at the University of Wisconsin, together with efforts to protect the last vestiges of true prairie landscape. Peter Schramm's 'Prairie restoration: A twenty-five year perspective on establishment and management' in the *Proceedings of the Twelfth North American Prairie Conference: Recapturing a Vanishing Heritage*, published in 1992, summarized these attempts to understand, protect and recreate prairie communities.

Parallel efforts were made in England, where 97 per cent of species-rich grasslands had been destroyed by ploughing or fertilizer treatment since the Second World War. Dr Terry Wells at the Institute of Terrestrial Ecology at Monks Wood, in Cambridgeshire, began his research on methods of selecting and establishing wild flowers and especially on recreating wildflower meadows in the late 1970s. His *Creating Attractive Grasslands using Native Plant Species* (1981), expanded with co-authors in 1982, provided clear guidance and inspiration for landscape architects working on motorway, reservoir and other large-scale civil engineering projects as well as for amateurs with private gardens, large or small. His research led a fellow botanist, Duncan MacIntyre, to set up Emorsgate Seeds, a company collecting, growing and selling seeds of native wild flowers of known provenance. My own work at the University of Reading, where both Wells and MacIntyre had been students, on adapting the then-novel techniques of raising vegetable plants in small cells, or plugs, to the production of wildflower plants was quickly taken up by commercial companies, so that it became possible to sow and/ or plant wild flowers in many different situations, large and small.

The work of Terry Wells, Duncan MacIntyre and their colleagues was aimed primarily at reversing the loss of native species-rich grasslands on a large scale: in land reclamation, in the ecological landscapes of new towns such as Warrington and Milton Keynes, on roadsides and other civil engineering projects, but it quickly found application in domestic gardens. The other source of inspiration for gardeners was in the gardens and writings of Beth Chatto (1923–) at Elmstead Market, near Chelmsford in Essex, and Christopher Lloyd (1921–2006) at Great Dixter, Northiam in Sussex.

Beth Chatto and her husband, Andrew, were fruit farmers in Essex. In 1960 they built a new bungalow, White Barn, and began making a garden around it. The garden, in the middle of the family farm, began as a wilderness of brambles and nettles with a few large oaks, land long-abandoned as useless for farming. The soil was primarily heavy acid clay with a small stream trickling through the bottom of the hollow, but the house was built on a gravel ridge, a parched spot in the driest part of England. Andrew Chatto, who had moved with his parents to Laguna Beach, California, at the age of 14, was a knowledgeable ecologist with a particular interest, stimulated by his American experience, in the adaptation of garden plants to the environment. He shared his wife's enthusiasm for the garden, and she absorbed from him the wisdom of suiting her planting to environmental conditions rather than trying to adapt the garden to suit particular plants, as Repton had advocated in his 1803 *Observations* and as gardeners had been spending vast amounts of time and money ever since.

Beth Chatto was a keen flower arranger and teacher of flower arranging. She found that the plants she wanted for her arranging, those with interesting leaves or seed heads or undefinable 'presence', were not readily available so, like Constance Spry before her, she began to grow her own. With the aid of machinery from the farm, the clay was shaped into a series of large ponds fringed with water-loving marginal plants, while the gravel bank only metres away became a sun-baked Mediterranean garden. Beth Chatto was also inspired by the artist Cedric Morris, who lived nearby at Benton End on the edge of Hadleigh in Suffolk. Morris was a keen and discerning gardener, breeding his own range of bearded iris as well as painting beautiful plant portraits. Chatto acquired many interesting plants from him and developed a life-long friendship. This artistic link and her own abilities as a flower arranger showed in the design of her garden, with plants displaying their beauty in an apparently natural but carefully considered way.

The garden soon began to attract visitors, and as Andrew's health forced him to retire from farming, his wife started a nursery, beginning with a typed plant list in 1967. In 1976 she arranged an exhibit of her plants at the Chelsea Flower Show. The catalogue entry for the display, 'Unusual garden plants arranged for shade, sun and damp conditions', was the garden understatement of the century. The array, carefully blending from Mediterranean grey-leaved plants to the translucent pale greens of shade-tolerant and moisture-loving plants – the whole exhibit a restful contrast to nearby mounds of roses, orchids, tulips and begonias – caused a sensation. Between 1977 and 1987 Chatto was awarded ten gold medals for her Chelsea exhibits. In 1978 she published *The Dry Garden* and in 1982 *The Damp Garden*. In 1983 and 1984 she gave lecture tours in the United States and Canada, and in 1987 in Holland and Germany. More books, lectures and magazine articles followed; the nursery flourished and Beth Chatto became internationally renowned.

In 2000 the small and awkwardly shaped triangular car park at White Barn, by now 'the Beth Chatto Garden', proved far too small, and a larger adjacent field was adopted for the purpose. The old car park was ploughed up and a new garden, the Gravel Garden, was created. Meandering gravel paths flowed between irregular, curved beds of plants – all to be seen and bought in small pots in the nearby nursery. There was, and is, no irrigation in the dry garden despite the area's low rainfall. The planting is managed by careful selection. If something dies the gap is filled by another plant. If something seeds the seedlings are left where appropriate but weeded out if they threaten to become too invasive. In 2008 Beth Chatto was the subject of a retrospective exhibition of her work at the Garden Museum in Lambeth, a key figure in English gardening in her own lifetime.

While Beth Chatto created her garden from a blank sheet in 1960, Christopher Lloyd was born in a room overlooking the garden in which he was to carve out his lifetime's work. Great Dixter, near Northiam in East Sussex, was a mid-fifteenth-century farmhouse, enlarged in 1909 by Edwin Lutyens, who added on a similar sixteenth-century house from

Kent and a new wing of his own design to create a delightful rambling house surrounded by a characteristically Lutyens garden of carefully interlocking compartments. Nathaniel Lloyd, Christopher's father, was keen on topiary, which still features significantly. His *Garden Craftsmanship in Yew and Box* (1925) was severely criticized by William Robinson (half a century later Christopher wrote that people who do not like topiary have no sense of humour), but Daisy Lloyd, Christopher's mother and the hands-on gardener of the pair, used her copy of Robinson's *English Flower Garden* as a constant source of information.

Daisy passed her love of gardening on to her son, introducing him to Gertrude Jekyll when he was a child. His studies in modern languages at King's College, Cambridge, begun in 1939, were interrupted by the war. In 1945 he continued instead with a degree in horticulture at Wye College, an outpost of Imperial College, London, based near Ashford in Kent. He graduated in 1949 and stayed on at Wye as a lecturer until 1954, when he returned to Great Dixter to manage the garden. He inherited a garden of many parts: a Lutyens plan, Nathaniel's topiary, and Daisy's roses, borders and meadows set in a much older landscape including the dry remnant of a moat. Daisy Lloyd was a well-known 'character' in Northiam, usually dressed in Austrian peasant costume. Christopher inherited her studied eccentricity, never afraid to air his opinions.

His interests in the garden were catholic, from hardy cacti and exotic foliage plants to the meadows studded with wild orchids and bulbs that his mother had carefully nurtured for more than half a century. In 1957 he published *The Mixed Border in the Modern Garden*, criticising what he saw as the obsolete herbaceous border mistakenly attributed to Gertrude Jekyll and William Robinson. In 1970 *The Well-Tempered Garden* appeared, a delightful idiosyncratic ramble through many different aspects of gardens and gardeners. His writings, including weekly contributions to *Country Life* magazine for many years, his lectures, his nursery and garden made Great Dixter a mecca for gardeners from all parts of the world. In recent years the conversion of the old and tired rose garden into an exotic or subtropical garden in partnership with head gardener Fergus Garrett has excited most visitors, but the meadows at Great Dixter have continued to exert a powerful interest. In *The Well-Tempered Garden* he wrote with amusement of visitors who commented that the poor old chap had not been able to mow his lawn as they walked along the path to the front door between panels of bulb-strewn and orchid-flecked meadow. *Meadows* (2004, latest edition 2016) summed up his experiences and illustrated the enviable spectacle of the waving sea of grass thickly studded with hardy orchids and other wild flowers.

Not surprisingly, Beth Chatto and Christopher Lloyd became firm friends, and their friendship was catalogued in correspondence published as *Dear Friend and Gardener* in 1998. Both were artist gardeners of a very high order working across the whole spectrum of garden styles from the highly exotic to seemingly purely natural. Their gardens are visited and their numerous books and articles are read on both sides of the Atlantic and across Europe by a following which spans the gulf which had long existed, in England especially, between the amateur gardener, the professional garden designer and the landscape architect.

The other cornerstones of the northern Europe/England/United States triangle in the twenty-first century are marked by the work of Piet Oudolf in the Netherlands, James Hitchmough and Nigel Dunnett at the University of Sheffield in England, and the partnership of the German Wolfgang Oehme and the American James van Sweden in the USA – although, as always, there have been and are many others making significant contributions.

Piet Oudolf (1944–) was born in Haarlem, the centre of the Dutch horticultural industry. In 1982, with his wife, he started a nursery in the small village of Hummelo near Arnhem. Early in the development of the nursery he found a chance seedling, *Salvia* 'Purple Rain', and excited by its discovery, he began a long process of breeding, finding and marketing new plants and those outstanding old plants which had disappeared from the nursery industry because of changes in fashion. Inspired especially by the designs of Mien Ruys, Oudolf began his own garden at Hummelo as an experimental area, demonstration garden and private retreat. He has captured the spirit of the age with the freedom and sophisticated naturalism of broad sweeps or intricate mixtures of herbaceous plants and grasses in his commissions across the western world: Pensthorpe in Norfolk; Scampston Hall in Yorkshire; Trentham in Staffordshire; Potters Fields in the shadow of Tower Bridge in London; and long borders at the Royal Horticultural Society's Wisley Garden, long the home of conventional gardening; a roof garden on West Broadway and waterside planting in Battery Park in New York; the spectacular Lurie Garden, a huge roof garden over Millennium Park in Chicago, jointly with Kathryn Gustafson; a misty waterside garden on the shore of Nantucket Island off Cape Cod in Massachusetts; and most notably the High Line in New York. Oudolf has also designed gardens in his native Netherlands, Germany, Sweden, Italy and Spain.

It would be unfair to attribute to Piet Oudolf the invention of the 'New Wave' planting design, as he would be the first to admit. Many people (who also became close friends) evolved the idea of using wild flowers and a limited range of tough, low-key and low-maintenance plants in carefully planned and artistically inspired but seemingly natural communities, but Oudolf – more than any of his contemporaries – took the new style around the temperate world.

James Hitchmough (b. 1956) studied horticulture in England and then spent five years from 1983 in Australia at the University of Melbourne, where he became involved in the restoration of fragile natural habitats and in the use of the remarkable plants from those habitats in garden and landscape designs. Returning to the UK he was appointed, after a brief period in Scotland, to a post in the Department of Landscape Architecture at the University of Sheffield in 1995, later becoming Professor of Horticultural Ecology. At Sheffield Hitchmough met Nigel Dunnett, now also a professor, who shared his interests in plant ecology, planting design and the establishment of naturalistic plant communities in challenging situations. Hitchmough's interests lie particularly in the creation of prairie-like communities from seed. Dunnett has worked especially on the creation of colourful, floristically rich plant communities, but also on roof gardens and vertical wall gardens as means of mitigating the effects of urban development by delaying the run-off of storm water and thus reducing flood risk. Both have been involved in revitalising run-down public parks, replacing tired shrubberies and former flower beds grassed over in times of economic difficulty by colourful meadows of annual and perennial species. Their most notable collaboration was in the Queen Elizabeth Olympic Park of the 2012 Olympics in London.

Wolfgang Oehme (1930–2011) was born in Chimnitz in East Germany. After apprenticeship in a nursery and a short period with a garden design practice employing the ideas of Karl Foerster, he studied landscape architecture in Dahlem and then worked for the long-established English nursery of John Waterer, Sons & Crisp in Bagshot, Surrey. In 1957 he emigrated to the United States where he worked as a landscape architect for Baltimore County. Unlike many landscape architects he retained a deep interest in plants and their cultivation. Frustrated by the lack of good plants, he imported plants from Germany and collected seeds of wild plants, establishing a nursery of his own.

James van Sweden (1935–2013) was raised in a Dutch community in Grand Rapids, Michigan, and graduated in architecture from the University of Michigan. After postgraduate studies in city planning and landscape gardening in Delft, in Holland, he returned to the United States as an urban designer in Washington, DC. In 1970 he bought a house in the Georgetown area of the capital and commissioned Wolfgang Oehme, whom he had heard of through Dutch friends, to design his garden – no lawn and no bare-stick roses but swathes of perennials. Van Sweden was so impressed with Oehme's work that he suggested a partnership in 1977, setting up their office in an old bank building on Capitol Hill. A severe winter had devastated the 2-acre public garden adjacent to the Federal Reserve building, and someone in the building, noting the spectacular planting outside the Oehme van Sweden office, contacted them and they were engaged to repair the garden.

In some ways their partnership resembled that of Lutyens and Gertrude Jekyll, except that van Sweden's garden architectural structure was much lighter and more elegant than that of Lutyens, and Oehme's planting was simpler and bolder in its massing. Their work, illustrated in *Bold Romantic Gardens* (1991), was clearly inspired by the breadth of scale of the American prairies but was much simpler in its composition, with huge drifts of a few species of herbaceous plants and grasses. In his many lectures internationally van Sweden advised to plant not in threes but in three hundreds. Their work for Oprah Winfrey's garden required 70,000 herbaceous perennials. Their schemes were expensive to install, usually involving automatic irrigation equipment and tons of mulching material, so were very different in some ways from the low-input gardens of Rosemarie Weisse or Beth Chatto, but they created much the same sense of breadth and, after installation, were very low maintenance.

The fusion of ideas which all these people represent was captured by two symposia organized by Brita von Schoenaich, a German landscape architect practising in England, and her partner Tim Rees at the Royal Botanic Gardens, Kew. 'Designing with Perennials: New Trends in Planting Design' in 1994 included lectures from Klaus Wittke on Hansen's work at Weihenstephan, Beth Chatto on reinterpreting Gertrude Jekyll and the English tradition, James Hitchmough on naturalising perennials, and Rosemarie Weisse on 'Nature and art: The steppe and rock garden in Munich's Westpark'. The lecture theatre was full to overflowing. The 1997 symposium included Wolfgang Oehme, Hein Koningen from the influential man-made 'natural' Heempark in Amsterdam and Beth Chatto again, with similar standing-room-only success.

The work of these and many other designers of the late twentieth century on both sides of the Atlantic has bridged the divide between nature and fine art in much the same way as William Kent and Capability Brown strove to do in the eighteenth century, except that now people from all walks of life are able to derive joy by crossing that divide.

17
A fair exchange

I N EARLY DAYS the American colonies were small, thinly populated extensions of English society, linked by family ties and governed from Westminster as if they were English counties. In the twenty-first century the situation is almost reversed, with England as a small island to the east of the great American landmass with over three hundred million people. Although England is not ruled from Washington, echoes from Wall Street and Congress ring loud on the eastern shores of the Atlantic. Because of this close association, this special relationship of two nations divided by a common language, it became easy by the middle of the twentieth century for the two countries to share their ideas and practice in relation to gardens and gardening as in many other aspects of life. Indeed, it has already been argued in chapter 11 that the most famous 'English cottage garden' was made by an American born in Paris, Lawrence Johnston, and it is beyond dispute that American money brought new life to the Cotswolds and saved many country houses and their gardens from ruin. While English gardeners offered a sense of history and refinement to an American clientele, Americans in England provided a certain sense of casual glamour.

The English garden designer Russell Page (1906–1985) was born a gardener, expressing a keen interest in plants and nature from an early age. He had various small gardening jobs as a young boy. His boarding school days at Charterhouse in Surrey were not happy: he was not a gregarious child, but his mother sent him regular parcels of plants and one of his teachers fostered his interests in painting and music, none of which endeared him to his fellow pupils. Gertrude Jekyll, who lived only a few miles from Charterhouse, had designed a garden for the headmaster around his Lutyens house in 1898, and Page was able to visit the elderly Jekyll at Munstead Wood. From Charterhouse he went to the Slade School of Art in London and then to Paris to pursue his studies in art. While at the Slade, Page met the elderly Mark Fenwick, owner of a fine old garden at Abbotsbury in Gloucestershire, and Fenwick introduced him to Lawrence Johnston at Hidcote. In Paris he met André de Vilmorin, one of the great dynasty of French nurserymen and seedsmen, and Amos Lawrence, a wealthy American with a small château near Paris. Lawrence introduced Page to French gardens and found him occasional work in some of them. His love of plants and his admiration of French garden geometry formed the basis of Page's future career.

In 1932 he met Henry Thynne, Viscount Weymouth and the future 6th Marquess of Bath, and collaborated with him in reshaping the run-down gardens of the ancestral home at Longleat in Wiltshire. The family estates included Cheddar Gorge with its mysterious limestone caves. Viscount Weymouth commissioned Geoffrey Jellicoe to design visitor facilities there, and Russell Page was asked to collaborate with advice on planting. Jellicoe's knowledge of and interest in plants was famously limited. The two men went into partnership until 1939, working together at Ditchley Park for Ronald and Nancy Tree, at the Royal Lodge in Windsor Great Park and at Page's old school, Charterhouse. Page also lectured on garden design for the landscape architecture course at the University of Reading from 1937 to 1939. At Ditchley Page met the Trees' interior designer, Stéphane Boudin, and the two struck up a long-term friendship, each bringing in the other on many of their later commissions. In 1948 Henry became the 6th Marquess of Bath, inheriting vast estates and enormous death duties. He decided to open the house and grounds to the public, later going into partnership with the owner of Chipperfield's Circus to bring the lions of Longleat into a large enclosure in the Capability Brown park. Page simplified and diversified the gardens around the house to accommodate the flow of thousands of visitors.

In the impoverished post-war years Page was stranded in Paris, but his friend André de Vilmorin, now head of the family firm, suggested a need for new labour-saving gardens by the French elite and offered him the use of an office in Paris. From here he designed many gardens in France, Belgium, Holland and Italy, combining the simple lines of paths, terraces, steps and pools with restrained planting schemes of box, roses and especially grey-leaved plants. Some of these gardens were illustrated in house and garden magazines, attracting wide international interest. His first American garden was in the mid-1950s for Mrs William Paley at Kiluna Farm on Long Island: an oval pool in an elliptical hollow with concentric paths and banks of softly coloured rhododendrons. Mrs Albert Lasker, wife of a well-known philanthropist, asked Page to design her New York garden in the 1960s, and she introduced him to First Lady Ladybird Johnson. There followed a flurry of schemes to beautify the capital and to create a federal botanic garden, but the Vietnam War intervened. President and Mrs Johnson had other matters on their minds, but Page went on to design gardens in St Louis, Palm Beach, New York, Connecticut and eventually California, Washington State, Texas, Maryland, Ohio and Alabama.

In 1972 the Frick trustees planned to pull down Widener House in New York City in order to build a new wing for the Frick Collection. There were loud protests and Page was called in to design a 'temporary' garden for 10–15 years to quell the protests. Mrs Paul Mellon, a member of the board, flew her retired gardener up from Washington, DC to advise her, and he recommended that Page be brought in. It took 10 years of steady evolution to create an oasis – as it transpired a permanent oasis – of green serenity.

The 'shrubby starworts', asters or Michaelmas daisies, were introduced to England from North America by the younger John Tradescant, but it was William Robinson who claimed to have rescued them from botanic gardens to use as an edging to his shrubberies.

ABOVE Twin borders of Michaelmas daisies in Gertrude Jekyll's garden at Munstead Wood. LEFT 'Marie Ballard', a modern hybrid developed at the Old Court Nurseries near Malvern, where Percy Picton, formerly gardener to William Robinson, joined forces with Ernest Ballard.

Carnation, Lily, Lily, Rose was painted by John Singer Sargent in 1885–6 in the garden of *Harper's Magazine* illustrator Edward Abbey in Broadway, Worcestershire, centre of the American Anglophile colony in the Cotswolds.

*Orange Lilies, Broadway, c.*1911, by Alfred Parsons, the artist turned garden designer who distilled the idea of England for the American readership of *Harper's Magazine.*

ABOVE The garden of Hidcote Manor, Gloucestershire, created from 1907 by Lawrence Johnston, an American born in Paris who became a British citizen in 1900.

ABOVE Cliveden, Buckinghamshire. Sir Charles Barry's great house (top) was embellished by William Waldorf Astor after his years as United States Minister to Italy. The Shell Fountain (bottom), by the American sculptor Thomas Waldo Story, replaced the statue of the Duke of Sutherland on the main avenue at Cliveden.

ABOVE AND LEFT Hever Castle, Kent, ancient castle and sometime home of Anne Boleyn, provided much scope for Astor's architectural and garden-making activities when he moved from Cliveden.

RIGHT When the American heiress and widow Dorothy Straight married the Yorkshireman Leonard Elmhirst in 1925 the couple moved to Dartington Hall, Devon, where Beatrix Farrand and later Percy Cane advised on the gardens.

Sunnie Holme, Connecticut, where Annie Burr Jennings was much inspired by the work of
Gertrude Jekyll and the English cottage garden tradition.

Thomas Church's garden for Dewey and Jean Donnell in Sonoma, California, signalled a new era in garden design, a garden primarily for people rather than plants.

BELOW John Brookes's *Room Outside* of 1969
brought the concept of the modern garden to a
wider English readership.

RIGHT This garden Brookes designed in 1964
for Penguin Books, Harmondsworth, was
inspired by Mondrian paintings of the 1920s.

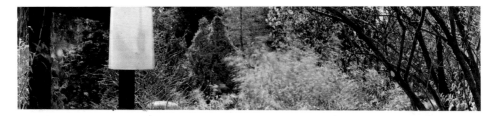

Room Outside
a new approach to garden design by JOHN BROOKES

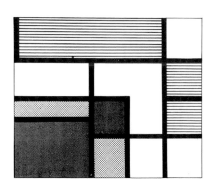

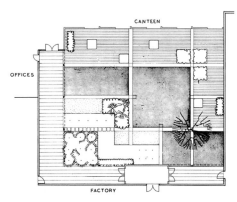

XXVII

LEFT Rosemary Verey's garden at Barnsley House, Gloucestershire, with its iconic laburnum tunnel underplanted with pale purple alliums.

ABOVE The charm of Rosemary Verey (left), her cardigan and pearls and her home-grown experience of garden making endeared her to an American audience, while Nancy Lancaster (right) brought an elegant reminder of Virginian shabby chic to many English interiors and gardens.

The High Line in New York City was officially opened on 8 June 2011.

Swathes of 'prairie planting' shared public interest with the sporting events at London's Queen Elizabeth Olympic Park in 2012.

The Liz Christy Community Garden in Lower Manhattan, a pioneer of the realization that gardens could have wide social benefits.

Page's philosophy was summed up in his comments on the Frick Garden: 'A garden striking to the casual visitor is not usually a garden to live with and I try to avoid trick effects … since even a mild shock of surprise is opposed to the idea of tranquillity which I consider more than ever essential in a city garden.'[119] These words bear a striking resemblance to Olmsted's philosophy that park carriage roads should avoid any sudden turns or changes of gradient in order to achieve a spirit of calm, a comment he repeated forcefully when he visited England for a second time and saw his much-loved democratic parks polluted by colourful bedding schemes.

Budd Harris Bishop, director of the Columbus Museum of Art, was greatly impressed by Page's work for the Frick and asked him to design a garden for his museum. Page came in 1977, and the garden was opened to the public in June 1979. Thomas Vail, publisher and editor of the *Cleveland Plain Dealer*, and his wife, Iris, also admired Page's work. Vail met Page at the Berkeley Hotel in London in 1976. Page flew to Cleveland, simplified an over-stuffed garden, and created eight new gardens in all with occasional visits and six years of correspondence. In 1981 he flew to Texas to design a rose garden for Anne Bass outside Fort Worth. He was concerned about coping with the climate and culture of Texas and was less than enthusiastic about the Basses' ultra-modern Paul Rudolph house. At White Birch Farm in Connecticut he was faced with an up-scaled replica of George Washington's Mount Vernon.

His health was starting to fail when he was asked to advise on his last major scheme, the Donald M. Kendall Sculpture Gardens at the Pepsi Corporation headquarters in Purchase, New York. Pepsi moved from Manhattan to Purchase in 1965 into E. D. Stone's seven three-storey buildings set in a 144-acre estate landscaped by Stone's son, Ed Stone junior. In 1981 Page was commissioned to transform the corporate estate into a park and sculpture garden. He created lakes (all Page gardens had to have water in one form or another) and a meandering golden path to unify the landscape, then planted to provide appropriate settings for each of the sculptures. He helped to choose and to site the varied sculptures which populated the park, spending three months every spring and three months every autumn for five years alone in a hotel (his second wife died in 1962) while suffering from advancing cancer. He died in January 1985.

Page's gardens were simple, classical and restrained, requiring relatively little maintenance. They were ideally suited to the latter part of the twentieth century, designed for discerning wealthy people who admired the international flavour of his English, French and Islamic-inspired gardens but who had little time for gardening themselves.

While Page was building his reputation in America, an American began his garden design career in England. Lanning Roper (1912–1983) was born in New Jersey and graduated with a degree in fine art from Harvard in 1933. He first came to England as a naval officer in the D-day campaign. After returning briefly to America, he came back to England on business but resigned to study at the Royal Botanic Gardens in Kew and Edinburgh. He married the artist Primrose Harley, former wife of garden designer John Codrington, and the couple settled in Kensington, in the fashionable heart of London's West End. In 1951 Roper joined the staff of the Royal Horticultural Society as assistant editor of its journal, a post which he held until 1957. The RHS in the 1950s had a few thousand members, many of whom lived in the south of England, especially in the rhododendron territories of Kent, Surrey and Sussex, and gardened on a few acres with the help of a full-time or part-time gardener. The wealthier members of the RHS had substantial estates and often came from renowned gardening families. In his writing and publishing activities Lanning Roper came into contact with many of this gardening elite.

The Ropers' garden developed into a luxuriant oasis of foliage and flowers in the centre of London. It featured in *Vogue* magazine and was illustrated in his first book, *Successful Town Gardening*, in 1957, the year in which he also published his book on Henry du Pont's Longwood Gardens. In 1960 Roper wrote *Hardy Herbaceous Plants*, one of a series of small books published in a collaboration between the RHS and Penguin Books. The early books in the series, on rock gardens, dahlias, chrysanthemums, roses and so on, followed well-trodden horticultural paths. *Hardy Herbaceous Plants* seemed to begin in that same vein, but there were important signs of change. There were indeed chapters on digging and planting, staking and dividing, pests and diseases followed by appendices on irises, delphiniums, peonies, lupins, perennial asters (Michaelmas daisies) and phlox, stalwart denizens of the conventional herbaceous border. In his opening remarks, though, Roper wrote: 'At the outset I want to make it plain that this book is not intended solely for the devotees of herbaceous borders. The gardener of today may well prefer to abandon this limiting form of gardening in favour of the mixed border containing shrubs, roses, herbaceous plants and perhaps quantities of bulbs as well. This will extend the range of interest and may better conform to the size of his property, the depth of his pocket, and the labour available.'

There is a short section on ground-cover plants, not the dull institutional evergreens of vinca, ivy and pachysandra used in America as substitutes for lawns where grass was difficult to manage, but ajuga, epimedium, tiarella and other flowering carpets. The appendices also extended to 'Flowers and Seed Heads for Drying for Winter' and perennials for chalk, for dry sunny positions, for shade and damp soils – sound advice on ecological aspects of gardening in the same year that Beth Chatto started her new garden in Essex. During his time with the RHS and in his many conversations with garden owners who were members, Roper became very aware of changing times, of smaller gardens and much smaller garden staffs; and his own garden in Kensington, a paradise in the middle of a great city, appealed to the many owners of country estates who also owned townhouses in London or other major centres.

From 1962 to 1974 he designed the garden of the Old Vicarage in Bucklebury, Berkshire, for Sir Robert and Lady Sainsbury, family partners in one of England's major supermarket chains. The garden was designed to accommodate the Sainsburys' sculpture collection, including two Henry Moores, and it featured a long mixed border with old roses spilling over grey-leaved lavenders and other relaxed, low-maintenance plants. Beyond a giant yew across the lawn from the rose border was a pool garden with a modern fountain embowered in the luxuriant foliage of golden *Robinia* 'Frisia', gold-variegated *Elaeagnus pungens* 'Maculata', dusky purple-leaved *Rosa glauca* and foaming carpets of yellow-green *Alchemilla mollis*: plants which provided the colourful effects usually associated with flowers but in a more lasting manner.

Lanning Roper developed a long-lasting association with Sir Winston and Lady Churchill at Chartwell in Kent, again providing a setting for sculpture but clothing banks below the house with grey-leaved shrubs and designing a gold garden to accommodate roses bought to celebrate the couple's golden wedding anniversary. He went on to design major gardens in England, Ireland, France, Italy, Switzerland and his native America, always in conversation with owners and often developing life-long friendships. Among his dozens of English gardens were Haseley Court for Nancy Lancaster (1968–70); a collaboration with Geoffrey Jellicoe on the new pool garden at the RHS Wisley garden in 1969; Folly Farm, a Lutyens house with a run-down Jekyll garden for the Hon. Hugh and Mrs Emily Astor (1971–7); a garden bordering the Thames at Swan Walk in London for the Hon. Michael Astor; North Mymms Park for Mrs W. S. Morgan Burns in 1975, following in the footsteps of William Robinson; and the Manor House at Yattendon (1977–81) and then Basildon Park (1982), both in Berkshire, for Lord and Lady Iliffe. In 1981 he was asked to advise the Prince of Wales on his new garden at Highgrove in Gloucestershire, but by this time he was too ill to accept the commission. His work at Scotney Castle in Kent for Lady Rosse and the National Trust continued from 1970 to 1982. A streamside walk in the garden was named after him, and his ashes were scattered there after his death in 1983.

Other outstanding contributors to this Anglo-American exchange were two English women, Penelope Hobhouse (1929–) and Rosemary Verey (1918–2001), both gifted amateurs turned professional. Born into a distinguished Anglo-Irish family, Penelope Hobhouse is the daughter of James Lenox-Conyngham Chichester-Clark and sister of Lord Moyola and Sir Robin Chichester-Clark. After graduating with a degree in economics from Girton College, Cambridge, in 1951, she went on a walking tour through Tuscany, studying the many beautiful villas and their gardens. In 1952 she married Paul Hobhouse and began to implement her ideas on garden making around the Hobhouse family's Hadspen House in Somerset. Her successes at Hadspen led to a career in writing and garden design, initially on planting and garden design but later on garden history, including the gardens of Persia (Iran) and Afghanistan. In 1983 the marriage was dissolved, and Mrs Hobhouse moved to Tintinhull in Wiltshire with her new husband, Professor Edward Malins, whom she had met at a Garden History Society meeting. As a tenant of the National Trust at Tintinhull, a delightful seventeenth- and eighteenth-century farmhouse turned modest manor house with a garden created by its owner Phyllis Reiss from 1933, Hobhouse revitalized the garden and continued her writing and consultancy. Her tall form, confident character and the combination of firm structure and exuberant planting in her gardens had wide appeal, and she worked in England, Scotland, France, Italy, Spain, Germany and the United States, including designing an 'English cottage garden' for Steve Jobs's Tudor-style home in Palo Alto, California, in 1996, the year in which she also hosted a television series for Home and Garden Television in the United States and in which the RHS awarded her the Victoria Medal of Honour. In addition to the herb garden for the New York Botanic Garden, she designed gardens in New York, Maine, Connecticut, New Jersey, California and Texas. In 1993 she received an Award of Excellence for *Gardening through the Ages* from the Garden Writers Association of America, and in 2001 she designed a Mediterranean-type garden for the Philadelphia Flower Show, where she also lectured.

In many ways Rosemary Verey epitomized a certain type of English mother with her flower-embroidered cardigans, strings of pearls and brood of four children, but most English mothers did not study economics at University College London nor have a passion for flying, horses and hunting. Rosemary Isabel Baird Sandilands gave up her studies in economics and social history to marry David Verey in 1939 on the eve of war. He was away for most of the war years, but on his return Rosemary resumed her role as a dutiful wife and mother. When he was appointed as architectural historian to the Ministry of Housing to investigate historic buildings in Gloucestershire, they moved to Ablington, near to Barnsley House where his parents lived. In 1951, when the parents moved to a smaller property in the village, David and Rosemary moved into Barnsley House, a large seventeenth-century stone manor house where they spent the rest of their lives.

By 1960 the children were away from home, Rosemary Verey was at a loose end, and although she had expressed no interest in gardening as a child, she decided to do something about the rather neglected garden. When David invited the well-known garden designer Percy Cane to Barnsley without consulting his wife, she was outraged and determined to make her own garden. With David's collaboration (echoes of Vita Sackville-West and

Harold Nicolson at Sissinghurst), she created a space of formal structure but free planting, becoming particularly skilled at successional planting in which alliums followed tulips that followed narcissi in a sea of emerging herbaceous perennials. In 1962 David bought a classical temple from Fairford Park which he re-erected by the lily pool. It was Rosemary, though, who spent long hours in the garden digging, planting and planning.

David Verey always had a deep interest in books and bought old books on gardening for his wife. Early on in her gardening life she was given a little book on the magical properties of the mandrake, a herb with powerful properties but with the awkward challenge that, if its vaguely man-shaped root were to be pulled out of the ground, it would utter a shriek turning the offender to stone. The solution was to tie the plant to a dog's tail, to go out of earshot and call the dog, whereupon the dog would be turned to stone but the owner would have the magical root – and would presumably look for a new dog. This interesting little book spurred an interest in other old garden books, and as her garden and her library of old books grew, Verey used historical precedents not in a twee false-historical manner but in a fusion of old and new.

Armed with her books and with some brief ideas sketched out by Percy Cane on his one fleeting visit, she set to work with a vigour characteristic of all her activities, whether hunting, dancing or gardening. The garden soon began to attract attention. In 1970 it opened once for the National Gardens Scheme, opening more and more frequently in subsequent years to meet the demand from visitors, until it was open six days a week during the growing season, with a plant sales area to boost income for the garden.

In the early 1970s she developed an interest in the 'potager', a decorative vegetable garden such as Louis XIV had had in his Potager du Roi, the king's potager, at Versailles. At Barnsley a pattern of brick and stone paths spanned by arches supporting beans, gourds and other climbers was created in a former yard by the cattle barns outside the main garden. The new potager was planted with parsley, dwarf beans, strawberries, coloured-leaved lettuce, fern-leaved carrots and other ornamental edible plants. Later the fence around the potager supported fruit trees trained as espaliers, cordons and in more elaborate shapes.

The Barnsley House potager was developing nicely when the great drought of 1976 arrived and vegetable supplies in the shops dwindled. The thought that one could have a beautiful garden which would also supply fresh vegetables and fruit, free of unknown pesticide sprays, created waves of interest. The potager was illustrated in gardening magazines and on television. Visitor numbers to Barnsley House increased sharply, and 'the potager' entered the garden vocabulary. Even John Brookes, the archetypal modernist at that time, designed a garden for the 1971 Chelsea Flower Show in which he included a small knot of box within which beans, carrots and strawberries were grown.

In 1980, when she was 62, Rosemary Verey co-wrote *The Englishwoman's Garden* with Alvilde Lees- Milne. It was a large format book with what were for the time remarkably good colour illustrations. She set off at once to America to publicize her book and her garden. To her American audiences she was the archetypal English lady, white hair elegantly coiffured, dressed in flowery tops and sensible skirts, always with something blue to match her eyes, and with a distinctly crisp accent. She had a genuine interest in other people, a warm personality, and although she suffered agonies of insecurity throughout her life from her lack of formal training, she exuded a sense of competence derived from her very hands-on approach to her garden. She conveyed her ideas and experience with great enthusiasm, encouraging her listeners with the thought that they, too, could garden like her. All these characteristics endeared her to an expanding group of people who, with growing affluence, were becoming interested in their 'yards'. *The Englishman's Garden* soon followed, and then *The Scented Garden*, an idea suggested by Ethne Clarke, an American publisher living in London. The subtitle, 'Choosing, growing and using the plants that bring fragrance to your life, home and table', conveyed a sense of traditional home-making that readers found immensely appealing, and there were a great many readers. In 1981 she gave a lecture at Wave Hill, the historic garden on the Hudson River, at the invitation of Henry Cabot, a renowned gardener and philanthropist, and she used her trip to visit the PepsiCo headquarters garden with Russell Page, to meet the du Ponts at Longwood and Winterthur, and to see other influential gardens – always with her notebook in hand for any useful tips. She crossed the continent to San Francisco and was inspired by the three-dimensional knot garden at Filoli, where the hedges were trimmed to appear to flow over and under each other. On her return to Barnsley she quickly copied the idea in her own previously flat-topped knots.

Rosemary Verey was always generous with plants and advice, but in 1980 her first proper design commission arrived. Karen and James Lowther had just bought Holdenby Hall, a great Elizabethan house in Northamptonshire built by Elizabeth I's lord chancellor, Sir Christopher Hatton. They wanted a garden to reflect the history of the house, using only plants available before 1580, so their choice of designer was particularly appropriate. In 1981 Prince and Princess Michael of Kent moved to Nether Lypiatt Manor near Barnsley. Verey gave advice, as she did to many other friends and acquaintances, but the princess then commissioned a design for a circular garden. The American financier Arthur Reynolds and his wife, Catherine, moved to London for his work, but Catherine was a keen horsewoman and they both wanted a weekend retreat. They bought The Little House in Barnsley, very close to Barnsley House. This was Verey's first complete garden design, with four square box-hedged parterres and apple trees trained in arches, borrowing from the potager at Barnsley House.

Her next book, *The American Woman's Garden*, written in collaboration with Ellen Samuels, brought her widespread recognition in America. The idea was inspired, making it clear that Americans, too, had gardens and that they had no need to feel inferior to their English counterparts. Also, by including a gathering of notable American women gardeners to contribute to her book, she widened her network of American friends, many of whom eventually found their way to tea at Barnsley House. In 1984 David died of prostate cancer. Rosemary had not travelled during his illness, but on his death, partly to compensate for the gap left in her life, she poured herself into her garden, her writing and her travels.

In 1988 she was asked by the Prince of Wales to advise on the garden he was making at Highgrove, near Tetbury in Gloucestershire, only a few miles from Barnsley. He had already consulted Dame Miriam Rothschild, a remarkable member of the Rothschild dynasty and a leading figure in the development of wildflower meadows, and Lady Salisbury, whose gardens at Cranborne Manor in Somerset and Hatfield House in Hertfordshire were renowned for their historically inspired but relaxed patterns. Verey was asked to create a cottage garden, a project which began a friendship lasting for the rest of her life. The prince was guest of honour at her eightieth birthday party. Another near-regal commission also came in 1988 when Elton John sought her advice on his garden at Woodside in Berkshire, where she worked for the next five years. Elton John was, as he remains, a frantically energetic personality. For once Verey had a more or less unlimited budget, but she suffered from her client's demands for instant results and his impulsive changes of mind. Her white garden on the terrace below Elton John's bedroom windows was scrapped just as it was coming to maturity because he had been to Italy, had fallen in love with Italian gardens, and decided to bulldoze the white garden to make way for his own Italian garden.

Meanwhile, with the trusty pair of Andy and Les Bailey to keep the Barnsley House garden going at home, she criss-crossed the Atlantic. In 1990 *The American Man's Garden* was published, with the same format as her *American Woman's Garden* and with the same effect of widening still further her list of American friends. In 1994 she crossed America on a lecture tour with Christopher Lloyd, standing in for Beth Chatto, whose husband was seriously ill. It was an unlikely but, as it transpired, a very successful partnership. In 1997 she was asked by the New York Botanic Garden to design a potager. Her reception was such that she decided to bequeath the archive of her work to the garden rather than arranging for it to be kept in England. In 1998 she was awarded the G. R. White Medal, the highest honour awarded by the Massachusetts Horticultural Society.

George Robert White (1847–1922) gave five million dollars to the city of Boston to establish a conservation centre. In 1909 he gave 7,500 dollars to the Massachusetts Horticultural Society to endow the George Robert White medal, the interest from the endowment to be used to award an annual medal, weighing 8.5 ounces of coin-grade gold, to someone who had made an outstanding contribution to horticulture. Several of these medals were awarded to British horticulturists, a recognition that horticulture on its highest plane spanned the globe.

Sir Harry Veitch, then head of the Veitch dynasty of nurserymen and the person responsible for sending Ernest Wilson to China via the Arnold Arboretum, was the first Englishman to be awarded the medal, in 1914. In 1916 it went to William Robinson. Charles Sprague Sargent, who recommended him for the medal, wrote to him from the Arnold: 'I do not suppose that you care about such things but as awards go this is the best thing in the United States in its way.'[120] Sadly, the medal never arrived, presumed lost at sea in a ship sunk during the war.

In 1920 the award went to the plant collector George Forrest. In 1924 it went to John McLaren (no relation of the McLarens at Bodnant in Wales), a horticulturist at the Edinburgh Botanic Garden. In pursuit of his ecological interests he studied the grasses which were colonising and stabilising the sandy shores of the Firth of Forth, the sea inlet on the south shore of which Edinburgh sits. He later emigrated to America and undertook the design and planting of Golden Gate Park in San Francisco, a project declared impossible by the Olmsted office because of the unstable sandy soils but one which McLaren triumphantly achieved because of his Scottish experience. He continued to manage the park until his death at the age of 94. McLaren had a great dislike of statuary, and whenever a statue was erected in the park he did his best to conceal it with trees and shrubs.

Gertrude Jekyll was the first Englishwoman to be awarded the medal, in 1929, three years before her death. The next Englishman was Francis Kingdon-Ward, a prolific plant hunter who undertook 25 expeditions to the Himalayas over a span of 50 years. In 1940 the medal was awarded to Sir Arthur William Hill, director of the Royal Botanic Gardens at Kew, and in 1948 to another McLaren, Charles McLaren, 3rd Baron Aberconway of Bodnant Garden, son of the 2nd Baron Aberconway, who was then, from 1931 to his death in 1953, president of the RHS.

In 1951 Sir William Wright Smith, Regius Keeper of the Royal Botanic Garden, Edinburgh, received the medal. It was to Wright Smith that Beatrix Farrand wrote seeking help in finding a gardener for Garland Farm, to which she retired after the sale of her Reef Point home.

In 1999, the year after her White Medal, Verey was recognized in England by the highest award of the RHS, the Victoria Medal of Honour. By this time she was becoming increasingly frail. In 1999 a bad fall, complicated by an injury she had sustained in a horse-riding accident many years earlier, necessitated two painful operations. She fell again later, leaving her face black and blue, but insisted on continuing a tour of Long Island gardens and a punishing routine of gardening, travel and writing. In March 2001 she travelled to Kentucky to design a walled garden potager for Antony and Angela Beck. In May she died. Tributes flowed in from all parts of the world and from all levels of society but particularly from her many American friends.

Rosemary Verey brought to America the charm, vivacity and down-to-earth wisdom of a lady gardener with mud under her fingernails and a message that Americans had nothing to be ashamed of in the realm of good garden making. Towards the end of her life, fashions were changing to a much more naturalistic and ecologically driven style, but when she went to the 1994 symposium at Kew with one of her protégés and co-organizer of the symposium, Tim Rees, she said, 'I don't know what all the fuss is about. Why, that's what I have been doing all along!'[121] In one sense she was right, but the new wave of Dutch, German, American and English designers were eliminating the patterned hedges and box balls, allowing the looser contents of her carefully detailed knots and parterres to spill out over the landscape.

While garden designers criss-crossed the Atlantic, opportunities for landscape architects were more limited by national rules of professional competence and registration. With rare exceptions, such as the Princess Diana Fountain, a necklace of Cornish granite in Hyde Park designed by the American Kathryn Gustafson, landscape architects tend to communicate with each other at international conferences and by their publications, but their practice is confined to home territory.

The one English landscape architect whose practice has spanned the Atlantic is Geoffrey Jellicoe (1900–1996), working on one major scheme in America but also for several Americans and former Americans in England. Jellicoe set out to become an architect, enrolling at the Architectural Association in London in 1919. The award of a British Prix de Rome enabled him to travel with a fellow student, John C. (Jock) Shepherd, to Italy to study its famous gardens, as a result of which he became more interested in the landscape setting of buildings and in landscape architecture than in architecture itself. Jellicoe and Shepherd's book, *Italian Gardens of the Renaissance*, was published in 1925 and helped to stimulate English interest in Italian gardens. Jellicoe was a founder member of the Institute of Landscape Architects in 1929, ensured the survival of the young institute during the war by accommodating it in his office, and became its president from 1939 to 1949. In 1948 he also became the instigator and first president of the International Federation of Landscape Architects. It was as an architect with a sensitivity to the landscape that Viscount Weymouth commissioned him to design a restaurant in Cheddar Gorge (1934–6) in Somerset, and it was here that he met Weymouth's friend and garden advisor, Russell Page.

In 1964–5 he was commissioned to design the Kennedy Memorial Garden, a philosophical design on a symbolic acre of Runnymede, the field by the Thames at Windsor where in 1215 the Magna Carta was signed, a great charter limiting the power of the king. Jellicoe was much influenced by the writings of psychoanalyst Carl Jung. The Kennedy Memorial consisted of a long, shallow flight of steps made from small granite setts, symbolizing the thousands of people who would climb the slope to pay their respects to the late president. At the top the path opened to the sky to reveal a simple memorial stone.

In 1980–86 he worked at Sutton Place in Surrey for the American recluse John Paul Getty, again an elaborate and philosophically driven design with a large lake and earth mound, an intricate maze-like garden near the house, and a Ben Nicholson sculpture reflected in an existing rectangular lily pond.

In 1984 came his one significant commission in America, a master plan for the Moody Gardens in Galveston, Texas. His design, on 126 acres of sea marshes on the Gulf of Mexico, was intended to invoke the whole history of landscape with a biblical Garden of Eden, Egyptian and Roman gardens and areas representing China and Japan, with other gardens, 15 in total, including waterfalls, caves and monsters, all to be seen from boats cruising silently along canals while visitors listened to a broadcast commentary. The gardens were not begun before his death in 1996, but they have since developed as a major educational and entertainment centre with a 12-storey high Aquarium Pyramid housing 10,000 marine animals and fish, a 10-storey Rainforest Pyramid and a Discovery Pyramid for temporary exhibitions.

18

A southern belle in England

Oⁿᴱ ᴼᶠ ᵀᴴᴱ ᴹᴼˢᵀ ᴵⁿᵀᴱᴿᴱˢᵀᴵⁿᴳ of all the accounts of transatlantic hopping must be that of Nancy Perkins/Field/Tree/Lancaster. Nancy Perkins was born in 1897, the granddaughter of Colonel Chiswell Langhorne and Nancy Witcher Keene. Her grandfather had been an odd-jobber and then, from 1885, a railroad contractor. In 1903, at 60, he retired as a multimillionaire. He remained something of a rough diamond, declaring: 'Etiquette is for people with no breeding. Fashion is for people with no taste,' but he acquired the old Mirador estate in Virginia.[122]

Colonel Langhorne had three daughters, all renowned for their beauty and wit, but Elizabeth, the eldest daughter and Nancy's mother, did not marry well. Her husband was Thomas Perkins, a meat packer, and the Perkins family lived in a shack on the Mirador estate. Not surprisingly, it was a troubled marriage. The couple separated in 1910, and Elizabeth took her children to France. They returned on the outbreak of war to find Thomas terminally ill. He died in 1914, and his wife collapsed and died weeks later. At 16 Nancy was an orphan, and she was taken in by her aunt. She came out in the 1915–16 debutante season and married Henry Field, the grandson of Marshall Field, founder of Chicago's leading department store. Tragically, her new husband went into hospital for a minor tonsil operation five months later, developed septicaemia and died. At 22 Nancy Field was a widow.

The five-year-old Nancy with her father, Thomas Perkins.

One of the Langhorne sisters, another Nancy, had married William Waldorf Astor. In 1918 Nancy Field went to spend Christmas with her aunt Nancy Astor at Cliveden. On board the *Mauretania* she met Ronald Tree, a cousin of Henry Field. Tree was rich, well educated and cultivated, born in England of American parents. Nancy and Ronald married in 1920. The couple returned to New York so that he could go into politics, and he bought Mirador, which had changed hands and, like so many southern homes, was falling into ruin. Nancy was able to return 'home', and she set about transforming her house with that unique taste which was later dubbed 'shabby chic'. She loved old furniture, faded fabrics and subtle colours which captured the mood of the South in the aftermath of the Civil War.

With his English background, Ronald Tree made no headway in American politics, so the couple moved back to England in 1925. In 1926 he became joint master of the Pytchley Hunt in Northamptonshire, becoming about as English as it was possible to be. In Northamptonshire they leased Kelmarsh Hall from Colonel Lancaster. It was a run-down Palladian house described later by the architectural historian Nikolaus Pevsner as a 'perfect, extremely reticent design done in an impeccable taste'.[123] With its beautifully proportioned central block and two advancing wings Kelmarsh Hall bore a considerable likeness to George Washington's Mount Vernon, Jefferson's Monticello and other American houses of the period. Its reticent taste was perfectly attuned to Nancy's ideals. The Trees lived in dignified discomfort until the house was remodelled by Paul Phipps, a pupil of Edwin Lutyens and Nancy's uncle by marriage to the third Langhorne sister, to include bathrooms and other modern comforts.

While at Cliveden Nancy had been overwhelmed by the beauty of the borders planned by Norah Lindsay. Lindsay was engaged for Kelmarsh, and the two women created a garden to match the house: comfortable, dignified and discreetly opulent. In 1929 came the Wall Street Crash. Ronnie resigned from the hunt and relinquished Kelmarsh, and the couple retreated to their London home.

In 1933 Ronald discovered Ditchley Park, deep in the Oxfordshire countryside and three miles from the Duke of Marlborough's estate at Blenheim. He fell in love with the house – a run-down but supremely elegant house with a central block and two advancing wings as at Kelmarsh, and bought it two weeks later. He bought furniture and pictures while Nancy determined how the house would look, consulting the renowned Belgian interior designer Stéphane Boudin but injecting her own taste. In London the Trees lived opposite Edward Hudson, the publisher of *Country Life*. Hudson knew Geoffrey Jellicoe and Jock Shepherd's *Italian Gardens of the Renaissance*, and he recommended the young Jellicoe to advise on their garden. Jellicoe designed a new forecourt for the house, created a long grass terrace terminated by an eighteenth-century temple brought from an outlying part of the estate, and with his partner, Russell Page, made a parterre terminated by an ornamental

Parterre at Ditchley Park, Oxfordshire, designed by Geoffrey Jellicoe for Ronald and Nancy Tree (later Nancy Lancaster).

pool which, at the press of a button, brought forth a line of fountain jets to obscure the pool from the house, turning it into a secluded swimming pool. In 1937, to celebrate the completion of the house and the coronation of George VI, the Trees had a spectacular party in which all the female guests were asked to wear red and white, the prevailing colour theme of the event and Nancy's favourite colours in dress.

The Trees played an important role in the war which broke out in 1939. On moonlit nights the prime minister's official weekend residence at Chequers became a conspicuous target for German bombers so Churchill and his war cabinet decamped to Ditchley, a practice captured in Ronald Tree's memoir, *When the Moon was High* (1975).

In 1943, with a now-English husband and two sons fighting in the British army, Nancy renounced her American citizenship and was forced to sell Mirador. Although this had not been her main home since 1925, the loss was a severe blow in a life troubled by misfortunes from its beginning. She had a nervous breakdown. Ronald suggested buying the interior design firm of Sybil Colefax Ltd to occupy her mind. Founded in 1929 and flourishing in furnishing homes of taste with restrained but distinguished furniture and subtle colours, the business developed the art which Nancy had been practising in her own homes for more than 20 years. Sybil Colefax's partner, the decorator John Fowler, was part of the firm so, under its new owner and driving force, Colefax & Fowler invaded every English mansion and stately home, in London or in the country.

Although the new career was a success, her marriage was not. The couple divorced in 1947, and in 1948 she married Colonel Claude Granville Lancaster of Kelmarsh Hall. That marriage ended in 1953, after only five years. Nancy Lancaster said wryly that she was better at choosing houses than husbands, and it seems probable that she married Kelmarsh Hall rather than its owner (she only left the house when her ex-husband disconnected the electricity).

She needed a new home. In a prolonged search she stumbled on Haseley Court on the edge of the village of Little Haseley to the south-east of Oxford, across the county from Ditchley. She telephoned her solicitor and bought Haseley Court with 80 acres of land for £4,000. The house had no roof, no bathrooms, no heat or electricity and was riddled with dry rot. With her usual flair she roofed the house, added eight bathrooms and furnished the interior with the offhand perfection characteristic of Colefax & Fowler directed by Nancy Lancaster. Geoffrey Jellicoe was engaged again to provide a dignified approach, a gravelled drive around a central panel of lawn with wide steps up to the terrace on which the house sat. Initially, the most remarkable feature of the garden was a topiary chess set clipped in box and planted in the 1850s. While the house had fallen into serious decay, an old man in the village had taken it upon himself to cycle out regularly to trim the box. While lawns and borders degenerated into hayfields and thickets, the chess set survived.

In her earlier homes Nancy had focused mainly on the interiors, but she had worked with Norah Lindsay at Kelmarsh and, in dealing with her Colefax & Fowler clients, would have been exposed to their gardens, many created with the help of Russell Page, Lanning Roper, John Codrington or other distinguished garden designers but all directed by interested and knowledgeable owners. Her shabby chic interiors and the Lutyens/Jekyll/Parsons/Lindsay garden with its luxuriant planting spilling over a strong architectural framework went hand in hand. At Haseley Court Nancy consulted Lanning Roper in 1968–70, but she evolved her own garden plan. In the topiary chess garden an intricate pattern of grey-leaved santolina and lavender contrasted with the dark green of the box. Darker yews surrounded three sides of the sunken garden with steps on the fourth side leading up to a white garden. East of the house ancient foundations were too numerous to permit normal planting, so clipped yews with skirts of ivy were raised on mounds of topsoil. An old moat stretched away from the house, lined by woodland and coppiced hazels forming a green tunnel in summer, thickly underplanted with bulbs and hellebores for winter and spring.

In the partially walled kitchen garden the enclosure was completed on the remaining two sides by hornbeam tunnels, again underplanted with early bulbs to flower before the hornbeam leafed out, and with a mirror placed at 45 degrees to the tunnels so that both arms, reflected in the mirror, seemed to continue into the distance. This square garden was quartered, with fruit trees in grass in two quarters, alternate beds of iris and strawberries around a central apple tree in the third, and a complex pattern of box hedges, weeping mulberries and grey foliage in the fourth, modelled on a Roman mosaic on the Venetian island of Torcello – a pattern also used by Gertrude Jekyll in the herb garden at Knebworth, Hertfordshire, and by Lutyens in his sunken 'Dutch' garden at Folly Farm in Berkshire.

Nancy Lancaster had impeccable taste, but this was allied with a wicked sense of humour. Her son, a successful racehorse trainer, once gave her a tip for a horse which was bound to win – and it lost. At the terminus of a poplar avenue which she had planted as a windbreak, she erected a triumphal arch of light timbers and painted canvas. When her son came to visit, mother burst into tears as she showed him how he had ruined her: she had spent the fortune she should have won on this magnificent 'stone' arch.

Haseley Court suffered severe fire damage in 1970, for which she was not insured. The house was sold in 1971, and she moved to the Coach House where she continued to live in reduced circumstances but great style until her death in 1994 at the age of 96.

19

Botanic gardens

A N AREA in which America has made a notable contribution to English gardens is in the realm of the public–private interface, in which one can clearly detect historical differences between a democratic republic and an inherited monarchy. This is particularly noticeable in the development of botanic gardens and in education. The early English botanic or physic gardens were the private gardens of physicians such as William Turner in the sixteenth century. Although the owners of such gardens would undoubtedly have derived pleasure from surveying their medicinal herbs arranged in orderly sequence, there is no evidence that the gardens were arranged for aesthetic effect. When the physic garden became more public, as in Pisa (1544) and Padua (1545) in Italy, and later in England's first such garden at Oxford (1621), they were attached to universities and were arranged in the manner of the medieval gardens, orderly rectangular beds facilitating access to the plants for teaching and collecting medicinal samples, with access restricted mainly to students of medicine and later taxonomic botany. Other members of the university might be admitted, but this was an exclusive community in which academic interests had quite loose boundaries. Professors of law, for example, would have a general interest in natural philosophy (a precursor to modern science) as it related to the workings of the world, while theologians would wish to enumerate the creations of the Maker. England's second institutional botanic garden was the renowned Chelsea Physic Garden, founded by the Society of Apothecaries in 1673 on the banks of the Thames. It, too, was arranged in an orderly array of rectangular beds. Admission was restricted to members of the society and its students.

By far the most famous English botanic garden is that at Kew, a royal property from the early seventeenth century which became a national botanic garden in 1841. As noted in earlier references to Kew, after the death of the Prince of Wales in 1751, his widow, Princess Augusta, expanded the garden with the help of the 3rd Earl of Bute, John Stuart (1713–1792), who was tutor to her son, George, Prince of Wales, and later an ineffective prime minister to his pupil, by this time George III. William Chambers, the architect and fierce rival of Capability Brown, added many buildings to the garden – Merlin's cave, a ruined 'Roman' arch, a classical orangery and Chinese pagoda among them – and in 1759 the princess began to plant a 9-acre botanic garden. When Bute died Joseph Banks succeeded him, advising Princess Augusta and, on her death, George III. Under Banks's direction Kew became a hub of botanical exploration in an expanding British empire. With the death of George III the garden fell into decline. George IV, the feckless leader of fashion and womanizer, had no interest in it, and his successor, William IV, who came to the throne at 65 and died at 71, had no time to express an opinion.

When Queen Victoria came to the throne in 1837 she had no interest in the garden either, but realizing that Kew had a particular place in the hearts of Londoners and an important economic role, she set up a commission to decide on its future. In 1841 the Royal Botanic Gardens, Kew, became a national, rather than a royal, institution with Sir William Hooker (from 1841 to 1865) and his son Joseph Dalton Hooker (from 1865 to 1885) as its first directors. Under the Hookers Kew became an institution of world renown, a clearing house for the transmission of cocoa, quinine, rubber, tea, coffee, spices and other economic crops from their native homes to establish plantation economies in various parts of the British empire, the parent of botanic gardens in other parts of the empire, and the trainer of botanists and gardeners who would make their mark throughout the world, including in America, where, as Marion Cran noted, the employment of a Kew-trained gardener was the most treasured possession of her cultured readership.

Sir William Hooker also developed Kew as a pleasure garden. The great Palm House (1844–8), the icon which most symbolizes Kew, was built to house plants that would not survive in the open in England, but it was also a beautiful building set above a parterre and among radiating axes designed by William Andrews Nesfield, one of the leading landscape gardeners of the day. However, the research, collecting and teaching aspects of the garden were of primary importance. There had always been struggles between the Crown and the general public over access to the garden, as there had been in the royal parks for centuries, and Joseph Hooker looked upon the public with disdain sometimes bordering on disgust.

In 1825, when the garden was still a royal possession, John Lindley, secretary of the Horticultural Society of London and a very distinguished horticulturist and author, spoke of knocking on the dark mahogany door on Kew Green: 'You entered unwelcome, you rambled about suspected, and you were let out with manifest gladness at your departure.'[124] All visitors were accompanied by a gardener, so every visitor was an impediment to normal work. In the 1830s, entry to Kew was allowed only to gentlemen wearing a tall black hat and a black or white neckerchief. Coloured neck scarves were forbidden, as were dogs and gentlemen's servants. When Sir William became director in 1841, the practice of escorting visitors was abandoned, relieving the gardeners to get on with their work. By the end of his first year 9,000 people had visited Kew. With steamboats from London to Richmond making regular stops at Kew to meet public demand and with the spread of the suburban railway system to new stations at Kew Junction and Kew Gardens, the number of visitors increased dramatically – to 180,000 by 1850 – but the gardens were only open in the afternoon, leaving students and scholars to work undisturbed in the morning.

In the face of mounting pressure from a growing public as Kew became a favourite and increasingly accessible haunt of Londoners, Joseph Hooker raised the outer wall and closed entrances, fearing a dilution of its scientific integrity and the transformation of Kew into a public park. In 1877 Hooker, now Sir Joseph, gave in to pressure by opening the gardens at 10 a.m. on Bank Holidays but argued: 'If opened the whole day the Gardens will be regarded as a Park. Park-licence will insinuate itself & demands for luncheons, pic-nics & bands of music will follow.'[125] Sir Trevor Lawrence, Member of Parliament, plantsman and son of the Mrs Lawrence who thwarted the Duke of Devonshire by being the first to flower *Amherstia nobilis* (see chapter 14), found Hooker 'full of what I cannot but call inveterate prejudice'.[126] He deplored the director's reference to 'a swarm of filthy children and women of the lowest class [who] invaded the Gardens' and his 'serious charge against the people that they resorted to the woods for immoral purposes in great numbers'.[127] Kew was, and is, exceptional in many respects, but the attitude of its senior scientific and horticultural staff to the defence of their gardens against the public – an attitude present later even in public parks themselves with their 'keep off the grass' notices – was evident in the management of many botanic gardens in the early years.

In America, apart from the botanic and nursery garden of John Bartram in Philadelphia, the first botanic garden in the modern sense was that in St Louis, Missouri, created by Henry Shaw. Shaw was born in England in 1800, in the industrial city of Sheffield. At 18 he went to New Orleans to study cotton production but soon moved on to Missouri to set up in business as a hardware supplier. His success was such that he was able to retire at 40, building himself a splendid Italianate villa, Tower Grove in St Louis, in 1849. His garden, initially of 10 acres north of the house, was inspired by his visits to Chatsworth, the Duke of Devonshire's palatial estate near Sheffield, to Paxton's Crystal Palace and to Kew. Shaw wanted to combine a display garden and one in which serious botanical research could be conducted. In creating the garden he sought advice from Sir William Hooker at Kew, Asa Gray at Harvard and George Engelmann, a German-born botanist and physician who had emigrated from Germany to America in 1832 and who, after long and arduous botanical exploration of the country, set up in medical practice in St Louis in 1835. The garden continued to expand and, on Shaw's death in 1889, was bequeathed to the city of St Louis as the Missouri Botanic Garden.

The Arnold Arboretum in Jamaica Plain, on the edge of Boston, was the next major garden to be created, in 1872, and was the one in which Anglo-American cooperation was most marked. Its first director, Charles Sprague Sargent, asked Olmsted to advise on the layout, but Olmsted agreed only reluctantly and after several requests. Olmsted's concept of an arboretum, with individual trees dotted across the terrain, did not accord with his ideal of a tranquil pastoral landscape, but he did design the serpentine road network providing access to the collections, and an immensely pleasurable means of exploring the garden. From its beginning the Arnold Arboretum combined the roles of internationally respected research institution and much-loved public park, the second-largest link in Olmsted's 'Emerald Necklace' (see chapter 9), open every day of the year free of charge.

As director of the Arboretum, Sargent had many links with England. The best known of these is Ernest Henry Wilson (1876–1930). Wilson was born in Chipping Campden in the heart of the Cotswolds that were later to become the centre of a colony of American Anglophiles. He left school early to work for a local nursery and at 16 went to work in the Birmingham Botanic Garden. Evening classes in the nearby technical college equipped him to move to Kew in 1897, where he won the Hooker Prize for an essay on conifers. At Kew he was spotted by Harry (later Sir Harry) Veitch of James Veitch and Son, by far the most notable nursery of the day, and Veitch engaged him to travel to China to find the handsome dove or handkerchief tree, *Davidia involucrata*, with small clusters of green flowers set in the large white bracts that gave the tree its common names. Veitch's orders were direct. As with his later expedition to collect the yellow-flowered *Meconopsis integrifolia* Wilson was told: *'this object is the object* – do not dissipate time, energy and money – on any other.'[128]

Wilson spent six months in the Veitch nursery at Coombe Wood in Surrey and then travelled west towards China, spending five days at the Arnold Arboretum learning to pack plants for long-distance travel. From there he went by train to San Francisco and hence by ship to Hong Kong, arriving in June 1899. On Sargent's advice he then went on to Szemao to meet Augustine Henry, a British doctor working as assistant medical officer for the Imperial Customs Service. Henry had been stationed in Shanghai but was transferred in 1882 to the isolated province of Hupeh in central China to study plants used in Chinese medicine. To relieve his boredom in this isolated post Henry began collecting plants and, in 1886, sent his first consignment of herbarium specimens to Kew. This began a long correspondence, with Henry eventually sending over 15,000 herbarium specimens and parcels of seeds to Kew and awaking botanists and gardeners to the spectacular beauty of the Chinese flora.

When Wilson went to the site where Henry had seen the dove tree 12 years earlier, he found that it had recently been cut down to build a house. Undaunted, he travelled nearly 400 miles to where the French Jesuit priest Père David had first seen and described the tree named after him and found a precious grove. He spent two years collecting in Hupeh, returning to England with seeds of over 300 species plus 35 cases of bulbs, corms, rhizomes and tubers. His many introductions included the paper bark maple *Acer griseum* with beautiful peeling orange bark and spectacular autumn colour, *Clematis armandii*, the vigorous evergreen climber

ABOVE AND RIGHT
Ernest Henry Wilson
in China, collecting for
the Veitch Nurseries
in England and the
Arnold Arboretum in
Massachusetts.

with masses of scented white flowers in spring, *Davidia* of course, and *Primula pulverulenta*, one of the so-called pagoda primulas with tiers of pink flowers. Staying in England only long enough to get married, he returned to China in 1903, discovering there many plants including the beautiful and fragrant regal lily. On his later expeditions he worked jointly for Veitch and for the Arnold Arboretum; he then moved to America as a full-time member of the Arboretum staff, although initially he spent more time away from the garden than in it. He went to China in 1907, 1908 and 1910. On the 1910 journey his leg was crushed in a rock fall. He continued his exploration carried in a sedan chair and then, when he was fit enough once again to walk, he used his camera tripod as a splint. He went to Japan from 1911 to 1916, introducing to the West 63 varieties of the flowering cherries so revered in Japan and 'Wilson's Fifty', a selection of the best varieties of the evergreen Kurume azaleas. He travelled to Korea and Formosa in 1917–18 and to Australia, New Zealand, India, Central and South America and East Africa in 1922–4. In 1919 he was made associate director of the Arboretum and, on Sargent's death in 1927, he became its director.

Ironically, after travelling the world and facing numerous life-threatening hazards, Wilson was killed, with his wife, in October 1930 in a car accident in Boston. His inheritance lives on, though, in his many plant introductions, his photographs (he was a keen photographer and carried large quantities of photographic equipment on his expeditions) and his books. *A Naturalist in Western China, with vasculum, camera and gun* (1913) conveys both the challenges and the joys of his work. A steady stream of more specialized books followed, including *America's Greatest Garden: The Arnold Arboretum* (1925), *Plant Hunting* (1927) and *China, Mother of Gardens* (1929).

Like Wilson, William Purdom (1880–1921) worked for Veitch and the Arnold Arboretum. After a spell with Veitch at their Coombe Wood nursery, from 1902 he went to Kew as under-foreman in the arboretum and then became a Kew student. In 1909, with Wilson expected back from China, Purdom was sent by Sargent to its north-eastern provinces to look for plants tolerant of climates even more challenging than that of New England. Sargent was disappointed with the number of plants he brought back, but the botanical riches of the north-east were far fewer than in the regions explored by Wilson and Purdom faced enormous challenges in escaping from native uprisings and other hazards. He was, though, a skilled photographer, and a rich photographic archive and his published tales of adventure amply compensated for the paucity of his plants.

A much less well-known figure in the Arnold's history is William Judd (1888–1946), its chief propagator. Born in Preston Brook, Cheshire, Judd was the son of the head gardener to Charles Jones, a wealthy Manchester cotton merchant. Deciding to follow in his father's footsteps, William worked in gardens, studied hard and was offered a post at Kew as a propagator. His Kew training in systematic record keeping stood him in good stead, and his notes, correspondence and an autobiographical sketch – all now in the archive of the Arnold Arboretum – give an almost day-by-day account of his life, travels and many contacts.

In 1913 Judd was recommended by William Jackson Bean (1863–1947), the great authority on trees and shrubs at Kew, to Sargent, and he was appointed as assistant propagator to Jackson Thornton Dawson at the Arnold. With typical thoroughness Judd recorded in his diary that the crossing had taken 7 days 1 hour and 54 minutes. When Dawson died in 1916, Judd was promoted to propagator of trees and shrubs. With his new post assured he married Lucy Smith, a young English girl who had emigrated from Aldershot in Hampshire to Boston in 1912. The two were very close – he recorded late in her life that she had gone on holiday without him, leaving him alone for the first time ever. They hosted an international stream of visitors in their home and in the arboretum.

Judd was highly skilled in coaxing difficult seeds to germinate and generous in sharing his plants and his knowledge with the hundreds of professional and amateur gardeners who consulted him. With the influx of many hundreds of seed collections from Wilson's many expeditions and from other Arnold explorers, it was Judd who propagated those seeds and ensured that they survived to furnish gardens on both sides of the Atlantic. He travelled widely in the United States and in Europe, and as a member of the Association of Kew Gardeners in America, he met up with other Kewites whenever he could, as well as attending the association's annual dinner held before one of the spring shows in New York, Boston or Philadelphia. He had a close relationship with Wilson. Judd and his wife travelled with Ernest and Ellen Wilson throughout New England to find and photograph native trees.

In the Arnold archive there are letters dated between 1936 and 1944 from Lord Aberconway at his famous garden of Bodnant in North Wales with reference to mutual visits, and a letter from F. C. Puddle, one of three generations of Puddles who were head gardeners at Bodnant. James Comber, himself a renowned plant collector at Nymans in Sussex, exchanged letters from 1936 to 1945, the year in which Judd was awarded the Veitch Memorial Medal by the RHS (although he was unable to collect it in person because the war had not yet ended). There were three letters from Lawrence Johnston from Hidcote between 1938 and 1943. He corresponded with Sir Frederick Moore, director of the National Botanic Garden in Dublin, inviting Moore to a Kewite dinner and making arrangements for a visit to Dublin. There were letters from Edwin Hillier, Charles Notcutt and John Waterer, proprietors of the most notable nurseries in England. He sent seeds to David Trehane, the leading grower of camellias and blueberries on his acid soil in Dorset, and there were seven letters from horticulturalist Sir Frederick Stern from his Highdown garden in a chalk quarry in Sussex thanking Judd for his plants, asking him for more and, in 1931, sending his sympathies on hearing of the death of

Ernest and Ellen Wilson the previous autumn. Plants went, too, to Lionel de Rothschild for his Exbury garden on the Hampshire coast. There was an extended exchange of letters with Beatrix Farrand from 1932 until 1945, inviting him to visit the Huntingdon Botanic Garden, seeking his advice on her Reef Point garden.

On 25 May 1928 Judd recorded the first flowering of the handkerchief, ghost or dove tree, *Davidia involucrata*, which had first taken Wilson to China for Veitch and the Arnold Arboretum, 'four flowers and not very laudable ones'.[129] However, his diaries record much more than his working life. He lists the books he has read – commenting early on that he had not had time to read other than horticultural works until his entry to America – his first American train journey, his first flights, the various social events and the succession of housekeepers that looked after him after the death of his wife in 1932. In January 1932 he attended a Horticulture Club meeting 'where Mr Charles Birdseye gave a talk on the new quick freezing of food'. On 4 and 11 May 1946 there are diary entries of his garden visits with social events in the evenings. Less than two weeks later he died suddenly.

William Judd's name lives on in *Viburnum × juddii,* a hybrid between *V. carlesii* and *V. bitchiuense*, a shrub of bushy habit with sweetly scented pink-tinted flowers, of better constitution than *V. carlesii* and less prone to aphid attack. His meticulous attention to record keeping, begun at Kew, has left us with probably the best account of the complex web of communications between gardeners of all sorts on both sides of the Atlantic in the first half of the twentieth century.

The New York Botanical Garden in the Bronx was incorporated in 1891 and opened in 1902. Olmsted's partner, Calvert Vaux, and Samuel Parsons junior advised on the plan, and many of New York's philanthropists – Carnegie, Vanderbilt and Morgan among them – supported the scheme. Other gardens followed in the twentieth century: Brooklyn Botanic Garden in 1901, Morton Arboretum in Chicago in 1922, Huntingdon Botanic Garden in 1925, Morris Arboretum in Philadelphia in 1932, Fairchild Tropical Botanic Garden in Miami in 1938 and Santa Barbara Botanic Garden in 1939. Chicago Botanic Garden, created by the Chicago Horticultural Society in 1965 and opened to the public in 1972, is a more recent addition.

Most of these gardens began as the private domain of an individual or couple: Joy Morton, Henry and Arabella Huntingdon, John and Lynda Morris or Robert Montgomery commemorating the life's work and extensive world travels of his friend David Fairchild. In Brooklyn the philanthropist Alfred White raised 25,000 dollars to convert 39 acres of rubbish-strewn wasteland into a garden of which the citizens of Brooklyn would be proud. Olmsted Brothers, the practice founded by Frederick Law Olmsted, laid out the site, and in 1912 Harold Caparn, an English landscape architect trained at the École des Beaux Arts in Paris, took over the more detailed design of garden features.

While all of these gardens undertook rigorous programmes of botanical research, most of world stature, the elitist attitude discernible in the early history of Kew and to a lesser extent in other English gardens was entirely absent. Plants of wild origin collected from known habitats were important for scientific research, but the use of garden plants for display, the trials of commercial cultivars of plants potentially useful for the gardens of the region, and the incorporation of sculpture, fountains and other ornamental features were all seen as valid functions of a botanic garden. Furthermore, those to be educated were the general public, not solely the students of botany, medicine and related disciplines. Educational displays, interpretative signs, guided trails and in some instances educational departments within the garden's management structure all made the casual visitor welcome. Refreshment facilities, even places designated for the 'pic-nics' that Hooker so abhorred, allowed the visitor to stay longer – and incidentally provided a useful source of revenue to support the garden's activities.

Another aspect in which American botanic gardens have led the world is in their welcoming public participation, most notably in the Children's Garden in the Brooklyn Botanic Garden. Created in 1914 by the schoolteacher Ellen Eddy Shaw, Brooklyn's Children's Garden has hundreds of small plots in which local children can grow food and flowers in a safe and supervised environment away from the pollution and dangers of its streets. This concept is further developed in the New York Botanical Garden where, in addition to the 'Children's Garden' designed by professional adults encouraging children to explore the senses of sound, sight, smell and touch, there is a large 'Family Garden' in which children have a freer rein to grow food and flowers in their own small plots, as in Brooklyn, but whole families are then encouraged to gather for barbecues and other social events using produce from the garden plots, thus developing a sense of social cohesion and community identity often lacking in a city of anonymous apartment blocks.

A third important aspect of the American botanic garden was in a focus on its own backyard. In old England – in gardens in general as well as in botanic gardens – chance variants of its own meagre repertoire of native plants were collected in early gardens. In Parkinson's *Paradisi* he delighted in double primroses and plantains with green rosettes instead of long-tailed green spikes, but it was the strange, the exotic, that excited the collector and garden maker. Plants from the Americas, South Africa, Australasia and later especially from the Far East filled gardens and nursery catalogues. In botanic gardens it was necessary to build stoves and palm houses if they were to encompass the entire flora of the world. America, by comparison, is a vast country spanning a whole continent. To garden in New York, Florida, Chicago, Los Angeles or San Francisco posed entirely different challenges. Accepting the need to be helpful to its citizens, each botanic garden developed a particular interest in plants which would survive in its own environment: tropical plants in the Fairchild garden, dry land plants in the Huntingdon, plants from China and Japan in Philadelphia's Morris Arboretum and the Brooklyn Botanic Garden. With the transformation of the prairies into endless fields of waving corn, no intelligent person could be oblivious to the loss of the prairie landscape. In 1963 the Morton Arboretum converted large areas of its pasture land to a reconstructed prairie plant community. In 1965 the newly formed Chicago Botanical Garden to the north of the city also established a 15-acre prairie.

In England the Cambridge University Botanic Garden, established on its new site in 1831 and opened to the public in 1846, had the usual range of glasshouses and order beds, though the latter were arranged in free-form beds representing the size of each plant family rather than in serried rectangular ranks. From the beginning, though, Cambridge also had displays of plants native to the region in simulated native habitats. Cambridge, the second oldest university in England, is in East Anglia, an area of great biodiversity from extensive heaths on wind-blown sandy soils to the intricate landscape of the Norfolk Broads with its lakes, rivers, peaty reed-covered fens and scattered woodlands of willow and alder. These varied communities, rich in beetles, butterflies, birds and the plants that support them, had long been studied by Cambridge dons, and this interest was reflected in the design of the new garden. A mound of limestone furnished with plants of the chalk hills stood across the path from a fen of reeds and other marginal aquatic plants around a pool (now replaced by a much more impressive and wheelchair-friendly design). A native hedgerow with plants of the hedgerow bottom flanked a miniscule field of cereals and other crops of the agricultural landscape. Cambridge, though, was unusual in paying attention to the landscape on its doorstep as well as giant Amazonian waterlilies and North American conifers.

By the late twentieth century botanic gardens had developed an international network. Annual conferences in various parts of the world, visiting academics from one institution to another, collaborative projects and papers in the professional journals allowed rapid communication of ideas. A growing acceptance in England of the need to tolerate, even to welcome, the general public is partly a home-grown development of increasing democratisation. A desire to educate the public about the importance of plants to the health of the planet and to human survival has also become a major focus of activity in English botanic gardens, and the fact that nature starts at the back door and not in the distant Amazon rainforest has influenced the design of all botanic gardens in recent years.

In 2001 the Eden Project, created in a disused china clay pit in Cornwall, opened. It has never claimed to be a botanic garden in the conventional sense, but it has set the standard in England for 'edutainment': that seamless blend of educating by entertaining, by engaging people in scenes combining art, plants and theatre. As budgets in public gardens as a whole are reduced year by year, the common sense of welcoming the public to spend money in cafés, plant centres, gift shops and other commercial facilities of the garden's operations, as well as the less tangible political support which comes from a welcoming approach, have all shaped attitudes by successive directors of English botanic gardens, but examples from the more advanced American gardens have been of great help in accelerating that evolution.

A similar conspicuous lack of elitism applies to the development of the Cooperative Extension Service and the Master Gardener programme in America. Although England is often regarded as a nation of gardeners, the profession of horticulture has not been well regarded either in amateur or in academic circles. Perhaps in a society in which Aunt Jane seems to know all there is to know about plants and gardens, what is the purpose of a Professor of Horticulture? J. C. Loudon was well aware of the stigma attached to gardening as a career on the large estates, despite the fact that the head gardener was usually widely read and often fluent in more than one language. In traditional universities the old-established subjects of law, medicine, classics and (until the twentieth century) theology have been the most respected courses. 'Pure' sciences have come next in the pecking order, with anything 'applied' being regarded with disdain, a similar reaction that those in 'trade' might have experienced at an aristocratic luncheon or school.

In America the 1862 Morrill Act, introduced to Congress by Representative Justin Smith Morrill of Vermont, provided individual states with a substantial tract of federal land to endow the creation of land-grant colleges or universities to undertake research and teaching in practical agriculture, science, military science and engineering, although explicitly 'without excluding classical studies'.[130] Kansas State University was established in 1863, and Michigan State and Pennsylvania State, both existing institutions, were given land-grant status in the same year. Iowa State followed in 1864, then other states, particularly those in the agricultural Midwest. In all the land-grant universities and colleges agriculture was a central academic activity with most having large experimental farms. Allied subjects such as forestry, horticulture and landscape architecture also featured prominently in their offerings.

In 1914 the Smith Lever Act established a cooperative extension link between the United States Department of Agriculture in Washington, DC and the land-grant universities. The Cooperative Extension Service (now the Cooperative State Research Education and Extension Service) offered advice to farmers and to the public in general, passing on research information and current best practice in relation to agriculture, food, the home and family, environment and similar topics. It was anticipated that each county in every state would have its own Cooperative Extension office, and although some disappeared or were amalgamated, there are still nearly 3,000 throughout the country. In the Midwest in the 1960s and 1970s, for example, Cooperative Extension offices might produce pamphlets on garden planning, on preserving fruits and vegetables, on control of particular pests and diseases, on selection of shrubs and trees for the region and other domestic matters.

This open-ended commitment to engage in research, teaching and extension in matters spanning the whole professional and domestic scene obviously had its challenges. At Washington State University, with its early interest in urban horticulture, staff were overwhelmed with requests from the public on matters great and small: how to organize a group to combat loss of urban trees or how to prune a rose bush. In order to manage demand, staff of the Center for Urban Horticulture at Washington State organized a 'Master Gardener' training programme in which volunteers, themselves usually keen and knowledgeable gardeners, would follow courses in the science, technique and practice of gardening to become Master Gardeners, able and willing to pass on their experience and learning to other people. The programme was launched in 1972. It quickly caught on in other areas, and by 2009 there were 95,000 Master Gardeners in all 50 states and 8 Canadian provinces, contributing an estimated 5 million service hours. Thus, there is a continuum from the high-powered researcher at the forefront of molecular science to the citizen wanting to know how to prune that rose.

To a considerable degree the Royal Horticultural Society is now adopting the mantle of science-to-practice in England. When the Horticultural Society of London was established in 1804, it quickly developed an experimental garden at Chiswick and a training programme for young gardeners, but the benefits of these endeavours were confined to its (usually wealthy) subscribers. By the mid-twentieth century the (now) Royal Horticultural Society with its garden at Wisley in Surrey had a broader membership but one still focused especially in the south of England. Wisley offered, as it still does, an advisory service and the monthly journal gave information on what and how to plant, based on trials at Wisley, but again for its members, or 'fellows'.

Towards the end of the century, under the guidance of a succession of far-sighted directors, the RHS widened its horizons to include collaboration with universities on climate change, with schools to encourage gardening by children, and with the general public on greening of the environment and on the social, mental and physical advantages of gardening in the community. Its educational programmes are increasingly widely accessible to the general public, both at Wisley and through horticultural colleges across the country.

Not for the first time, England has benefited by taking a leaf from its American friends' book.

20

Professional parallels

~~~~~~~

NOTHER AREA in which American and English practice has differed widely, but in which they are drawing closer together to the benefit of the latter, is in the profession of landscape architecture. When the American Society of Landscape Architects was formed in 1899 in Washington, DC, there were 11 founder members, including Beatrix Farrand as the only woman, Frederick Law Olmsted junior, his stepbrother John Charles Olmsted, and Downing Vaux, the son of Olmsted senior's partner Calvert Vaux. Samuel Parsons junior, successor to Calvert Vaux as chief landscape architect of New York City's parks department, was another founder member. It was Parsons with whom the irascible William Robinson crossed swords over the 'absurd name of "landscape architecture"'.[131]

The world's first academic course in landscape architecture only began in the following year at Harvard, so founder members of the professional body had all found their way into the profession by various other routes: farming, nursery practice and garden design, forestry, painting, engineering, architecture and travel or any combination of these. As university courses proliferated and spread – especially to the land-grant institutions – the curriculum included a whole spectrum of related subjects from engineering to plant science and art history. For the first quarter century of landscape architecture courses, much of the work of its graduates remained in the realm of garden design for wealthy clients. As gardening did not form part of the DNA of the average American (if there ever was such an animal), professional advice on the making of gardens was needed and respected, and sought after even by clients of moderate wealth. In England the vast majority of garden owners would create their own gardens, with only the wealthiest consulting a professional designer.

Only during and after the Wall Street Crash of 1929 and the subsequent Depression did this primary source of employment in the United States dry up and the profession turn its attention to public works: the parkways and other National Park infrastructure built under the auspices of the Civilian Conservation Corps introduced under President Roosevelt's New Deal to provide work for the unemployed. In post-Depression decades the scale of garden making was reduced, but the numbers of people seeking advice on the design of their gardens increased dramatically. Most landscape architects would deal with a range of projects from public to private, but a proportion of most offices' work was in the design of gardens. The doyen of garden designers, Thomas Church, trained in landscape architecture at Harvard, devoted his entire career to private gardens, often of modest dimensions, and his associate Lawrence Halprin shared in that work until he became involved in larger scale commercial and institutional schemes.

In England the Institute of Landscape Architects was formed in 1929 (not an auspicious year given the Wall Street crash later that year), after a meeting of garden designers at the Chelsea Flower Show. The assembled group wanted to raise the status of garden design and designers, and the initial proposal was to form a Society of Garden Designers. The whole idea was not well received by Thomas Mawson or Percy Cane, the two leading practitioners of the day, who thought that such a society was unnecessary. They could deal with all the commissions that were to be had. However, an alternative view was put forward by a few people in the group who were aware of what landscape architects were doing in America and who saw their own futures as doing more for society than designing large private gardens for rich people. They won the day, and the new body became the Institute of Landscape Architects.

Much of the work of the newly designated landscape architects, though, remained in the sphere of private garden design. Several members were employed by nurseries to design gardens for clients who, if they sourced their plants from that nursery, would have the design fee waived. The first academic course in landscape architecture began at the University of Reading in 1930, and the first generation of academically trained landscape architects emerged from Reading between 1933 and 1962. The programme had a tenuous existence. It was a diploma course, not a degree. Frank Clark, who ran it, was a half-time lecturer at the university with half of his half-time in the Department of Horticulture, with its rigorously scientific outlook, and the other half in the Department of Fine Art, where anything as earthy and useful as landscape design was deeply suspect. In 1962 Frank Clark moved to the University of Edinburgh where both he and his course flourished.

The decade of the 1960s was a period of rapid development in Britain, finally shrugging off the scars of war. New housing developments, motorways (modelled on the American freeways), reservoirs, power stations and quarries required skilled professionals to integrate the new development into the intricate landscape patterns of a densely populated island. In 1962 there was one landscape architecture course in Britain, at the University of Edinburgh. By 1970 there were 10 courses, mainly in the north and west of the country in the old industrial cities but with others in London and Gloucester/Cheltenham. There was suddenly a great deal of work to be done and a new wave of young, trained but not experienced landscape architects to do it. The profession had something of an identity crisis. It did not command the respect given to architects, whose status had long been recognized in the establishment of the Royal Institute of British Architects in 1837, but the new landscape architects did not want to be confused with landscape gardeners, the people who might turn up in their muddy boots once or twice a week to mow the lawn and prune the roses.

An attitude seemed to develop within the institute that landscape architecture was a noble calling and that it had nothing to do with gardens or gardening – or even garden design. After all, again, in a nation of gardeners in which Auntie Jane felt perfectly capable of creating her own garden, who needed someone with a degree in landscape architecture to tell them what to do? Furthermore, to prepare detailed designs and planting plans for a modest private garden might take as much expensive professional time as the broader plan of a housing estate or stretch of motorway, and the English, in the main, were not accustomed to spending large sums of money on their gardens. In order to reinforce their hoped-for sense of superiority, new graduates emerged from their universities with only the most basic list of plants (after all, learning all those Latin names was a tedious task); they have often been caricatured as thinking they could solve all the world's environmental problems with 20 species of plants. This notion of the importance of Design, with a capital 'D', elevated almost to religious status, and the unimportance of the green stuff of landscape was not confined to the new generation. Geoffrey Jellicoe, a founder member of the institute, its president from 1939 to 1949 and first president of the International Federation of Landscape Architects, famously shocked young students at the University of Texas when, on being asked what trees he proposed to use in the scheme he was discussing with them, said that he had no idea. It was the philosophy underpinning the design that mattered: which species to plant was a technical detail. It helped with his practice, of course, that he married Susan Pares, herself a landscape architect, garden designer and photographer with an encyclopaedic plant knowledge.

By the latter part of the twentieth century the neurosis attached to the English profession of landscape architecture had dulled. The scope of the profession encompassed by the institute widened when, in 1983, it became the Landscape Institute, a small change in name but one which signified a change of mission from caring for landscape architects to caring for the landscape. The renamed institute offered membership in Design, Management and Science. Members have since become increasingly recognized for their contribution to ecological design, sustainability and the creation of green infrastructure, using balancing lakes, green roofs and other methods of alleviating the adverse effects of development instead of relying on hard civil engineering solutions. As the numbers of landscape architects have increased and the demand for public works from successive governments eager to contain expenditure has declined, at the same time the wealthier segment of the population has accepted that garden design services are worth paying for, so the divide between landscape architecture and garden design has gradually closed.

All this revolves around sweeping generalizations, of course. There were many landscape architects whose work involved private garden design, but the general tenor of the post-1945 landscape profession in England was of a studied separation from the horticultural, the garden-keeping, world.

Not until 1985 was a Society of Garden Designers formed. Initially, it evolved in much the same way as the Institute of Landscape Architects. Its founder members emerged from various walks of life with an interest in gardens and plants, perhaps working in nurseries, and they read books on garden design, visited gardens and tried out their art in the gardens of relatives, friends and friends of friends. As they grew in experience they wanted to separate themselves from run-of-the-mill landscape gardeners who might be skilled at erecting fences and pergolas or making terraces and patios but often had only a rudimentary knowledge of plants and design. Membership was achieved by peer review of work and by interview with a panel of existing members.

Gradually, privately run courses in garden design began to appear, perhaps because established designers had a mission to pass on their knowledge to others, or perhaps because the practice itself did not provide sufficient income so the teaching supplemented the practice. Finally, the horticultural colleges and newer universities realized the potential demand and produced their own academic courses in garden design. The Society of Garden Designers is now firmly established. It hosts regional and national conferences, sometimes with international speakers. It offers particular advantages for women who want a creative but part-time career. Entry to the profession can still be achieved by personal effort. Many courses are part-time to fit in with other responsibilities. It is possible to extend from design into construction and maintenance services, becoming an advisor and friend to one's clients, and although it is very difficult to make a garden design business generate sufficient income to support a family, it can provide useful supplementary income. Perhaps, like landscape architecture, garden design will become a graduate-entry profession, but the willingness of keen amateurs to help relatives and friends with their gardens is unlikely to disappear.

21

The public park revisited

~~~~

URING THE LATTER PART of the twentieth century the public parks which had
cheered, and probably extended, the lives of the poor in the nineteenth century fell
into a parlous state of neglect. On both sides of the Atlantic the voting and taxpaying
majority had moved to the suburbs. They had their own gardens and their cars to take
them off to the national parks, coasts and other scenic areas, so they had no use for the
man-made nature of the urban park, a drain on local taxes. As budgets were cut and
standards fell, even those who might make use of their local park were discouraged.
Parks were populated by the very poor, the homeless and drug addicts, deterring the
general public still further. In England the privatization of park maintenance and other
public services by Margaret Thatcher's Conservative government in the 1980s resulted
in the loss of permanent staff as contractors moved their maintenance crews from one
park to another to fulfil their duties in the most financially efficient way. The plight of
the parks, and of the inner city dwellers for whom parks represented their only healthy
escape from crowded living conditions and noisy streets, seemed dire.

Rescue came first in New York, a city with extremes of deep poverty and immense
wealth. Central Park had always had a special place in the hearts of New Yorkers, but in
the 1960s the city faced financial crisis. Budgets were slashed. In the park, maintenance
was reduced, repairs stopped, Olmsted's carefully graded hills (increasingly denuded
of vegetation) eroded, and the eroded soil turned water bodies into weed-infested
swamps. Vandalism was rife and graffiti covered every surface. Ironically, the 1960s and
1970s were decades of public protests and public events – rallies against the Vietnam
War and in favour of gay rights, marathons and concerts – and Central Park was the
obvious location for these mass gatherings. Public pressure grew to do something about
the park. In 1978 the new mayor, Edward Koch, appointed Gordon Davis as Parks
Commissioner. For the first time parks had a champion in City Hall. In 1979 a Central
Park Administrator was appointed. The park now had one person overseeing its day-
to-day management and long-term conservation. A patchwork of improvements began
to take place, and each smart new patch threw the poor state of the rest into sharper
focus. In 1981 a restoration planning team began a three-year survey of all aspects of
the park, and out of this came a policy and strategy for complete restoration using
public money and private benefactions. Today Central Park is once again a jewel in the

crown of New York and a fitting monument to Olmsted's contribution to America and the rest of the world.

In England the movement to save Victorian parks came from several directions. By the 1980s the Victorian era was sufficiently far removed that its heritage could be appreciated, and the image of garish mixtures of bedding, wiggly paths and shrubberies covered in soot and dust could be separated from the true value of the best aspects of Victorian design, prominent among them the public parks. The Garden History Society campaigned vigorously for a better deal for parks.

Support for their campaign came from the more far-sighted directors and former directors of the parks, especially Alan Barber, former director of Bristol Parks. He pointed to the original purpose of the parks in alleviating the living conditions of the poor, a need still clearly evident in the centres of most major towns and cities, but also in the value of parks for improving the health of the population as a whole. Barber developed the concept of the 'Natural Health Service' as an inexpensive adjunct of the National Health Service. There was growing evidence of the role of 'nature', of green spaces, in reducing heart attacks, depression and other mental and physical conditions. When the psychologist Roger Ulrich published his paper linking the view from the hospital window with patient recovery rates in the American journal *Science* in 1984, he reported that, in carefully controlled comparisons over the period 1972 to 1981, patients with a view of green plants from their hospital window recovered, on average, a day earlier than those with a view of brick walls, needed less painkilling drugs and had fewer post-operative complications. This spurred a raft of further studies in environmental psychology. In 1989 the partnership of Rachel and Stephen Kaplan at the University of Michigan published *The Experience of Nature: A Psychological Perspective*, a wide-ranging review emphasizing the point that humans were products of nature and that separation from the natural environment brought stresses which could lead to mental and physical health problems. Parks offered a venue for reconnecting with nature – for jogging, for dog walking, for organized sports perhaps, but also simply for being in a calming, quiet and green space with fresh air.

A third strand of the rescue campaign came from a growing awareness of climate change. To the average English citizen the year-long drought of 1976, the devastating storms of 1987 and 1990, and increasing incidences of severe flooding in various parts of the country made it seem as if the weather was not behaving in its usual genial manner. Within the scientific community there were deeper concerns that the increasing levels of carbon dioxide in the atmosphere, a result of the burning of fossil fuels from the beginning of the Industrial Revolution onwards, was creating a 'greenhouse effect'. As the sun's energy reaches the earth, it warms the surface and part of the absorbed energy is radiated back into space as infra-red radiation. Carbon dioxide strongly absorbs infra-red, retaining the energy within the atmosphere instead of radiating back into space, causing the planet to warm up. By 1988 widespread concerns about the potential impacts of climate change led the World Meteorological Organization and the United Nations Environment Programme to set up the Intergovernmental Panel on Climate Change. Since then it has been literally a hot topic with scientists warning that a 2-degree Celsius (3.6-degree Fahrenheit) rise in global temperature will lead to irreparable damage to life on earth. At the December 2015 international meeting in Paris more than a hundred countries set out their strategies for reducing global warming and for coping with climate change.

One strategy for reducing warming and its effects on a local scale, and by cumulative effect nationally or internationally, is to 'green' the environment. Buildings and roads absorb solar energy and radiate it as heat, causing the 'urban heat island' effect. Heating and transport systems produce waste heat and carbon dioxide, which traps much of that heat in the atmosphere. The centres of cities are therefore several degrees warmer than their rural surroundings. Buildings and roads also shed rainwater that rushes off across paved surfaces or in drains to cause a rapid rise in streams and other watercourses, leading to flooding. If the land is covered with grass, shrubs and trees, as in a park, rain soaks into the soil and gradually replenishes the water table which supplies watercourses with their steady flows, evening out wet and dry seasons. Some of the water is taken up by plants and evaporated. The energy needed to evaporate water is very considerable. It takes three times as much energy to turn boiling water into water vapour as it does to turn ice into boiling water, so evaporation cools the atmosphere – the plants act literally as air conditioners.

This is by no means a new idea. In his mammoth opus *Man and Nature*, published in 1864, George Perkins Marsh warned that uncontrolled loss of forests would lead to soil erosion, an increase in global temperatures and environmental degradation which could threaten human existence. In 1871 Olmsted's *Report to the Staten Island Improvement Commission of a Preliminary Scheme of Improvements* included proposals for wide green verges to roads to accommodate rain run-off which would be directed into a chain of ponds, stocked with fish to prevent the risk of malaria, and providing a green matrix within which the borough would develop on healthy lines. Much more recently, in the 1960s, a visionary member of the school board in Ann Arbor, Michigan, persuaded other members of the board that planning new schools should begin with the landscape before an architect was commissioned to design the buildings. At its Clinton School, built on the edge of town to serve a new housing development, much existing woodland was retained, the school grounds were extended to the edge of a balancing lake designed to accommodate sudden run-off from houses, drives and roads and feed it more slowly into the river downstream, and a simple amphitheatre of logs was created overlooking the lake so outdoor classes and environmental education could form an integral part of the curriculum. The lake served as an invaluable wildlife reserve and also saved hundreds of thousands of dollars in piped drainage (which would have served only to move the flood risk downstream).

In 1972 the U.S. Department of the Interior National Parks Service and the American Society of Landscape Architects published *Plants, People and Environmental Quality* by the executive director of ASLA, Gary Robinette. Much of the focus of the report was on the benefits of living in an aesthetically pleasing landscape, but there were chapters on the engineering uses of plants (for erosion control, sound reduction, atmospheric purification and traffic control) and on their climatological uses (for solar radiation control, wind reduction and the control of rain and temperature). There was, as yet, no mention of the health-sustaining attributes of plants later identified by Ulrich and the Kaplans.

The role of green spaces in lowering temperatures in summer and raising them in winter by reducing wind speeds and in lessening run-off during heavy rain has led to the concept of 'green infrastructure': using green spaces and green roofs to ameliorate urban conditions rather than relying on the 'grey infrastructure' of heaters, air conditioners and piped drains. Plants not only cool the atmosphere in summer and reduce wind chill in winter, but they convert carbon dioxide into oxygen during photosynthesis and trap dust particles from the air until they can be washed off into the soil during rain. Combined with their health-improving potential, plants are increasingly recognized as 'good things' rather than merely 'nice things', and the urban public park is one means of bringing plants into close proximity with large numbers of people.

In 1994 the National Lottery was introduced in the United Kingdom, somewhat controversially as many people objected to the idea of state-sponsored gambling. A proportion of the profits from the lottery was set aside to fund charitable purposes, and in 1996, as part of that scheme, Parks for People was launched, offering grants of between 100,000 and five million pounds, to be matched by local authorities and other groups, for the revitalization of public parks. The scheme proved very popular, and to date nearly a billion pounds has been distributed in grants. This funding has had benefits beyond the rescue of valued local green spaces. Because each grant application required a thorough historical survey and conservation plan, it has given employment to landscape architectural and other practices with an interest in historic landscape conservation. It has given some hope to beleaguered parks staff who saw the parks to which they had devoted much of their lives being dismembered in the name of financial economy. But more than this it has stimulated the equivalent of the community garden throughout the country. Heritage Lottery funding required demonstration that the park would benefit the community and would engage the community in its restoration and care. Matching funding was required from the local authority, but that could include contributions in kind as well as actual monies. Friends' groups soon formed around each park, and the Friends engaged in fund raising, in voluntary activities in the park, and in evolving their own programme of events to attract other members and to cement their sense of friendship and purpose.

This public support for parks has stimulated bolder schemes. The Mayor of London has given his support to London's Green Grid, a plan or ideal clearly based on Olmsted's Emerald Necklace in Boston. The aim of the grid is to link the many small green spaces in Greater London by new land acquisition where possible, street tree planting and other tinkerings to amalgamate the separate components of scattered green spaces into a London-wide grid for walkers, cyclists, joggers and for the wildlife and environmental benefits that a network of green spaces would bring.

Now the future of public green space is on the cusp. The post-2008 economic gloom has resulted in a mood of austerity. Unlike health and education, parks are not a statutory responsibility of local government. As budgets are cut, the spending on parks, libraries and other community resources is the easiest to reduce. Life for many people seems grim. At the same time, we are increasingly aware of the benefits that can accrue from looking after our green spaces, not only the tangible benefits to health known to the Victorians, to climate amelioration and to biodiversity, but a general sense of well-being, of the joy of being in a green and pleasant land and having the opportunity to meet other like-minded neighbours. Who will win this battle remains uncertain, but given the evidence of the economic benefits of an attractive environment and the assertion by some economists that confidence is an important factor in stimulating the economy, perhaps England can take inspiration from the United States in harnessing public and private investment to improve life for everyone.

One of the areas in which English people with an interest in the public landscape envy their American cousins is in the way in which wealthy Americans fund that landscape. Is it that wealthy Americans are more numerous and richer than those in England? Is it that donations receive particularly favourable tax benefits? Is it that Americans lack the history which aristocratic inheritance has conveyed to the English so they seek to buy immortality in their sponsorship? Is it that the American 'aristocracy' consists of shrewd business people who recognize the benefits that public giving can offer to their 'brand'? Or is it simply that the new elite is following in the tradition of the first presidents in seeking to make America a civilized and peaceful nation in a beautiful landscape? For whatever reason, all American cities have benefited from this generous spirit and probably none more so than New York City, together with a Parks Department now well endowed by its share of the property taxes arising from breathtakingly expensive real estate.

Battery Park, for instance, extends for over a mile along the shore of the Hudson River down to the tip of Manhattan. Strung along the shore is a series of gardens designed by notable landscape architects. The idea for Battery Park City evolved in the 1960s in attempts to reverse the decay of the old waterfront and to dispose of mountains of landfill created by huge construction projects in the financial district. A master plan was completed in 1979, with landscape architects and artists playing leading roles. The 8-acre Rockefeller Park, completed in 1992, was designed primarily for active sports, but a series of berms sheltering the playing fields and giving structure to the park was designed by Wolfgang Oehme and James van Sweden. Their trademark use of grasses – recalling the grasses used to stabilize sandy shores throughout the world, creating a dynamic feature throughout the often windy site and marking the seasons by their changing colours – was particularly appropriate.

To the south of Rockefeller Park is North Cove Harbor, and below that is a small garden by M. Paul Friedberg, well known as an early exponent of the modern movement. Islands of paper birch uniting in distant view as a small woodland are surrounded by hedges of Japanese holly and underplanted with colourful annuals. Farther south still is South Cove, a landscape designed by environmental artist Mary Miss, architect Stanton Eckstut (one of the authors of the 1979 master plan) and landscape architect Susan Child. The intention was to recreate the idea of the Hudson River shore in the eighteenth and early nineteenth centuries. Huge boulders fringed by wooden pilings of a lost waterfront are backed by a thin woodland of oak, robinia and amelanchier through which paths wind and in the shelter of which benches are sited. This sophisticated interpretation of a lost natural landscape epitomizes what the collaborative efforts of creative professionals are capable of, and seemingly much more capable than can be seen in the old country.

Perhaps the most remarkable recent example of the resurrection in the public realm is New York City's High Line. In 1847 a railway was constructed on the Manhattan's West Side to serve the factories and warehouses along 10th and 11th Avenues close to the Hudson River docks. By 1866 there was a conflict between the railway and burgeoning volumes of street traffic to the extent that cowboys were employed to ride in front of the trains waving flags to warn other traffic. By 1908 congestion was strangling the area, and in 1927 an elevated line was proposed. In 1931 construction began on the line and the vast St John's Park Terminal, capable of taking 190 wagons directly into the upper floor of the terminal. The first trains ran in 1933, and the elevated line was officially opened in 1934 at an estimated cost of 85 million dollars. The line was busy from 1934 to 1960, by which time the rapid increase in lorry (truck) transport led to a decline in rail. Sections of the line were demolished as rail companies were merged or folded, and the last train ran in 1980.

For the next 20 years the structure rusted and fell into decay. In 1983 a local architect, Steven Holl, proposed a scheme to convert it into houses, commercial property and open space, but he failed to attract support. In 1991 further demolition took place as the rail companies were consigned to history and the area degenerated, with undesirables of many sorts occupying the dark recesses beneath the tracks. In August 1999 there was a public meeting to debate the future of the emasculated elevated railway. Two young men, Joshua David and Robert Hammond, decided that the 'High Line', as they later named it, should be saved. With no experience whatsoever of the political, economic or design expertise required, they each hoped the other would take the lead, but they finally worked together to create the Friends of the High Line.

A decade followed of meetings with planners, fund-raising events, exhibitions, pleadings and wrestlings. Donors pledged a million dollars here, 10 million dollars there, until it was finally clear that the High Line project would go ahead. Eventually, there was a design competition in which 51 entries were narrowed down to seven, then to four, with each of the four teams being given $25,000 to draw up detailed proposals. The winning team was the New York firm of James Corner Field Operations, including the Dutch plantsman Piet Oudolf as part of the team. The end result was a spectacularly successful blend of old and new. Old railway lines emerged from new grassy meadows and faded back into the undergrowth. New stairs and light wells punctuated the structure.

The High Line was officially opened at a small ceremony on 8 June 2011. In the words of its co-inventor, Joshua David:

> We hadn't publicized the ribbon cutting, but people on the streets below had heard the speeches and gone to the stairs to wait. The word had also traveled quickly online – *the High Line is opening, right now!* – and people who'd been following the project for years rushed over to be the first to visit the park. [Suddenly] the High Line was full of people looking down from the railings, trying out the benches, sipping coffee from paper cups, taking photographs of one another. Among them were a bride and groom in full wedding regalia. They'd heard about the ribbon cutting on the radio, thrown on their tux and gown, and run over to do their photos.[132]

More than four million visitors came in the following two years, about half from New York and half from out of town and overseas.

The end was in many ways the beginning. The success of the High Line brought investment into the formerly run-down area. New hotels, apartments, cafés and shops opened, with the highest priced properties looking on to or giving access to the High Line. Joshua David and Robert Hammond had reinvented the promenade or *passegiata*, with people strolling to look at other people in a city in which it had long been the custom to look the other way.

The phenomenal success of the High Line has excited professional designers around the world. In England the Landscape Institute launched its High Line for London competition in 2012, not intending to replicate a high-level park but looking for landscape ideas that would do for London what the High Line had done for New York and bring a sense of social cohesion. There were 170 entries, of which 20 were short-listed. Joshua David and Robert Hammond were among the judges. The winning entry was a proposal by Fletcher Priest Architects, 'Pop Down', to convert the unused 'Mail Rail' tunnels under Oxford Street, London's major shopping street, into a mushroom garden illuminated by glass-fibre 'mushroom' lights, an idea that would surely have appealed to William Robinson, whose book calling for the wider cultivation of mushrooms was published in 1870. The runner-up was a scheme to create a clean water channel along the Regent's Canal, linking Little Venice, near Paddington station to the north of the city, with the Thames-side Limehouse Basin in the east. Other short-listed proposals were for 'Bus Roots' ('roots' and 'routes' are pronounced in the same way in England), creating green-roofed bus shelters with sparrow colonies, insect hotels and wildflower meadows, and for a linear park floating on barges by the old docks at Canary Wharf. These were all well-meaning – if at times somewhat zany – proposals, but nothing could quite match in scale and potential city transformation the brilliance of the High Line.

22

A sense of community

⌒

O LDER AND ON A SMALLER SCALE than the High Line, but arguably having a
wider sphere of influence in the realm of transforming the city, is the idea of the
community garden. This idea again springs from many sources but it had its most notable
origin in what is now the Liz Christy Community Garden, barely a mile from the High
Line. The junction of Houston and Bowery streets to the east of Greenwich Village is near
the northern edge of that part of New York City where an old pattern of always straight
but irregular streets gives way to the characteristic American grid of north–south avenues
and east–west streets. The area of relatively low-rise brownstone houses 'was populated
with an eclectic mix of immigrants, artists and students, these last two groups attracted
as much by the lively atmosphere as by the cheap rents. In the 1960s the area was blighted
by rubbish-strewn streets and vacant or derelict building sites. It had the vitality of street
life that so appealed to Jane Jacobs when she wrote *The Death and Life of Great American
Cities* (1961), but it also had the overlay of desolation that encouraged well-meaning city
planners and less well-meaning property developers to flatten the 'slums' and replace them
with shiny new office blocks.

While recent immigrants, at the bottom of the social heap, might accept their living
conditions as inevitable – conditions that they might eventually escape by moving out
– many of the artists who had moved here came from very different social backgrounds.
They were accustomed to more salubrious surroundings, were socially active and vocal,
and would not tolerate the mess for long. They began to clear up the litter and to plant
flowers at the base of the struggling street trees and in window boxes. In 1973 Liz Christy
and Hattie Carthan launched their Green Guerrilla campaign. They climbed over broken
fences to commandeer empty building sites to plant flowers. Where fences were too difficult
to climb, they tossed balloons filled with water and wildflower seeds over the fence. The
Green Guerrillas persuaded the city to rent the plot at the junction of Bowery and Houston
to them for a dollar a year. At first the Bowery Houston Farm, cleared of rubbish and with
imported topsoil, grew vegetables in raised beds, but soon flowers and trees were added
and the farm became a community garden, which not only served the community but
helped to create it by attracting neighbours from their apartments into this public green
space. In 1986 the farm was renamed the Liz Christy Bowery-Houston Garden in memory
of its founder. By the end of the century the garden boasted more than a thousand species

of plants, and the working area at the back was giving away a quarter of a million dollars' worth of seeds, plants, compost and services each year.

The idea of the community garden spread rapidly throughout the city and beyond. There are hundreds in the five New York boroughs alone, each with its own history and distinctive character, and thousands worldwide. The West Side Community Garden, between West 89th and West 90th streets on Columbus and Amsterdam also had its origins in the early 1970s when the whole block was razed for a development that was then aborted. Local residents commandeered the site and began gardening, each with their own small raised bed. When the economy improved, the developers wanted to build, but instead of the usual acrimonious battle, an agreement was reached whereby building went ahead on part of the site but the gardeners were given nearly half an acre of land on which the permanent garden developed. Part of the new garden retained individual raised beds as before, but the other part had elegant fencing, arbours, pergolas, seats and an amphitheatre of borders around a green lawn, half paid for by the developers, who also facilitated the design and supervised the construction. The result was a very beautiful garden in which adults could sit and read in the shade of birches, oaks and dogwoods while children played on the lawn or raced around the paths of the amphitheatre and parents tended the vegetables in their own plots – a truly civilized existence.

The 91st Street Garden on Manhattan's Upper West Side began in 1977 when local residents planted bulbs in a vacant lot on Broadway. The colourful spring flowers excited great interest and stimulated further plantings. When developers decided it was time to build on the plot, the now coherent community asked the city for replacement land, and despite some controversy they were given a site within Riverside Park on public land. In 1981 the active group, now incorporated as Garden People, created the octagon and in 1982 the rectangle, both overflowing with colourful flowers of a distinctly domestic rather than institutional character. The freshness of the area cast the gloomy park surroundings into a less than flattering light, and a programme of general improvement began with resurfaced paths, unusual shrubs replacing dusty evergreens and a refurbished playground.

There is no blueprint for community gardens: some are tiny, some seemingly untidy, some more or less artistic installations, but all are idiosyncratic and much-loved magnets of community involvement. To the simple joys of growing plants and being in the open air is now added an awareness that this green environment has great health benefits and potential benefits in adding to the green infrastructure of urban areas.

England also has its community gardens and guerrilla gardeners. Indeed, the idea of guerrilla gardening in England dates back to the seventeenth century and to the activities of Gerrard Winstanley (1609–1676). Winstanley was born in Lancashire but moved to

London as an apprentice and then a freeman in the Merchant Tailors' guild. In 1643 he went bankrupt as the Civil War ruined his business, and he moved to Surrey as a cowherd. Outraged by the inequalities between the landowning gentry and peasants dispossessed by the Enclosures, he became leader of the 'True Levellers' or what his opponents dubbed 'the Diggers'. In 1649 Winstanley and his followers took over vacant land, grubbed up hedgerows and filled ditches to grow food which was distributed to the poor, but not everyone was in favour of this redistribution of property. Thugs destroyed crops and attacked the Levellers. Despite Winstanley's protests to the authorities he was unable to win against the landed gentry, and the movement died almost as soon as it was born.

Twentieth-century guerrilla gardening did not have the political motivation of the Levellers and to a very large extent it avoided confrontational politics, but the guerrillas did take over unused and unkempt parcels of land in the 1980s. They threw wildflower 'bombs' on to roundabouts (traffic circles) and encouraged the concept of community gardening. One of the important precursors of the community gardening movement is the work of Chris Baines (1948–). Baines began life in Sheffield, where he worked in the local parks before studying horticulture and landscape architecture. After graduation his early career was in greening the desert in the Middle East, but he returned to England to work in a very different desert, the dull green gang-mown and litter-strewn desert around many urban housing estates. Grass was ploughed up and areas replanted with flowering shrubs, bulbs and wild flowers. The effect on the local communities in fostering a sense of pride in their surroundings was remarkable. Baines's interest evolved into a particular focus on the wildlife supported by many of his planting schemes. In 1985 he designed a wildlife garden at the Chelsea Flower Show, a hugely popular exhibit demonstrating that wildlife gardens need not be untidy assemblies of coarse weeds. In the same year he presented a television series called 'Bluetits and Bumblebees' and published *How to Make a Wildlife Garden*. He was still teaching postgraduates in landscape architecture, and in 1986 was awarded a professorship at Birmingham Polytechnic, a combination of events leading to his becoming known as 'Professor Bumblebee'.

The Royal Horticultural Society has had an interest in education since 1822 when, as the Horticultural Society of London, it began a two-year course for gardeners in its new Chiswick garden. Joseph Paxton was one of the first students. Throughout the nineteenth and twentieth centuries the RHS has continued its involvement in the education of professional gardeners with its National Diploma in Horticulture, now the MHort, and lower level introductory courses. In the latter part of the twentieth century these courses have been increasingly available to serious amateurs as well as to people following a career in horticulture. More recently, in common with other botanic gardens, the RHS has developed an Education Department within its structure, and there is now a dedicated Schools Officer to develop programmes of education for visiting children, for assisting teachers in setting up gardens in their own schools, and for organizing competitions and other events to encourage children to care for the environment, to know where their food comes from, and to work together.

These diverse strands of wildlife gardening, engaging children in healthy outdoor exercise and developing a sense of community through neighbourhood gardens have woven together to bring the joys and benefits of gardening to a much wider constituency. In February 2012 a leading article in *The Garden*, the monthly journal published by the RHS, proclaimed 'Gardening helps to reduce crime', pointing to case studies in which the tidying up of run-down housing estates by volunteers has led to a greater sense of community, to more activity in streets and courtyards as people garden, and to reduced crime rates. There are even cases of local police forces offering advice on gardening: gravel paths to make noisy approaches to the house, spiky plants under windows and other techniques to discourage burglars. Clearly, the garden has many benefits.

The widely reported success of the High Line and the exchange of ideas on community gardening are but two indicators of the all-pervasive nature of communications in the early twenty-first century. Newspapers, magazines, professional journals and especially the Internet have made it possible to see what the rest of the world is doing, but the wealth of the more fortunate has made it possible for many people to travel to see for themselves. English people travelling to America are mainly interested in the spectacular natural scenery of its national parks and coasts, in the un-English climate of Florida and southern California, or in the peculiarly specific aspects of American culture such as Las Vegas and Disney World. Americans are mainly interested in the fact that England is very old. They visit Stonehenge, Shakespeare's Stratford-upon-Avon, the old university cities (where 'New College' in Oxford dates from 1379), the sights of London, and perhaps more recently places familiar to viewers of Harry Potter or Downton Abbey. A discerning few will seek out the quieter charms of the Cotswolds or Devon and Cornwall, but a steady stream are also interested in English gardens.

For nearly half a century the University of Oxford has organized summer schools for the alumni of various American universities. The Oxford/Berkeley summer school has been offered since 1970, at Worcester College and more recently at Merton. Michigan State's 'Odyssey to Oxford' began in 1984, and other summer schools have been organized with Florida, Iowa State, Kentucky and Duke universities and with the Smithsonian Institution. The topics covered are wide-ranging: Shakespeare, Jane Austen, spies, history of science, architecture and music, for example, but many of the summer schools have offered a garden history course, so many hundreds of Americans have pursued their interest in English gardens over the decades. And many of them have taken English ideas back to incorporate, or perhaps just to reminisce about, in their own 'yards'.

In May and August 2005 I was invited to lecture on the then new *Queen Mary II* sailing from New York to Southampton. Each of the four lectures on the five-day crossing was attended by up to 200 people. The first crossing, with its arrival in Southampton coinciding with the Chelsea Flower Show in London, had large numbers of individuals and garden groups heading for Chelsea, an indication of the annual migration of Americans to this scene of horticultural splendour. American accents are to be heard in most major open gardens, especially those such as Hidcote with strong American connections and Sissinghurst with romantic literary associations.

Of course, all these courses and tours appeal mainly to the generation with the spare time in retirement and with the financial resources to participate in two or three weeks of travel, although the Oxford/Berkeley summer school now has an arrangement with St Thomas Aquinas College in Sparkill, New York, to include young students in the programme.

The Royal Oak Foundation was started in New York in 1972, specifically, though not exclusively, to support the work of the National Trust in England. Its lecture series and other activities across the United States are both fund-raising and social events. Much of the money raised is used for the care and repair of English houses, always an expensive task, but in 2012, for instance, the late Christopher Lloyd's garden at Great Dixter, now in the care of the Great Dixter Charitable Trust (and not a National Trust property), received over $25,000 to support trainee gardeners. These and innumerable other small-scale examples testify to the continuing warm relations between America and England in gardening matters.

One little known but continuing thread in the links between young people in England and America in matters horticultural for nearly 70 years is the scholarship funded by the Garden Club of America and a series of English institutions and individuals, initially the English-Speaking Union (ESU), to send one student from each country across the Atlantic each year.[133] The idea was launched by the Hillsborough Garden Club in California and by Lady Heald, a member and later president of the Guildford branch of the ESU in England. In 1948 the Hillsborough Garden Club raised money from a house and garden tour and agreed with the University of California at Berkeley and the ESU Garden Committee in London to create a Hillsborough Garden Club Study Grant in Horticulture. The first recipient, sponsored in England by the Fisons fertilizer and agro-chemicals company, was Daphne Vince. She went on to gain a PhD, and developed a distinguished academic career at the University of Reading in the study of photoperiodism, the effect of day length on the growth and flowering of plants, a field originating in studies at the United States Department of Agriculture in Beltsville, Maryland.

In 1950 the ESU offered a reciprocal fellowship to an American student. In 1951 the Woodside-Allerton and Piedmont garden clubs, also in California, joined Hillsborough, and in 1952 the Garden Club of America voted to organize a permanent US/UK fellowship to rotate among the twelve zones of the club. On the English side the fellowship was funded by Fisons from its inception to 1972. From 1973 to 1982 support came from the Stanley Smith Foundation. Sir George Taylor, former director of the Royal Botanic Gardens, Kew, and chairman of the trustees of the Stanley Smith Trust, acted as horticultural advisor to the interview panel. From 1984 funds came from the Martin McLaren Trust and the organization of the fellowship moved to the Institute of Horticulture. Martin McLaren was a great-nephew of Gertrude Jekyll and grandson of the first Lord and Lady Aberconway of the famous garden of Bodnant in North Wales, so horticulture featured large in the McLaren genes. Martin's widow, Nancy, is herself an enthusiastic and knowledgeable gardener, and has taken a personal interest in the interchange fellowship and its recipients following her appointment to the selection committee in 1980. In recent years the fellowship has been organized by the RHS.

For most of its existence the fellowship placed students in universities. As fees for overseas students in England rose steeply and as the bureaucracy involved in placing ad hoc postgraduate students in America became more arduous, major gardens became involved in the exchange programme. Under the auspices of the RHS the exchange is now primarily between major gardens on both sides of the Atlantic. The aims of the fellowship have always been to foster Anglo-American relations through studies in botany, horticulture and landscape architecture. Fellows are chosen on their ability to act as ambassadors of their host country, but the interview panels also try to select the person that they feel will benefit most from the award. In both these aims they have been remarkably successful.

Initially, the fellowship was open to women only, but in 1962 men were allowed to apply. I applied for the 1965 scholarship but failed. My timid manner was not a good recommendation for the role of an English ambassador, and apparently I put Capability Brown in the wrong century. However, there must have been some sympathy from the interviewing panel, because I subsequently received an invitation to study at the University of Illinois for a year and then, via the New York office of the ESU, an offer from the University of Michigan to complete my master's degree in landscape architecture while teaching horticultural aspects of the subject. That experience shaped the rest of my professional life.

James St John Wilson, the 1971 English recipient, studied in Syracuse, gaining an MLA from a horticultural background. One of the advantages of many American universities was that it was possible to study landscape architecture *and* horticulture (and forestry, environmental science and related disciplines). Wilson returned to England to make a distinguished career as a landscape architect, a contribution arising particularly from his ability to span that range of expertise.

Gerald Luckhurst, who graduated in horticulture from Reading in 1981, gained his MLA in America, returning to develop a career in historic landscape management in Portugal, where he has hosted members of the Brooklyn Botanic Garden and *Horticulture* magazine in tours of Sintra on the Portuguese mainland and Funchal on the island of Madeira.

Philippa Sargeant joined the Longwood Graduate Program in 1987–8 and returned to work for the RHS, becoming promoted to shows organizer.

In 1989–90 Nigel Dunnett studied at North Carolina State University but took advantage of his time in America, with the characteristic generous support and connections of his hosts in the Garden Club, to travel widely and immerse himself in the study of native plants and the naturalistic landscape movement then burgeoning in various parts of the country. He is now Professor of Planting Design and Vegetation Technology at the University of Sheffield, where he has developed an international reputation for his work on green roofs, pictorial meadows (using many American flowering plants in his mixes), naturalistic planting design and rain gardens. These are designed to accommodate sudden flows of surface water in ditches and hollows, allowing the water to seep gradually into the surface instead of causing damaging floods.

Paul Broadhurst studied in Washington State but found Seattle and the American way of life in the Northwest so appealing that he stayed to become a designer of elegant and beautifully detailed gardens for a clientele who appreciate his blend of English and American ideas.

In the other direction, Lawrence Skog, the American scholar in 1968, became Curator of Botany at the Smithsonian Institution in Washington, DC.

Judy Zuk came from America in 1976–7, studying at Kew, the RHS gardens at Wisley and at the University of Reading. She returned to America to head the horticultural team at Swarthmore College and then became president of the Brooklyn Botanic Garden. Sadly, she died of cancer while still young.

In 1978–9 Fred Blackley came to England with his wife, Nancy. They returned to North Carolina where Fred has developed a successful career as a landscape architect, working especially on private gardens but also contributing in many ways to the local community.

Todd Lasseigne came to England and the University of Reading in 1994–5. After gaining his PhD and filling several positions of increasing responsibility in botanic gardens, he has recently become the director and CEO of the new Tulsa Botanic Garden in Oklahoma.

Tony Aiello returned from his studies in England to become Head of Horticulture at the Morris Arboretum. He has returned to England since to collect witch hazels for the arboretum and more recently to collect DNA samples from *Acer griseum* trees throughout the British Isles to compare with material he has collected from trees in China, where the maple is now threatened with extinction.

Michael Dosmann returned to America after his 1998–9 year in England to complete his PhD at Cornell University and is now Curator of Living Collections at the Arnold Arboretum. He and Tony Aiello have recently been on a joint expedition to China, a good example of the horticultural network developed partly through the auspices of the Garden Club.

Many young people have obviously crossed the Atlantic in both directions to explore the other culture and sometimes to take root. As just one example, Matt Wells graduated with a degree in landscape management from the University of Reading in 1995. His first job after graduation was as training officer for the British Trust for Conservation Volunteers, but he then moved to New York where he became a forester in the City of New York Parks and Recreation Department, then Head of Forestry for the city. In 2009 he was asked to speak at the annual conference of the Arboricultural Association in Devon, repeating his lecture to London-based members of the association in the grand setting of Islington town hall in north London. His audiences listened to accounts of the closing of city streets in New York to turn them into green oases, and they were green with envy as he recounted that the mayor had decided New York needed more trees and had given the department an extra 10 million dollars to spend. Electronic databases are not new in the arboricultural world, but with the sophisticated resources of his department Matt was able to investigate where the city was least well provided with trees and where the incidence of child asthma was highest. The overlap of these two maps determined where trees would be planted. Perhaps the grass is always greener on the other side of the fence, but English tree officers were definitely left in awe of New York's enlightened environmental policy conveyed to them by a young English expatriate. Long may this Anglo-American special relationship in this most civilized and civilizing aspect of our lives continue.

Notes

1   'Whig' and 'Tory' were originally terms of abuse: 'Whig' was a Gaelic term for a horse thief and 'Tory' signified a Papist (Catholic) outlaw. By the eighteenth century Whigs were supporters of constitutional democracy with the king's power limited by Parliament. Tories were supporters of the Crown, the so-called 'King's Friends'.

2   Vivian Russell, *Edith Wharton's Italian Gardens*, London, Frances Lincoln, 1997, p. 9.

3   E. S. Rohde, *The Story of the Garden*, London, Medici, 1932, with a chapter on American gardens by Mrs Francis King, p. 240.

4   Rohde, *Story*, p. 241.

5   Prudence Leith-Ross, *The John Tradescants: Gardeners to the Rose and Lily Queen*, London, Peter Owen, 1984, pp. 66, 71, 91.

6   Leith-Ross, *The John Tradescants*, p. 184.

7   Ann Leighton, *Early American Gardens: 'For meate or medicine'*, Boston, MA, Houghton Mifflin, 1970, pp. 50–52.

8   Leighton, *Early American Gardens*, p. 16.

9   Ann Leighton, *American Gardens in the Eighteenth Century: 'For use or for delight'*, Boston, MA, Houghton Mifflin, 1976, p. 77.

10   H. R. Fletcher, *The Story of the Royal Horticultural Society 1804–1968*, Oxford University Press, 1969, p. 8.

11   Stephen Switzer, *Ichnographia Rustica*, 2nd edn, London, D. Browne, 1741; facsimile reprint New York, Garland, 1982, p. 81.

12   David Green, *Gardener to Queen Anne: Henry Wise, 1653–1738 and the Formal Garden*, London, Oxford University Press, 1956, plate 52 (after p. 232).

13   Elizabeth Barlow Rogers, *Landscape Design: A Cultural and Architectural History*, New York, Abrams, 2001, p. 224.

14   Fletcher, *Royal Horticultural Society*, p. 10.

15   Leighton, *American Gardens in the Eighteenth Century*, p. 91.

16   Leighton, *American Gardens in the Eighteenth Century*, pp. 110, 112.

17   Leighton, *American Gardens in the Eighteenth Century*, p. 421.

18   Anthony Ashley Cooper, *The Moralists* (1709), in J. D. Hunt and P. Willis, eds, *The Genius of the Place*, Cambridge, MA, and London, MIT Press, 1988, p. 124.

19   Horace Walpole, 'The Modern Taste in Gardening' (1771), in Hunt and Willis, *Genius*, p. 313.

20   Mavis Batey, 'The Way to View Rousham by Kent's Gardener', *Garden History* 11: 2, Autumn 1983, pp. 125–32.

21   For Whig and Tory, see note 1 above.

22   Sir William Chambers, *Dissertation on Oriental Gardening*, London, W. Griffin, 1772, pp. x, 11.

23   Dorothy Stroud, *Capability Brown*, 3rd edn, London, Faber, 1975, p. 201.

24   *Thomas Jefferson's Garden Book*, annotated by Edwin Betts, Philadelphia, American Philosophical Society, 1944, p. 109.

25   All descriptions below from *Garden Book*, pp. 111–14.

26   Fletcher, *Royal Horticultural Society*, p. 11.

27   All letter extracts above from Jefferson Papers Series 1, vol. 2, no. 246, in MS division of the Library of Congress, Washington, DC.

28   William Gilpin, *Observations relative chiefly to Picturesque Beauty, made in the Year 1772 on Several Parts of England*, 3rd edn, London, Blamire, 1792, and *Remarks on Forest Scenery and other Woodland Views*, London, Blamire, 1791.

29   Richard Payne Knight, *The Landscape* (1794), in Hunt and Willis, *Genius*, p. 345.

30   John Claudius Loudon, *The Landscape Gardening and Landscape Architecture of the Late Humphry Repton Esq.*, London, Longman, 1840, p. 103.

31   Loudon, *Humphry Repton*, p. 215.

32   Loudon, *Humphry Repton*, p. 215.

33   Loudon, *Humphry Repton*, p. 215.

34   Loudon, *Humphry Repton*, pp. 339–40.

35   Loudon, *Humphry Repton*, p. 559.

36   Fletcher, *Royal Horticultural Society*, p. 19.

37   Fletcher, *Royal Horticultural Society*, p. 20.

38   Fletcher, *Royal Horticultural Society*, p. 32.

39   David Douglas, *Journal kept by David Douglas during his Travels in America, 1823–1827*, London, W. Wesley & Son, 1914, p. 20.

40   Douglas, *Journal*, p. 23.

41   Fletcher, *Royal Horticultural Society*, p. 101.

42   Douglas, *Journal*, p. 102.

43   Douglas, *Journal*, p. 111.

44   Douglas, *Journal*, p. 128.

45   Douglas, *Journal*, p. 174.

46   Douglas, *Journal*, p. 181.

47   Douglas, *Journal*, p. 188.

48   Douglas, *Journal*, p. 293.

49   J. C. Loudon, *The Villa Gardener*, London, William Orr, 1850, pp. 35–6 (2nd edn of *The Suburban Gardener*, edited by Jane Loudon).

50   J. C. Loudon, *The Suburban Gardener and Villa Companion*, London, Longman, Orme, Brown and Green, 1838, p. 140.

51   The 'ancient or geometric[al] style' was a term used by Repton in his *Fragments* (Loudon, *Humphry Repton*, p. 520) and later by Loudon (*Villa Gardener*, p. 36) to indicate what would later be known as the 'formal garden'.

52   Violet R. Markham, *Paxton and the Bachelor Duke*, London, Hodder and Stoughton, 1935, p. 30.

53   Geoffrey Barraclough, ed., *The Times Atlas of World History*, London, Times Books, 1978, p. 221.

54   Chris Thompson, 'Tony's Trade Cards', *Farm and Horticultural Equipment Collector* 78, January/February 2005, pp. 14–15.

55 Andrew Jackson Downing, *A Treatise on the Theory and Practice of Landscape Gardening adapted to North America*, 4th edn, 1849; facsimile reprint Washington, DC, Dumbarton Oaks, 1991, p. vi.

56 Downing, *Treatise*, p. vii.

57 Charles Beveridge and Paul Rocheleau, *Frederick Law Olmsted: Designing the American Landscape*, New York, Rizzoli, 1995, p. 11.

58 Frederick Law Olmsted, *Walks and Talks of an American Farmer in England*, Ann Arbor, University of Michigan Press, 1967, p. 286; Beveridge and Rocheleau, *Olmsted*, p. 33.

59 Olmsted, *Walks and Talks*, p. 95.

60 Olmsted, *Walks and Talks*, p. 95.

61 Olmsted, *Walks and Talks*, p. 52.

62 Beveridge and Rocheleau, *Olmsted*, p. 17.

63 Olmsted, *Walks and Talks*, p. 90.

64 Frederick Law Olmsted, *The Spoils of the Park: With a Few Leaves from the Deep-laden Notebooks of 'A Wholly Unpractical Man'*, 1882; reprinted in Albert Fein, *Landscape into Cityscape*, Ithaca, NY, Cornell University Press, 1968, pp. 391–440.

65 Richard Tames, *William Morris*, Princes Risborough, Shire Publications, 1995, p. 5.

66 Aymer Vallance, *The Life and Work of William Morris*, London, Studio Editions, 1995, p. 490 (first published by George Bell, 1897).

67 Stephen Coote, *William Morris: His Life and Work*, London, Garamond, 1990, p. 196.

68 Coote, *William Morris*, p. 197.

69 Christopher Hussey, *The Life of Sir Edwin Lutyens*, London, Country Life, 1950; reprinted Woodbridge, Antique Collectors' Club, 1984, p. 24.

70 Gertrude Jekyll, *Home and Garden*, 2nd edn, London, Longmans Green, 1901, p. 17.

71 Herbert Baker, *Architecture and Personalities*, London, Country Life, 1944, pp. 15–16.

72 Gertrude Jekyll, *Wood and Garden*, London, Longmans Green, 1899, title page.

73 Hussey, *Lutyens*, p. 136.

74 Hussey, *Lutyens*, p. 96.

75 Charles Augustus Keeler, *The Simple Home* (1904), in Judith Tankard, *Gardens of the Arts and Crafts Movement*, New York, Abrams, 2004, p. 172.

76 Gertrude Jekyll, *On Gardening*, in Susan E. Schnare and Rudi J. Favretti, 'Gertrude Jekyll's American Gardens', *Garden History* 10: 2, Autumn 1982, p. 149.

77 Schnare and Favretti, 'Gertrude Jekyll's American Gardens', p. 152.

78 Reef Point Collection of Jekyll plans in the College of Environmental Design Library, University of California, Berkeley, File V, folder 120, 1914.

79 Schnare and Favretti, 'Gertrude Jekyll's American Gardens', p. 158.

80 Schnare and Favretti, 'Gertrude Jekyll's American Gardens', p. 160.

81 Schnare and Favretti, 'Gertrude Jekyll's American Gardens', p. 160.

82 Schnare and Favretti, 'Gertrude Jekyll's American Gardens', p. 163.

83 William Robinson, *The English Flower Garden*, 12th edn, London, John Murray, 1914, pp. vii–viii.

84 Letter from Charles Darwin in a box of Robinson correspondence in the RHS Lindley

Library, 5 May 1866, WRO/2/026 album 1.

85 Mea Allan, *William Robinson 1838–1935*, London, Faber, 1982, p. 50.

86 William Robinson, *Gleanings from French Gardens*, London, Frederick Warne, 1868, p. 101, and William Robinson, *The Parks, Promenades and Gardens of Paris*, London, John Murray, 1869, p. 76.

87 Robinson, *Gleanings*, p. 108.

88 William Robinson, 'Letters from Paris', *Gardeners' Chronicle*, 20 April 1867, pp. 405–6; Robinson, *Gleanings*, p. 94; Robinson, *Parks, Promenades*, p. 59.

89 William Robinson, 'Letters from Paris', *Gardeners' Chronicle*, 6 April 1867, p. 348.

90 Robinson, *Gleanings*, p. 109.

91 W. H. King and E. Charles Nelson, 'William Robinson in North America 1870', *Studies in the History of Gardens and Designed Landscapes* 24: 2, 2004, p. 118.

92 William Robinson, *Alpine Flowers for Gardens*, 4th edn, London, John Murray, 1910, p. 138.

93 King and Nelson, 'William Robinson in North America', p. 120.

94 Robinson, *Alpine Flowers*, p. 137.

95 King and Nelson, 'William Robinson in North America', p. 123.

96 G. C. Taylor, 'North Mymms Park', *Country Life*, 27 January 1934, pp. 38–44.

97 Anon., 'Nuneham Park', *Gardeners' Chronicle*, 4 January 1908, pp. 9–10.

98 Nicholas Alfrey, Stephen Daniels and Martin Postle, eds, *Art of the Garden*, London, Tate Publishing, 2004, p. 221.

99 Henry James, prefatory note to *Catalogue of a Collection of Drawings by Alfred*, London, Fine Art Society, 1891, in Alfrey, Daniels and Postle, *Art of the Garden*, p. 47.

100 Alfrey, Daniels and Postle, *Art of the Garden*, p. 47.

101 Graham Stuart Thomas, *Gardens of the National Trust*, London, Weidenfeld and Nicolson, 1979, p. 120.

102 Churchill/Astor dialogue taken from https://www.goodreads.com (Churchill and Astor quotes, accessed 29 April 2016).

103 Allyson Hayward, *Norah Lindsay*, London, Frances Lincoln, 2007, p. 65.

104 Hayward, *Norah Lindsay*, p. 111.

105 Jellicoe, personal communication with the author, *c*.1980.

106 Alfrey, Daniels and Postle, *Art of the Garden*, p. 47.

107 Vivian Russell, *Edith Wharton's Italian Gardens*, London, Frances Lincoln, 1997, p. 11.

108 Russell, *Wharton's Italian Gardens*, p. 11.

109 Russell, *Wharton's Italian Gardens*, p. 18.

110 David Ottewill, *The Edwardian Garden*, New Haven and London, Yale University Press, 1989, p. 150.

111 Mac Griswold and Eleanor Weller, *The Golden Age of American Gardens 1890–1940*, New York, Abrams, 1991, p. 18.

112 Griswold and Weller, *Golden Age*, pp. 87–8.

113 Rohde, *Story*, p. 268.

114 Louis Sullivan, 'The Tall Office Building Artistically Considered', 1896, in *Oxford Dictionary of Quotations*, 4th edn, Oxford University Press, 1992, p. 671.

115   J. M. Richards, *Modern Architecture*, Harmondsworth, Penguin, 1963, p. 38.

116   Christopher Tunnard, *Gardens in the Modern Landscape*, London, Architectural Press, 1938, p. 69.

117   Ebenezer Howard, *Garden Cities of Tomorrow*, London, Swan Sonnenschein, 1902, between pp. 16 and 17.

118   William Mason, *The English Garden: A Poem in Four Books*, York, A. Ward, 1783, Book 2, ll. 322–39.

119   Marina Schinz and Gabrielle van Zuylen, *The Gardens of Russell Page*, New York, Stewart, Tabori and Chang, 1991, p. 227.

120   Letter dated 9 January 1919 in box of letters to William Robinson in the RHS Lindley Library, WRO/2/177 album 2.

121   Barbara Paul Robinson, *Rosemary Verey*, Boston, MA, Godine, 2012, p. 178.

122   Martin Wood, *Nancy Lancaster: English Country House Style*, London, Frances Lincoln, 2005, p. 9.

123   Nikolaus Pevsner, *Buildings of England: Northamptonshire*, Harmondsworth, Penguin, 1961, p. 261.

124   Ray Desmond, *Kew: The History of the Royal Botanic Gardens,* London, Harvill, 1995, p. 167.

125   Desmond, *Kew*, p. 236.

126   Desmond, *Kew*, p. 237.

127   Desmond, *Kew*, p. 238.

128   Sue Shephard, *Seeds of Fortune: A Gardening Dynasty*, London, Bloomsbury, 2003, p. 247.

129   Arnold Arboretum Archives, Harvard University, Cambridge, MA, IV A-1 WHJ, p. 50.

130   The Library of Congress: A Century of Law Making for a New Nation: U.S. Congressional Documents and Debates 1774–1875: Statutes at Large 37th Congress, 2nd session, p. 504 of 1443 at https://memory.loc.gov/cgi-bin/ampage?collId=llsl&fileName=012/llsl012.db&recNum=535 (accessed 29 April 2016).

131   William Robinson, *Home Landscapes*, London, John Murray, 1920, p. 95.

132   Joshua David and Robert Hammond, *High Line: The Inside Story of New York City's Park in the Sky*, New York, Farrar, Straus and Giroux, 2011, p. 121.

133   Nancy McLaren and Ann Farrell, 'The Institute of Horticulture Martin McLaren Horticultural Scholarship and Garden Club of America Interchange Fellowship', *The Horticulturist* 7: 3, July 1998, pp. 7–14.

Select bibliography

Alfrey, Nicholas, Stephen Daniels and Martin Postle, eds, *Art of the Garden*, London, Tate Publishing, 2004

Allan, Mea, *The Tradescants: Their Plants, Gardens and Museum 1570–1662*, London, Michael Joseph, 1964

Ammann, Gustav, *Landscape Gardens*, Zurich, Verlag fur Architektur, 1955

Athelstan, George Harvey, *Douglas of the Fir*, Cambridge, MA, Harvard University Press, 1947

Bailey, Liberty Hyde, *The Standard Cyclopedia of Horticulture*, 3 vols, New York, Macmillan, 1947

Balmori, Diana, Diana Kostial McGuire and Eleanor McPeck, *Beatrix Farrand's American Landscapes*, Sagaponack, NY, Sagapress, 1985

Bardi, P., *Tropical Gardens of Burle Marx*, London, Architectural Press, 1964

Barraclough, Geoffrey, ed., *The Times Atlas of World History*, London, Times Books, 1978

Berner, Nancy, and Susan Lowry, *Garden Guide: New York City*, New York, Little Bookroom, 2002

Beveridge, Charles, and Paul Rocheleau, *Frederick Law Olmsted: Designing the American Landscape*, New York, Rizzoli, 1995

Bisgrove, Richard, *The English Garden*, Harmondsworth, Viking, 1990

—, *The Gardens of Gertrude Jekyll*, London, Frances Lincoln, 1992; Berkeley, University of California Press, 2000

—, *William Robinson: The Wild Gardener*, London, Frances Lincoln, 2008

Brookes, John, *Room Outside*, London, Thames and Hudson, 1969

Brown, Jane, *The Omnipotent Magician: Lancelot 'Capability' Brown 1716–1783*, London, Chatto and Windus, 2011

Calkins, Carroll, ed., *Great Gardens of America*, New York, Coward-McCann, 1969

Chadwick, George F., *The Park in the Town*, London, Architectural Press, 1966

Chatto, Beth, *Beth Chatto's Gravel Garden*, London, Frances Lincoln, 2000

—, *The Damp Garden*, London, Dent, 1982

—, *The Dry Garden*, London, Dent, 1978

Church, Thomas, *Gardens are for People*, New York, Reinhold, 1955 (the second edition (New York and London, McGraw Hill, 1983) and the third edition (Berkeley and London, University of California Press, 1995) have long introductions on Church's work)

Clarke, Ethne, *Hidcote*, London, Michael Joseph, 1989; New York, Norton, 2009

Cleveland, H. W. S., *Landscape Architecture as applied to the Wants of the West*, Chicago, Jansen McClurg, 1873; reprinted Pittsburgh University Press, 1965

Coats, Alice, *Flowers and their Histories*, London, A&C Black, 1968

—, *Garden Shrubs and their Histories*, London, Vista Books, 1963

Conway, Hazel, *Public Parks*, Princes Risborough, Shire Publications, 1996

Coote, S., *William Morris: His Life and Work*, London, Garamond, 1990

Curl, James Stevens, 'The Architecture and Planning of the Nineteenth-Century Cemetery', *Garden History* III: 3, Summer 1975, pp. 13–41

Daniels, Stephen, *Humphry Repton*, New Haven and London, Yale University Press, 1999

David, Joshua, and Robert Hammond, *High Line: The Inside Story of New York City's Park in the Sky*, New York, Farrar, Straus and Giroux, 2011

Desmond, Ray, *Kew: The History of the Royal Botanic Gardens*, London, Harvill, 1995

—, 'Victorian Gardening Magazines', *Garden History* V: 3, Winter 1977, pp. 47–66

Douglas, David, *Journal Kept by David Douglas during his Travels in America, 1823–1827*, London, W. Wesley & Son, 1914

Downing, Andrew Jackson, *A Treatise on the Theory and Practice of Landscape Gardening adapted to North America*, Washington, DC, Dumbarton Oaks, 1991

Droste, Magdalena, *Bauhaus*, Berlin, Taschen, 2011

Eckbo, Garrett, *Landscape for Living*, New York, Dodge, 1950

Evelyn, John, *Silva: or, a Discourse of Forest Trees, and the Propagation of Timber in His Majesty's Dominions*, London, Dodsley, Cadell, Robson and Durham, 1776 (first published 1664 as *Sylva* and with many later editions)

Fairchild, David, *The World was my Garden*, New York, Scribner's, 1938

Fein, Albert, *Landscape into Cityscape: Frederick Law Olmsted's Plans for a Greater New York City*, Ithaca, NY, Cornell University Press, 1968

Fell, Derek, *The Gardens of Frank Lloyd Wright*, London, Frances Lincoln, 2009

Fletcher H. R., *The Story of the Royal Horticultural Society 1804–1968*, Oxford University Press, 1969

Garden Museum, *Henk Gerritsen, Piet Oudolf and the Inspiration of the Dutch Wave Garden*, special issue of *Museum Journal* 24 (Autumn 2010)

Gilpin, William, *Observations relative chiefly to Picturesque Beauty, made in the Year 1772 on Several Parts of England*, 3rd edn, London, Blamire, 1792

—, *Remarks on Forest Scenery and other Woodland Views*, London, Blamire, 1791

Gleason, David King, *Plantation Homes of Louisiana and the Natchez Area*, Baton Rouge and London, Louisiana State University Press, 1982

Gloag, John, *Mr Loudon's England*, Newcastle on Tyne, Oriel Press, 1970

Green, David, *Gardener to Queen Anne: Henry Wise, 1653–1738 and the Formal Garden*, Oxford University Press, 1956

Griswold, Mac, and Eleanor Weller, *The Golden Age of American Gardens 1890–1940*, New York, Abrams, 1991

Hall, Andrew M., 'The History of the Lawnmower', *Chronicle of the Early American Industries Association* 52: 2, June 1999, pp. 43–50

Hansen, Richard, and Friedrich Stahl, *Perennials and their Garden Habitats*, trans. Richard Ward, 4th edn, Cambridge University Press and Portland, OR, Timber Press, 1993; first published in German 1981

Harvey, Sheila, and Steven Rettig, eds, *Fifty Years of Landscape Design*, London, Landscape Press, 1985

Hayward, Allyson, *Norah Lindsay*, London, Frances Lincoln, 2007

Hitchmough, James, and Nigel Dunnett, *The Dynamic Landscape*, London, Spon, 2004

Hobhouse, Penelope, *Flower Gardens*, London, Frances Lincoln, 1991

—, *Penelope Hobhouse on Gardening*, London, Frances Lincoln, 1994

Hopkins, John, and Peter Neal, *The Making of the Queen Elizabeth Olympic Park*, Chichester, Wiley, 2013

Howard, Ebenezer, *Garden Cities of Tomorrow*, London, Swan Sonnenschein, 1902

Hughes, Robert, *American Visions*, London, Harvill Press, 1997

Hunt, J. D., and Peter Willis, eds, *The Genius of the Place*, Cambridge, MA, and London, MIT Press, 1988

Hunt, Peter, *The Shell Gardens Book*, London, Phoenix, 1964

Hussey, Christopher, *The Life of Sir Edwin Lutyens*, London, Country Life, 1950; reprinted Woodbridge, Antique Collectors' Club, 1984

Jacobs, Jane, *The Death and Life of Great American Cities*, New York, Random House 1961; Harmondsworth, Penguin, 1965

Jefferson, Thomas, *Thomas Jefferson's Garden Book*, annotated by Edwin Betts, Philadelphia, American Philosophical Society, 1944

Jekyll, Gertrude, *Colour in the Flower Garden*, London, Country Life and George Newnes, 1908

—, *Home and Garden*, London, Longmans Green, 1900

—, *Wood and Garden*, London, Longmans Green, 1899

Jekyll, Gertrude, and Lawrence Weaver, *Gardens for Small Country Houses*, London, Country Life, 1912

Jellicoe, Geoffrey, *The Landscape of Civilisation as Experienced in the Moody Historical Gardens*, Northiam, Garden Art Press, 1989

Jellicoe, Susan and Geoffrey, *Modern Private Gardens*, London, Abelard-Schuman, 1968

Jourdain, Margaret, *William Kent*, London, Country Life, 1948

Kassler, Elizabeth B., *Modern Gardens in the Landscape*, New York, Museum of Modern Art, 1964

King, Mrs Francis [Louisa Yeomans King] *The Well-Considered Garden*, New York, Scribner's, 1915 (introduction by Gertrude Jekyll)

King, W. H., and E. Charles Nelson, 'William Robinson in North America 1870', *Studies in the History of Gardens and Designed Landscapes*, 24: 2, 2004, pp. 116–32

Kingsbury, Noel, *The New Perennial Garden*, London, Frances Lincoln, 1996

Knopf, Jim, *The Xeriscape Flower Gardener*, Boulder, CO, Johnson Books, 1991

Lawrence, Elizabeth, *A Southern Garden*, Chapel Hill, University of North Carolina Press, 1942

Leighton, Ann, *American Gardens in the Eighteenth Century: 'For use or for delight'*, Boston, MA, Houghton Mifflin, 1976

—, *Early American Gardens: 'For meate or medicine'*, Boston, MA, Houghton Mifflin, 1970

Leith-Ross, Prudence, *The John Tradescants: Gardeners to the Rose and Lily Queen*, London, Peter Owen, 1984

Lemmon, Kenneth, *The Golden Age of Plant Hunters*, London, Phoenix House, 1968

Leopold, Rob, ed., *Perennial Preview: Creative Ecology and Integral Landscape Design*, Amsterdam, Perennial Perspectives Foundation, 1996

Lloyd, Christopher, *Meadows*, London, Cassell, 2004; reissued as *Meadows at Great Dixter and Beyond*, intro. Fergus Garrett, London, Pimpernel Press, 2016

—, *The Well-Tempered Garden*, London, Collins, 1970

Loudon, John Claudius, *An Encyclopaedia of Gardening*, London, Longman, Hurst, Rees, Orme and Brown, 1822 (including in 3.IX.3: Gardening in North America)

—, *The Landscape Gardening and Landscape Architecture of the Late Humphry Repton, Esq.*, London, Longman, 1840

—, *On the Laying Out, Planting and Managing of Cemeteries and on the Improvement of Churchyards*, London, Longman, Brown, Green and Longmans, 1843

—, *The Suburban Gardener and Villa Companion*, Edinburgh, Longman, Orme, Brown and Green, 1838

—, *The Villa Gardener*, London, William Orr, 1850; reprinted Redhill, Ivelet Books, 1981

McLaren, Nancy, and Ann Farrell, 'The Institute of Horticulture Martin McLaren Horticultural Scholarship and Garden Club of America Interchange Fellowship', *The Horticulturist* 7: 3, July 1998, pp. 7–14

Marsh, George Perkins, *Man and Nature*, Cambridge, MA, Harvard University Press, 1965

Mawson, Thomas H., *The Art and Craft of Garden Design*, London, Batsford, 1900

Minter, Sue, *The Apothecaries' Garden: History of the Chelsea Physic Garden*, Stroud, Sutton, 2003

Montero, Marta Iris, *Burle Marx: The Lyrical Landscape*, London, Thames and Hudson, 2001

Morwood, William, *Traveller in a Vanished Landscape* [David Douglas], London, Gentry Books, 1973

Musgrave, Toby, Chris Gardner and Will Musgrave, *The Plant Hunters*, London, Ward Lock, 1998

Nichols, Rose S., *English Pleasure Gardens*, New York, Macmillan, 1902

—, *Italian Pleasure Gardens*, New York, Dodd Mead, 1928

Oehme, Wolfgang, and James van Sweden, *Bold Romantic Gardens*, Herndon, VA, Acropolis, 1991

Olmsted, Frederick Law, *Walks and Talks of an American Farmer in England*, New York, Putnam, 1852; Ann Arbor, University of Michigan Press reprint of 1859 edition, 1967

Otis, Denise, *Grounds for Pleasure: Four Centuries of the American Garden*, New York, Abrams, 2002

Oudolf, Piet, and Noel Kingsbury, *Planting: A New Perspective*, Portland, OR, and London, Timber Press, 2013

Pape, Christine, ed., *Always Growing: The Story of the Morton Arboretum*, Chicago, Morton Arboretum, 2010

Parkinson, John, *Paradisi in Sole Paradisus Terrestris*, London, Humfrey Lownes and Robert Young, 1629; facsimile reprint London, Methuen, 1904

Pearson, Graham S., *Hidcote: The Garden and Lawrence Johnston*, London, National Trust, 2007

Platt, Charles, *Italian Gardens*, London, Thames and Hudson, 1993 (first published New York, Harper, 1894)

Robinette, Gary O., *Plants, People and Environmental Quality*, Washington, DC, US Department of the Interior National Parks Service, 1972

Robinson, Barbara Paul, *Rosemary Verey*, Boston, MA, Godine, 2012

Robinson, William, *Alpine Flowers for Gardens*, 4th edn, London, John Murray, 1910

—, *The English Flower Garden*, London, John Murray, 1883 (with 14 further editions to 1933)

—, *Gleanings from French Gardens*, London, Frederick Warne, 1868

—, *God's Acre Beautiful*, London, The Garden Office, 1880

—, *Gravetye Manor, or, Twenty Years' Work round an Old Manor House*, London, John Murray, 1911

—, *My Wood Fires and their Story*, London, Country Life, 1917

—, *The Parks, Promenades and Gardens of Paris*, London, John Murray, 1869

—, *The Subtropical Garden*, London, John Murray, 1870

—, *The Wild Garden*, London, John Murray 1870; 2nd edn 1881; with new introduction by Judith Tankard and material written by William Robinson and sent to John Murray in 1932 for an 8th edn which was not published, Sagaponack, NY, Sagapress, 1994; with new chapters by Rick Darke, Portland, OR, Timber Press, 2009

Rogers, Elizabeth Barlow, *Landscape Design: A Cultural and Architectural History*, New York, Abrams, 2001

—, *Rebuilding Central Park*, Cambridge, MA, MIT Press, 1987

Roper, Lanning, *Hardy Herbaceous Plants*, Harmondsworth, Penguin, 1960

—, *Successful Town Gardening*, London, Country Life, 1957

Rose, James, *Creative Gardens*, New York, Reinhold, 1958

Russell, Vivian, *Edith Wharton's Italian Gardens*, London, Frances Lincoln, 1997

Schinz, Marina, and Gabrielle van Zuylen, *The Gardens of Russell Page*, New York, Stewart, Tabori and Chang, 1991

Schnare, Susan E., and Rudy J. Favretti, 'Gertrude Jekyll's American Gardens', *Garden History* 10: 2, Autumn 1982, pp. 149–67

Shephard, Sue, *Seeds of Fortune: A Gardening Dynasty* [Veitch], London, Bloomsbury, 2003

Shepheard, Peter, *Modern Gardens*, London, Architectural Press, 1953

Sitwell, Sir George, *On the Making of Gardens*, London, John Murray, 1909; reprinted Jaffrey, NH, Godine, 2003

Stroud, Dorothy, *Capability Brown*, London, Country Life, 1950; 3rd edn, London, Faber, 1975

Sunset Magazine, *Sunset Deck Plans*, Menlo Park, CA, Sunset, 1991

—, *The Western Gardens Book*, Menlo Park, CA, Sunset, 2001

Tankard, Judith B., *Gardens of the Arts and Crafts Movement*, New York, Abrams, 2004

Tate, Alan, *Great City Parks*, London, Spon, 2001

Taylor, G. C., *The Modern Garden*, London, Country Life, 1936

Taylor, Patrick, *The Oxford Companion to the Garden*, Oxford University Press, 2006

Tishler, William H., *American Landscape Architecture: Designers and Places*, Washington, DC, Presentation Press, 1989

Toole, Robert M., 'Picturesque Landscape Gardening in the Hudson River Valley, New York State', *The Picturesque* 10, Spring 1995, pp. 1–13

Tunnard, Christopher, *Gardens in the Modern Landscape*, London, Architectural Press, and New York, Scribner's, 1938

Vallance, Aymer, *The Life and Work of William Morris*, London, George Bell, 1897; reprinted London, Studio Editions, 1995

Verey, Rosemary, *The American Man's Garden,* New York, Little Brown, 1990

Verey, Rosemary, and Ellen Samuels, *The American Woman's Garden*, New York, Little Brown, 1984

Verey, Rosemary, and Alvilde Lees-Milne, eds, *The Englishman's Garden*, London, Allen Lane, 1982

Verey, Rosemary, and Alvilde Lees-Milne, eds, *The Englishwoman's Garden*, London, Chatto and Windus, 1980

Wells, T. C. E., S. Bell and A. Frost, *Creating Attractive Grasslands using Native Plant Species*, London, Nature Conservancy Council, 1982

Wharton, Edith, *Italian Villas and their Gardens*, New York, Century Co., 1904

Wood, Martin, *Nancy Lancaster: English Country House Style*, London, Frances Lincoln, 2005

Woudstra, Jan, and Ken Fieldhouse, eds, *The Regeneration of Public Parks*, London, Spon, 2000

Wulf, Andrea, *The Brother Gardeners*, London, Windmill, 2009

—, *The Founding Gardeners*, London, Windmill, 2012

Index

Picture credits

With the exception of those listed here, all the images in this book are in private collections or in the public domain. The publishers have made every effort to contact holders of copyright works. Any copyright holders we have been unable to reach are invited to contact the publishers so that a full acknowledgment may be given in subsequent editions. For permission to reproduce the images below, the publishers would like to thank the following:

COLOUR
123RF: VIII (above); **akg-images**: XVIII; **Alamy Stock Photo**: I (below left) Ferne Arfin; IV (above) Granger Historical Picture; VI (above) & XXI (above) The National Trust Photo Library; XVI Paul Fearn; XXV Peter Anderson; XXVIII MBP-one; XXXII New York City; **By courtesy of John Brookes**: XXVII; **Dartington Hall**: XXIII; **Florilegius/SSPL/Getty Images**: I (above right); **www.frustratedgardener.com**: IX (above); © **Andrew Lawson**: XXIX (left); **Library of Congress, Rare Book and Special Collections Division**: II; **Macplants** (www.macplants.co.uk): XVII (below); **New York Public Library**: XII; **Private Collection**: I (above left), X, XV (above), XVII (above), XXVI, XXIX (right); **Queen Elizabeth Olympic Park**: XXXI (photo Anthony Charlton); © **Royal Academy of Arts, London**: XIX (photo John Hammond; **Shutterstock**: III, V, VII (above), IX (below), XIII, XXI (below), XXII, XXX; **Wikimedia Commons**: VI (below) & XIV (below) Daderot; VII (below) Matt Kozlowski/Moofpocket; XI (below) Bostonian 13; XIV (above) Andrew Balet; XV (below) Agnieszka Kwiecien Nova; XX HARTLEPOOL MARINA 2014

BLACK AND WHITE
Alamy Stock Photo: Page 23 (916 Collection); **Shutterstock/Bubica**: compass rose decoration

THE EARLIEST WRINKLED PEA
FOR FORCING.

As early as SUTTON'S RINGLEADER, which is the forwardest Round White Pea.

Haulm only 10 inches high, thickly covered with fine pods, each containing from 7 to 9 peas of delicious flavour.

THE ILLUSTRATION IS FROM A PHOTOGRAPH, AND SHOWS THE HABIT OF GROWTH.

FOR DESCRIPTION OF THIS NEW PEA SEE REMARKS ON NEXT PAGE.

INVALUABLE FOR EARLY FORCING.

UNSURPASSED FOR SMALL GARDENS.

AMERICAN WONDER PEA.

SIZE OF POD.

SIZE OF POD.

CAUTION.—Sutton & Sons are the only English House to whom a consignment of this new Pea has been sent for sale by the raisers, Messrs. B. K. Bliss & Son, of New York. Every package will bear Messrs. Sutton's Registered Trade Mark.